Routledge Revivals

The Volunteer Force

Originally published in 1975, *The Volunteer Force* is a study of the part-time military force which came into being to meet the mid-nineteenth century fear of French invasion. It survived and grew for fifty years until in 1908 it was renamed and remodelled as the Territorial Force. Composed initially of middle-class and often middle-aged gentlemen who elected their own officers and paid for their own equipment, the Volunteer Force soon became youthful and working-class, with appointed middle-class officers, a Government subsidy, and a minor military role as an adjunct to the Regular Army. This book examines the origins of the Force, the transformation in its social composition, the difficulties in finding officers who were 'gentlemen', the ambiguous status, of the Force both in the local community and in the Regular Army, and the political influence which the Force exerted in the early twentieth century. Above all it is concerned with the reasons for and the implications of enrolment; publicists argued that the Force was the embodiment of patriotism, and an indication of working-class loyalty to established institutions.

The Volunteer Force

A Social and Political History 1859-1908

by Hugh Cunningham

Routledge
Taylor & Francis Group

First published in 1975
by Croom Helm Ltd

This edition first published in 2018 by Routledge
2 Park Square, Milton Park, Abingdon, Oxon, OX14 4RN
and by Routledge
711 Third Avenue, New York, NY 10017

Routledge is an imprint of the Taylor & Francis Group, an informa business

© 1975 Hugh Cunningham

All rights reserved. No part of this book may be reprinted or reproduced or
utilised in any form or by any electronic, mechanical, or other means, now
known or hereafter invented, including photocopying and recording, or in any
information storage or retrieval system, without permission in writing from the
publishers.

Publisher's Note
The publisher has gone to great lengths to ensure the quality of this reprint but
points out that some imperfections in the original copies may be apparent.

Disclaimer
The publisher has made every effort to trace copyright holders and welcomes
correspondence from those they have been unable to contact.

A Library of Congress record exists under LCCN: 75022126

ISBN 13: 978-0-367-23320-4 (hbk)
ISBN 13: 978-0-429-27967-6 (ebk)
ISBN 13: 978-0-367-23327-3 (pbk)

THE VOLUNTEER FORCE

THE VOLUNTEER FORCE

A Social and Political History 1859-1908

HUGH CUNNINGHAM

ARCHON BOOKS HAMDEN CONNECTICUT

Published in the United States of America and Canada
by Archon Books, an imprint of The Shoe String Press
995 Sherman Avenue, Hamden, Connecticut

Library of Congress Cataloging in Publication Data

Cunningham, Hugh.
The volunteer force : a social and political history,
1859-1908.

       Bibliography: p.
       Includes index.
       1. Great Britain.   Army.   Volunteers-History.   I.   Title.

UA661.C86 355.35 75-22126
ISBN 0-208-01569-8

© 1975 Hugh Cunningham

CONTENTS

	Preface	
	Abbreviations	
	Introduction	1
1.	The Formation of the Force	5
2.	The Volunteers and the Working Class, 1860-1870	18
3.	The Composition of the Force	33
4.	An Officer – and a Gentleman?	52
5.	Citizens and Soldiers	68
6.	Patriotism and Recreation	103
7.	The Politics of Reform, 1899-1914	127
	Conclusion	153
Appendix	The Irish and the Volunteers	156
	Bibliography	158
	Index	162

ILLUSTRATIONS

1. Dorchester Volunteers, 1863
2. Scottish Volunteers, Royal Review, 1881
3. Review and Sham Fight at Brighton, Easter Monday 1866
4. Female pressure
5. Patriotic employees
6. 'Who shot the dog?'
7. Volunteer humour
8. The Volunteer as hero: Lord Ranelagh
9. Volunteer Festival at Grimston Park, 1864

TABLES AND FIGURES

Chapter III
Table 1 Occupations of Rank and File Volunteers, 1904
Table 2 Occupations of 23rd Middlesex Volunteers, 1887
Table 3 Occupations of the Galloway Rifles, 1897
Table 4 Distribution of Lincoln and 36th Middlesex Volunteers
    by occupation categories
Table 5 Volunteers joining the Regular Army, Militia, or Special
    Reserve
Table 6 Distribution of Lincoln and 36th Middlesex Volunteers by age
    at enrolment
Table 7 Distribution of Lincoln and 36th Middlesex Volunteers by
    length of service
Table 8 The ages and length of service of Volunteers, 1895-1913
Table 9 Regional distribution of Volunteers as a percentage of the
    male population aged 15-49
Table 10 Volunteers and density of population, Scotland 1881
Table 11 Volunteers and density of population, England 1881

Chapter IV
Table 1 Occupations of London Volunteer Officers, 1860-72
Table 2 Previous Service of London Volunteer Officers, 1860-72
Table 3 Occupations of Volunteer Officers, 1904

Chapter VI
Figure 1 Number of Efficient and Enrolled Volunteers, 1860-1913

PREFACE

When I first became interested in the Volunteer Force some six years ago, I had the heady feeling that I had struck some rich vein of Victorian life, totally and unjustifiably neglected by the experts. It remains true that the Volunteers scarcely feature in general accounts of nineteenth-century Britain. Yet the more I worked, the more I discovered that other historians had an interest in and often a fund of knowledge about the Volunteers; and moreover were willing to share that knowledge. I have benefited from discussions and correspondence with the authors of two theses on the Volunteers which have been in progress while I have been writing: I.F.W. Beckett of King's College, London, and Mrs Patricia Morton of Ontario. Other scholars have helped me on particular points, especially Michael Allison, Alan Armstrong, Brian Bond, Gerald Flint-Shipman, Robbie Gray, Brian Harrison, Patrick Joyce, Richard Price, Raphael Samuel, and John Springhall. Ian Shiell and H.P. Dawton have kindly shared with me their reminiscences of the Force, John Pell drew the graph, and John Bevan and Eileen Mitchelhill have instructed and helped me in some elementary statistics. None of these, least of all the latter, bears any responsibility for the final outcome. Nor indeed does my wife, Diane, despite the considerable help she has given me both in the collection of archival material and in bringing to bear on the text the critical mind of a sociologist. She has also put up with my habit of disappearing into archives when supposedly on holiday. To all these my thanks.

Photocopies of material from the Royal Archives were made available by gracious permission of Her Majesty the Queen. I am grateful, too, to the many Librarians and Archivists who have made my life easier, and to the owners of private papers who have allowed me access to and given me permission to quote material in their possession, in particular W.F. Deedes Esq., Lord Esher, the Earl of Pembroke, and the Earl of Wharncliffe.

I am indebted to the Faculty of Humanities at the University of Kent which has met part of my research and travel costs.

The sources of the illustrations are: Plate 1, Military Museum, Dorchester; Plate 2, *Illustrated London News*, 27 August 1881; Plate 3, *Illustrated London News*, 14 April 1866; Plate 4, *Punch*, 28 May 1859; Plate 5, A. Larking, *History of the 4th VB East Surrey Regiment* (London, 1912), p.17; Plate 6, *Punch*, 28 April 1860; Plate 7 [J.L. Roget], *A Volunteer's Scrap-Book* (London, 1860), p.1; Plate 8, *Graphic*, 8 July 1899; Plate 9, *Illustrated London News*, 6 August 1864.

ABBREVIATIONS

BM – British Museum.

CAB – Cabinet.

Committee (1878-9) – Reports, Minutes of Evidence and Appendix of the Committee appointed by the Secretary of State for War to enquire into the Financial State and Internal Organization of the Volunteer Force in Great Britain, PP 1878-9 (C. 2235-I), XV.

HO – Home Office.

PP – Parliamentary Papers.

PRO – Public Record Office.

RC (1862) – Report and Appendix of the Commissioners appointed to inquire into the condition of the Volunteer Force in Great Britain, PP 1862 (5067), XXVII.

RC (1904) – Report, Minutes of Evidence and Appendices of the Royal Commission on the Militia and Volunteers, PP 1904 (Cd. 2061-4), XXX-XXXI.

SC (1894) – Report and Evidence of the Select Committee on Volunteer Acts, PP 1894 (224), XV.

SUSM – Scottish United Services Museum.

VSG – Volunteer Service Gazette.

WO – War Office.

INTRODUCTION

On 23 June 1860 21,000 members of the newly-created Volunteer Force, were present in Hyde Park to be reviewed by the Queen. 'It was enough', wrote the Earl of Malmesbury, 'to make an Englishman proud of his country to see this wonderful demonstration of patriotism and loyalty.'[1] Each man was there, as the *Annual Register* described it, 'at his own free will, and clothed and trained at his own expense.' The Volunteers assembled in Hyde Park without difficulty — 'The whole operation — one requiring the keenest exercise of one of the rarest military faculties — was performed with unerring precision and perfect ease, by the intelligent zeal of the men and the clear heads of the officers.' The Queen arrived at four o'clock and 'for an hour and a half corps after corps stepped before their Sovereign, offering the spontaneous devotion of noble and patriotic hearts.' It had been, as the *Annual Register* remarked, a scene 'worthy of note in a nation's history.' London had arranged 'a "general holiday" ' for this 'national spectacle', and 'to a late hour the streets were thronged with multitudes parading under the banners that floated from the houses.'

Such a scene a year before would have been unimaginable. Although authorised in May 1859, the Volunteers had not rated a mention in the *Annual Register's* 'Chronicle' for 1859 because they had not in that year become a 'great fact'. In 1860, however, 'the self-planted institution outgrew first the conception of the Government, and then the anticipations of its own most ardent advocates', so that by the end of the summer there were well over one hundred thousand Volunteers.[2]

That the Victorians should take so readily to arms is in itself perhaps cause for surprise. The briefest study of the Force, however, is enough to show that they did so for social as well as military reasons. The Volunteer Force was the military expression of the spirit of self-help, Victorian capitalism in arms in the year of the Cobden-Chevalier Treaty. Captains of industry became captains of companies, and drilled their employees in evenings and weekends in the complex steps of a mid-nineteenth-century army. To contemporaries it was a wonderful testimony to the improvement of class relationships since the days of Chartism, and to the maintenance of the physique of the people in an urban civilisation. The establishment of the Force offered opportunities without comparison: it would not only end the danger of invasion by striking respect if not terror into the hearts of foreigners; it would also impart unto the youth of the nation obedience, promptitude and self-respect, and provide a safe and salutary occupation for the increasing hours of leisure at men's disposal. Drunkenness, prostitution, gambling

1

and loitering would wane as Volunteering increased.

These hopes were at their zenith in the first decade of the Force's existence. During those ten years the Force had undergone a remarkable transformation. Originally envisaged as a military institution for the middle class, it had become largely working-class. Middle-class enrolment fell away as the working class joined the ranks. Although the Government gave financial assistance from 1863, there was no material incentive for anyone to join; the Volunteer was almost always out of pocket. Moreover as government financial aid increased, so also did government insistence on a greater approximation to Regular Army notions of military life. The club-like atmosphere of the early days, when officers were elected, was replaced by a stricter military discipline, and a closer identification with the Regular Army.

The Volunteer Force in the 1870s settled down as an accepted institution, some 200,000 in strength, and attracting into its ranks about one man in twelve. The majority joined the Infantry, but there was also a substantial Artillery section, and less numerous Light Horse and Mounted Rifles, Engineers, and Submarine Mining Engineers. The various branches, however, never cohered into an Army. Military historians can be forgiven for finding little of interest in such a Force for until 1914 its military achievements were minimal.* Some Volunteers saw service in the Boer War, and seem to have performed creditably the not too exacting duties assigned to them. But this apart there were no battle honours.

Critics were doubtful whether the Volunteers, with their lack of discipline and training, could play any useful role in preventing or defeating the invasion which the Victorians so feared. Home defence was the *raison d'être* of the Force, but the Volunteers never successfully laid to rest the invasion bogey. Conscription won an increasing number of advocates as the answer to the nation's military needs. So great however was the entrenched power of the Volunteer officers in Parliament and in society that they were able to withstand not only the demand for conscription but also the reform of their own body. In the twentieth century Haldane was able to present his reforms as a triumph, but in fact he was foiled in his attempt to convert the Volunteer Force into a reserve for the Expeditionary Force. Volunteers became Territorials, but continued to see their role as that of home defence.

The political strength of the Volunteer Force is one theme explored in this book. The Volunteers were both citizens and soldiers. As citizens

* The Volunteer Force ceased to exist on 1 April 1908. It was replaced by the very similar Territorial Force. In this history of the Volunteers I have occasionally taken evidence from the period 1908-14, and I have sketched in the history of the Territorial Force up to the outbreak of war in 1914.

2

many of them were prominent in their own right: Matthew Arnold, Thomas Hughes, George Cruikshank, Lord Leighton, J.E. Millais, Sir Henry Campbell-Bannerman, R.A. Cross, W.E. Forster, David Lloyd George, all served in the Force. Local leaders patronised or joined: John Laird in Birkenhead, Edward Akroyd in Halifax, T.D. Acland in Devon. No less than ninety Members of Parliament held commissions in the Volunteer Force in 1868.[3] Such a force could not but have political power, a power greater in many ways than that of the militarily much more significant Regular Army. Paradoxically, however, as the political role of the Force increased its social status declined. This was reflected in the chronic shortage of officers of the right quality. There could be no certainty that a Volunteer officer would be a gentleman.

For the social historian, however, the most intriguing feature of the Force is its working-class membership. What induced working-class men to join a Force which almost always entailed some financial outlay? The numbers joining were not insignificant. If patriotism was the motive for enrolment, then many preconceptions about Victorian society are shaken. To volunteer required commitment of time, effort and money; it was a more considered act than the celebration in the street of national victory or royal jubilee. It is therefore a chief aim of this book to explore the motives for and implications of enrolment, by looking both at the internal history of the Force and its relationship with the rest of society. Patriotism is but one among many factors going into the make-up of the Force. On the one side the recreation which the Force offered, and the desire for upward social mobility and respectability must be considered; and on the other the pressure which could be exerted by an officer who was also an employer.

The sources for the study of the Force are abundant. Much can be gleaned from the Reports and Evidence of the four major official inquiries into the progress of the Force, the Royal Commission of 1862, the Committee appointed by the Secretary of State for War in 1878, the Select Committee on Volunteer Acts of 1894, and the Royal Commission on the Militia and Volunteers reporting in 1904. Volunteer newspapers, headed by the semi-official mouthpiece of the Force, the *Volunteer Service Gazette*, are another essential source. But perhaps most valuable of all are the numerous histories of local corps. Some of them are factual guides with full information on the winners of the shooting competition in 1874 or the names of the commissioned officers in 1888, but others have more body to them, and are essential sources, the more so because of the paucity of central government records. Like other students who have worked on War Office records in recent years, I have found that the apparently indiscriminate process of 'weeding' has led to the destruction of some of the potentially most useful records. No one could construct a history of the Volunteer Force from the patchy papers that remain in the Public Record Office. This essentially local Force must be studied in the localities where the source material is plentiful. Scarcely a county archive, local history collection or military museum is without some material on the Volunteers, and I am uneasily aware that I have done no more than sample it. The value of much of this material is dependent on a full knowledge of local personalities and powers, and it is hoped that this book may at least provide a framework within which local historians can place their own corps.

Just as the *Annual Register* pronounced the Force to be a 'great fact' by 1860, so the journalist, G.A. Sala, felt it would 'be a great fact for a future Macaulay to chronicle, that the country, including men of every class and grade, were determined that the freedom and independence of these realms should be as unassailable as the island itself is deep and immoveable in its home of waters.'[4] This book has been written, not with any pretence to being a Macaulay, rather from the belief that the Volunteers were a 'great fact' in the second half of the nineteenth and early twentieth centuries. For too long social historians have neglected the rich sources to be found in military records. This study of the most civilian section of the armed forces touches on, and hopefully contributes to, the history of patriotism, of class and status relationships, of community consciousness both urban and rural, and of leisure. It comments, too, on the status and function of the armed forces in British society.

It would be a mistake, however, and an injustice to the Volunteers, to take them too seriously. Their history before 1914 belongs to comedy not tragedy. They provided their contemporaries with the occasion for flights of solemn rhetoric about patriotism and duty, but at the same time they were a rich target for the cartoonist's pencil and the urchin's mirth. It was the saving grace of the Volunteers, and has added considerably to the pleasure of studying them, that they were not unaware of the comedy of their own situation. One can laugh with them as well as at them.

Notes

1. The Earl of Malmesbury, *Memoirs of an Ex-Minister,* new ed. (London, 1885), p.524.
2. *Annual Register,* 'Chronicle', 1860, pp. 87-91, 27-9.
3. *VSG,* 2 Jan. 1869.
4. G.A. Sala, *A Narrative of the Grand Volunteer Review in Hyde Park, Saturday June 23, 1860,* 2nd ed., revised and enlarged (London, n.d. [1860]), p.34.

1 THE FORMATION OF THE FORCE

Victorian Britain was afflicted by a chronic anxiety about invasion. The fear that the British coastline lay open to a French descent was rarely absent from the minds of responsible statesmen, and it flourished like a weed in the imagination of a handful of publicists. The creation of a Volunteer Force was one response, initially by no means the most favoured one, to this anxiety about defence. This chapter describes the circumstances in which the Government came to accept offers of service from prospective Volunteers. Those circumstances arose partly from the defencelessness of the country, and were in part domestic, stemming from a belief that by 1859 it was safe to arm Volunteers.

The panics about defence began some fifteen years before the formation of the Volunteer Force was authorised. Their rational origin lay in technological advance, in the first instance the application of steam-power to ships. It was believed that steam would enable the French to throw up to 30,000 men across the Channel in a single night, and would allow the Navy no time to organise itself in opposition. Thus there came about renewed interest in fortifications and the organisation of an army of defence. Since over half the Regular Army was stationed overseas and likely to remain there, it was apparent that any substantial army of home defence must be recruited on a part-time or unpaid basis.

The anxiety about invasion first became of political importance in 1844 after the publication of a pamphlet by the Prince de Joinville, son of Louis Philippe, in which was outlined the possibility of a French steam navy inflicting heavy losses on British coasts. The publicity given to this pamphlet was followed quickly by a crisis in Franco-British relations in which the danger areas were Tahiti and Morocco. War was mentioned openly as a possibility, and from that time onwards the Prime Minister, Peel, was constantly concerned about the defences of the country and was prepared to spend money on them. He was under pressure on the one hand from the Foreign Secretary, Aberdeen, for being alarmist, and on the other from Wellington for doing too little. In August 1845 Wellington pronounced in favour of a revived Militia of 150,000 men, and only the Corn Law crisis prevented the Government from the introduction of a Militia Bill.[1]

This idea of reviving the Militia was the first resort of military thinkers as concern about the state of the defences continued. 'The Constitutional Force', as it proudly called itself, had been in a state of decay since the end of the Napoleonic Wars. The schemes for its revival envisaged it as a part-time paid force, with the ballot in reserve if the

5

numbers were not forthcoming voluntarily. It would be an army for home defence rooted in the counties, with the gentry raising and officering their dependents. Both in the section of society from which it recruited and in the fact that it was paid, it offered a contrast and indeed an alternative to any proposed Volunteer Force.

Palmerston, on his return to the Foreign Office in July 1846, more than shared the anxiety of the outgoing Government about the defences, and he too, in 1847, was pressing his Cabinet colleagues to revive the Militia. The Cabinet was alive to the necessity of doing something about defence, but considered the revival of the Militia too controversial.[2] That they had some reason for their belief was shown the following year, when the first of Cobden's 'Three Panics' was sparked off by the publication in January 1848 of Wellington's famous letter to Major-General Sir John Burgoyne on the defenceless state of the country. The country's alarm, as Cobden ironically noted, subsided rapidly when the Government proposed an increase in the income tax in order to pay for a reorganisation of the Militia.[3]

There followed a period of reduced estimates on both sides of the Channel, and it was not until Louis Napoleon's coup of 2 December 1851 that the invasion scare revived. 'From that day to the meeting of Parliament on the 3rd February,' wrote Cobden, 'a large portion of the metropolitan journals teemed with letters and articles of the most exciting character,' attacking Louis Napoleon and anticipating an invasion. In Parliament this abuse of Louis Napoleon and the attention drawn to the poor state of the defences was deplored; nevertheless the Government took steps both to prepare the Fleet for any aggressive moves by the French, and once again to introduce a Militia Bill, a Bill which, as is well known, met its fate in Palmerston's 'tit-for-tat' with Lord John Russell.[4] The incoming Conservative Government pressed ahead with a new Militia Bill which met with success and empowered the Government to raise a force of 80,000 men, or 120,000 in case of great emergency. The force would be paid, and would have twenty-one days' training a year. With the passage of the Militia Act the scare seemed over, but it revived again in the autumn with reports of hostility towards England from Paris, and only received its final quietus with the outbreak of the Crimean War.

One important outcome of the first two panics, therefore, was the final achievement of the long-mooted revival of the Militia. But that revival failed to lay to rest fears about the nation's defences. In 1857, when British resources were stretched in the quelling of the Indian Mutiny, there were those who feared that other nations would take advantage of the weak state in which Britain itself was left. And already at that time, the third of Cobden's 'Three Panics' was ready to break to the surface. Whereas in the earlier panics the actual danger

6

of a French invasion might reasonably have appeared to contemporaries, as it does to historians, to be slight, there were real grounds for alarm in the late 1850s. Once again it was technological advance that was at the root of it. During the Crimean War French ironclad floating batteries had proved themselves efficient against Russian shells, and it at once appeared that an ironclad fleet would hold an advantage against any defence it might meet. After the Crimean War the French pressed ahead with the development of such a fleet; indeed no wooden ship of the line was laid down in France after 1855. Britain was much slower to put her faith in ironclads, and by 1858 there was alarm that the French lead was positively dangerous to the security of the country. Together with the breech-loading rifled cannon, the ironclad gave a significant advantage to the attack.[5]

In these circumstances any signs of hostility from the French were likely to turn well-founded alarm into panic, and from early 1858 there was a succession of such signs. There was the French development of the port of Cherbourg, for which the British could see no other use than as a port of embarkation for an attack on Britain. There was the explosive French reaction to the fact that the bomb thrown by Orsini at Napoleon III had been made in England. There was the constant fear that France was seeking an alliance with her Crimean enemy Russia, an alliance which appeared formidable to the British. And finally, alongside the prevalent anti-Austrian feeling, there was suspicion of Napoleon's motives in his intervention in Italy, suspicion which seemed to receive its justification in 1860 with the annexation of Savoy and Nice.

The panic existed both in official circles and amongst sections of the public. It was initially focused on the inadequacies of the Navy, and these were openly stated by the First Lord of the Admiralty, Sir John Pakington, when he asked for increased supplies in February 1859.[6] But, as always, if the Navy was felt to be weak, it was not only the Navy which must be strengthened. Other means of defence must be looked to. The Government, while putting its main hope in the new naval building programme, began to look also to fortifications. Plans for increased fortifications had long been discussed by experts, but it was only in the crisis circumstances of 1859-60 that there could be secured authorisation and finance for their implementation.[7]

It was not so much the Government as a handful of interested enthusiasts who saw safety in yet a third remedy, the creation of Volunteer Rifle Corps. There was of course historical precedent for government authorisation of Volunteer Corps. At times of crisis in the eighteenth century, and particularly in the French Revolutionary and Napoleonic Wars, the Government had been glad to accept offers of service from Volunteers. To volunteer then, however, was seen partly as a means of escaping the Militia ballot, and was therefore less than a free and unimpeded act of patriotism. Towards the end of the Napoleonic Wars, indeed, the Government favoured the Militia as against the Volunteers, and the latter had been considerably reduced in numbers by the time they were disbanded in 1814. Moreover, their function while they did exist was not simply, as might be supposed, to defend their country against foreign invasion; it was also to preserve law and order in Britain.[8]

It is hardly surprising that some of the early nineteenth-century Volunteers were less than willing to forget their past soldiering at the fiat of the Government in 1814. In Greenock surviving Volunteers met triennially until 1841. In London the Duke of Cumberland's Sharpshooters, formed in 1803, seem to have continued to meet after 1814 as a rifle club, while retaining their old regimental name, and wearing uniform.[9] It is equally not surprising that at times of crisis in the first half of the nineteenth century the Government received offers of service from Volunteers. But it is notable that until the 1850s these were offers to preserve law and order. This was the purpose of the Leeds Volunteers of 1820, and of other Armed Associations in that year.[10] And that the distinction between an Armed Association and a Volunteer Corps was a blurred one became apparent in the response to Lord John Russell's circular letter of May 1839 urging the formation of Armed Associations in the face of Chartism. Many who came forward did so in the belief that they were being encouraged by the Government to form new companies of Volunteers or troops of Yeomanry, and the Home Secretary found himself obliged to refuse sanction to the formation at Cockermouth of 'The Derwentside Volunteer or Rifle Corps', and similarly to reject the offer of the principal tradesmen of Welshpool to form a Volunteer Rifle Corps.[11]

There are isolated examples of officially recognised Volunteer Corps at this time – a Corps of Volunteer Infantry at Salisbury disbanded in 1840, another at Uxbridge disbanded in 1842[12] – but in general the Government preferred to rely for the maintenance of law and order on an improving police, the Regular Army, the Yeomanry, and special constables. When the year of Chartist revival, 1848, produced another spate of offers to form Volunteer Corps, the reply from the Home Secretary, Sir George Grey, was that he did 'not think it would be expedient that armed Volunteer Corps should be formed in large cities or towns for the sole purpose of repressing internal disturbance.'[13]

Four years later there was a much more favourable government response to the offers of service, and in this case the offers included the defence of the country as well as the maintenance of law and order. In January and February 1852 Sir George Grey acknowledged fifteen offers to form Volunteer Corps by stating that the Government was 'prepared in certain cases to advise Her Majesty to accept the services of Volunteer Rifle Corps provided that the proposed formation of such corps is recommended by the Lord Lieutenant of the County', and that members provide their own equipment. He even sanctioned the formation of Corps at Cheltenham and Hull, but neither of these seems to have come into being.[14]

The change of government brought a change of policy. Spencer Walpole, the new Home Secretary, refused offers of service, stating that the Government would not consider offers of service from Volunteers until it had determined what the future of the Militia should be. The passing of the Militia Act meant the refusal of offers from Volunteers. This policy of refusal was continued during 1853-4 when twenty-two offers to form Volunteer Corps were received.[15] It may well be that General Sir William Napier was right when, in April 1852, he claimed that 'The Government has rejected the volunteers evidently from political feeling, fearing they would demand an extension of reform.' Socially and politically, the Militia, as 'a link between the gentry and the labouring classes', seemed safer.[16]

Two Volunteer Corps, however, did come into being in these years. The first was the Exeter and South Devon Corps whose services were accepted on 26 March 1852 as Walpole considered that Sir George Grey had already given an implied acceptance, and 'having regard to the particular district within which the Corps is intended to be raised . . .'; the Corps had a continuous existence from that date. Its establishment was raised to two Companies in December 1852, and to three in March 1854. From the beginning of 1853 the number of effectives never dropped below 135. Founded by Dr. J.C. Bucknill, Superintendent of the Exminster Lunatic Asylum, and a man of some distinction in his own profession, the Corps sought without success the support of the aristocracy and country gentry. Lord Churston said that he thought putting arms into the hands of the middle classes a very dangerous proceeding, and the country gentry were slow to come forward to take commissions. Equipment and uniform cost twelve guineas, so there was no question of anyone below the middle classes joining. The corps does not seem to have confined its activities to the defence of the realm, for a county magistrate, writing to *The Times* in 1857, testified

> to the value of our corps in domestic disturbances. Before its formation, during a bread riot, we had to send to Exeter for military in aid of the special constables. On a similar occasion, recently, it was quite sufficient to announce that the Rifles would assemble at the Town-hall on the night on which disturbance was threatened to swear in some members, and all was perfectly tranquil.[17]

The second Corps to come into being at this time, the Victoria Rifle

9

Corps, was likewise concerned with internal security. In 1835 a Royal Victoria Rifle Club had been founded, claiming a shadowy connection with the old Duke of Cumberland's Sharpshooters. In 1850 the officers had been licensed by the Middlesex magistrates, under an Act of 1819, to drill and exercise their members in arms. As early as 1848 the Club had been describing itself as a 'Corps', and by the Laws and Regulations of 1850 members engaged 'especially to promptly appear under arms whenever the Corps may be called upon for the purposes of assisting the civil power in maintaining tranquillity or suppressing riot.' Like others, the Royal Victoria Rifles sought to be accepted as a Rifle Corps by the Home Office in February 1852, at which time there were about fifty active members, but they were subject to the succeeding Conservative Government's refusal. Angry at this, and considering themselves a cut above other applicants, they continued their pressure on the Government, and in July 1853 were enrolled as a Volunteer Corps under 44 Geo 3, Cap. 54, with an establishment of 300 men, and with the Duke of Wellington as Lieutenant-Colonel. With at least four peers among its members, the Victoria Rifles seem to have been a more exclusive body that the Exeter and South Devon Rifles.[18]

These were the only two Rifle Volunteer Corps whose services were accepted by the Government in the years leading up to 1859. But in the 1850s there existed a number of clubs, some of them with paramilitary features, which were laying the groundwork for the 1859 Force. There were rifle clubs, for example in Edinburgh, Cheltenham, and Hastings, and drill clubs in Liverpool, Bury and Surrey.[19] It was in these years, too, that the advocates of Volunteers as a force for home defence began to find an audience. A.B. Richards, the first editor of the *Daily Telegraph*, promulgated the cause extensively in newspapers in the 1850s. Hans Busk, who had campaigned for a Volunteer Force ever since his undergraduate days in Cambridge, now began to find a market for his books and pamphlets; he seems to have had a considerable impact on the Victoria Rifles when he joined them in 1858, and between 1858 and 1861 travelled the country addressing 147 meetings on the idea of Volunteering. In Liverpool Nathaniel Bousfield, the originator of the drill club, was another persistent advocate of a Volunteer Force. These and others were later to have thrust upon them or to claim the title of 'Father of the Volunteers', a matter of considerable dispute in subsequent years.[20]

Perhaps more important than any of these claimants was the advocacy of *The Times*. In 1857 it supported those who were urging that Volunteers be sent to India, a proposal which was exceedingly distasteful to authority: 'They would be an armed and a very dangerous rabble,' wrote the Duke of Cambridge; 'The danger would be greater to their friends than their foes,' replied Panmure, Secretary of State for War.

The Times, however, saw beyond the immediate danger in India to the possibility of establishing a permanent Volunteer Force at home, and the reasons it gave for this proposal were social, not military. English youth, it believed, was peculiarly pugnacious and athletic; 'Compare with them the students of a French Lycée, strolling two and two along the Quartier Latin, and playing dominoes over their lemonade; or the pupils of a German professor, who accompany their instructor during the holydays in a botanical ramble.' Yet this national advantage was squandered, for there was no military outlet for this youthful energy, the Regular Army being 'a profession, if not a close corporation'. The security of the realm demanded that England should make use 'of all classes and conditions of its people . . . We must popularize the army and martialize the population. The gulf must be narrowed between the soldier and the citizen.'[21]

In its advocacy of a Volunteer Force *The Times* was suggesting more than a mere military reform. In the aftermath of the aristocratic mismanagement of the Crimean War it was voicing the aspirations of those members of the professional and business middle class who believed that they had a military role to play, and who were critical of the social isolation of the Regular Army and Militia, both of them officered by the aristocracy and its offshoots and manned by the lower working class. To such men the creation of a Volunteer Force seemed to be not only a cheap and efficient answer to the problem of national defence, but also a means of harnessing the energy of middle-class youth in a desirable and patriotic direction, and of making control of the Army less of an aristocratic monopoly.

It would be quite wrong, however, to suggest that the weight of public opinion in 1859 was such that the Government had no option but to authorise the establishment of the Force. It was, as has been seen, a time of considerable concern about the national defences, and of course the advocates of a Volunteer Force took the opportunity to present their case. But there was no sign of great public enthusiasm for the Force at this stage. St. Martin's Hall, Long Acre, was less than one-third full for a public meeting on the defences on 17 April 1859; and although it was A.B. Richards who organised the meeting, and the speakers included a number of prominent advocates of a Volunteer Force, it seems from the report of the meeting that there was as much stress on the necessity of maintaining a Channel fleet as on the potential use of a Volunteer Force. And this, as far as can be seen, was the only public meeting on the matter.[22]

The Times, it is true, gave strong support to the establishment of a Volunteer Force. On 19 April, after deploring the periodic panics, it declared that 'there can only be one true defence of a nation like ours; – a large and permanent Volunteer Force, supported by the spirit and

patriotism of our young men, and gradually indoctrinating the country
with military knowledge.' On 28 April a leading article strongly
criticised 'the old fogies of the Horse Guards' whose attitudes were
'likely to prevent all attempts at creating a cheap and efficient force
for service in these islands, unless the popular voice be loudly heard.' It
was *The Times*, too, which published Tennyson's famous poem,
'Riflemen Form', on 9 May.

It is not clear what effect such pressure as there was had on the
Government. Sharing with the country a concern about the defences, it
is possible it had simply concluded that no harm, and possibly some
good, might come from authorising the establishment of Volunteer
Corps when suitable offers were made. The terms under which Volunteer
Corps were authorised made it seem clear that the Government was
incurring neither social risk nor any substantial financial obligation. The
two indeed were connected for if a Volunteer had to pay for his own
arms and equipment it was inevitable that he should be a man of some
financial and therefore social standing. It was to be a Force for the
middle class and those above them, and social conditions and attitudes
had changed sufficiently since 1848 for there to be little fear in
government circles that the arms of the middle class would be turned
against the working class.[23]

Government authorisation for the Force was contained in a circular
from the Secretary of State for War, General Peel, to Lords Lieutenant
on 12 May 1859. The Force was to be raised under the provisions of
the Act of 1804 which had consolidated previous Acts relating to the
Volunteers. The circular set forth some of the conditions of the Act:
the Force was 'liable to be called out in case of actual invasion or
appearance of an enemy in force on the coast or in case of a rebellion
arising out of either of these emergencies'; 'members who did twenty-
four days' drill a year could be returned as effective; except when on
actual military service a member could quit a corps on giving fourteen
days' notice; all property of a corps 'is legally vested in the Commanding
Officer and subscriptions and fines under the rules and regulations are
recoverable by him before a magistrate.' These conditions were to be
modified but never substantially changed until 1908. They made it clear
that the Force was to be used for defence, not riot control. By giving
a member the right to quit on giving fourteen days' notice, they made
the maintenance of military discipline exceedingly difficult. And by
granting financial responsibility to the Commanding Officer they made
wealth a premium for high rank and the maintenance of financial
stability a prime concern for any corps. In further explanation of the
Act Peel stated that corps should be recommended by the Lord
Lieutenant of the county, and that members should 'undertake to
provide their own arms and equipments and to defray all expenses

attending the corps except in the event of its being assembled for actual service.' It was to the Lord Lieutenant, too, that Peel looked 'for the nomination of proper persons to be appointed officers subject to the Queen's approval.'[24] In thus giving to the Lord Lieutenant control over the formation of a corps and the appointment of its officers the Government seemed to be ensuring that the Force would remain socially and politically safe.

This circular must have mystified anyone who gave careful consideration to it. Nothing was said about the military function of the Force, its place in the general scheme of defence, or its relation to the Regular Army, Militia or Yeomanry. The kind of training which was expected of it was not stated. Everything points to the conclusion that the War Office acted without much forethought, and in reproducing the Act of 1804 gave little consideration to the military and social changes of the past fifty years. As General Peel stated later, the circular 'did not arise from any fear of invasion on their part, but solely in consequence of the numerous and urgent applications which were being made to them for permission to form rifle corps, on the express understanding that they were to be of no expense to the country.'[25]

It was not the War Office, but no less a figure than the Prince Consort, who sought to explain further the Government's intentions; a second circular issued from the War Office on 25 May was in fact his work.[26] Both its military and social assumptions were soon to be outdated, but it is an excellent indication of early thinking about the function of the Volunteers. Although stating as a first essential that any body of Volunteers should be amenable to military discipline, it went on to say that 'the conditions of service should be such as . . . to induce those classes to come forward for service as Volunteers who do not, under our present system, enter either into the Regular Army or the Militia.' To this end, 'the system of drill and instruction . . . should not be such as to render the service unnecessarily irksome.' Indeed the main emphasis should be not on drill, but on rifle firing, in small units 'composed of individuals having a knowledge of and thorough dependence upon each other personally.' Militarily the Volunteers were to act

> as an auxiliary to the Regular Army and Militia . . . The nature of our country, with its numerous inclosures and other impediments to the operations of troops in line, gives peculiar importance to the service of Volunteer Riflemen, in which bodies each man deriving confidence from his own skill in the use of his arm and from his reliance on the support of his comrades — men whom he has known, and with whom he has lived from his youth up — intimately acquainted, besides, with the country in which he would be called upon to act, would hang with the most

13

telling effect upon the flanks and communications of a hostile army.

The Artillery Volunteers were to have a quite different function, to man the batteries in coastal towns; they should be organised in even smaller bodies, 'ten or twelve men, all neighbours intimately acquainted with each other, in the charge and working of a particular gun mounted, so to speak, at their very door.'[27]

The Government, in issuing this circular, gave its blessing to the Prince Consort's vision of the Force as composed of small, independent, middle-class units, auxiliary to the Regular Army and Militia, and relying for any military achievements not on drill and discipline so much as skill in the use of rifle or artillery, knowledge of the countryside, and trust in each other. It is not reading too much into the circular to say that it envisaged the Volunteers emanating from a society which was essentially rural or small-town, and in which there was little geographical mobility. In fact the Volunteers were to become increasingly urban, working-class, subject to military discipline, and organised in large units.

In the following month the Conservative Government was toppled from power, and Sidney Herbert succeeded Peel at the War Office. Although fully alive to the danger posed by the French, he was less than enthusiastic about the Volunteers, primarily because it was one of his chief aims to reform the Militia as an army of home defence. It will be remembered that under the 1852 Act the Militia was envisaged as such an army, with its members doing twenty-one days' continuous training each year. Under the pressure of the Crimean War it had undergone two radical transformations. It had been embodied at a time when there was no danger of invasion of the United Kingdom, and it had begun to function not as an independent and self-sufficient force but as a recruit supplier to the Regular Army. Over 70,000 men passed from the Militia to the Line. It was Herbert's aim to restore the Militia to its original function. He failed in this, partly because his programme of disembodiment was halted in the spring of 1860 by renewed fears of a French invasion, partly because the recruitment of Militiamen into the Regular Army could not be stopped, and partly because the Volunteers increasingly appeared to be performing the same function as a Militia for home defence. Herbert, with some justice, believed that a Militia under military discipline and a five-year term of service was a more reliable force than the Volunteers, and he viewed with alarm the process whereby the Volunteers came to look more and more to government to meet their financial needs. 'My view', he wrote, '. . . is to keep up a fair standing Army, with a disembodied Militia behind it, and an auxiliary force of Volunteers, composed of men who will do the work *for the liking of it, and maintain themselves.* But the two first, one with a ten year and the other with a five year engagement, are the really dependable force.'[28]

It was fortunate for the nascent Volunteer Force that Herbert delegated the detailed work of organising it to his Under Secretary of State, Earl de Grey, who had considerable sympathy for the new force. As Under Secretary of State, but for a brief break, until April 1863, and Secretary of State from then until February 1866, he was to guide the Volunteers to the position of being an accepted and financially supported part of the military system.

Just as it has been impossible to say that there was any great pressure on the Government to form the Force, so it is hard to discern any rush to arms when it was authorised. There are unfortunately no reliable figures which would enable one to plot the early progress of the Force. Dudley Baxter, the eminent statistician, attempted to assess the numbers in January 1860, but his precise and accurate-looking total of 73,794 was arrived at only after a considerable amount of guesswork. The *Volunteer Service Gazette*, in commenting on Baxter's figures, thought that he had considerably underestimated, and that the true total was nearer 100,000. The first official figures, for 1 October 1860, give the total of enrolled Volunteers as 119,146.[29] All these figures are liable to a considerable margin of error. What does seem reasonably certain is that the first major spurt to volunteering came not in the summer of 1859, but in the late autumn and early winter of that year; half of Baxter's total enrolled in November and December, when *The Times* in particular was encouraging the Force and when there was renewed alarm as to Napoleon's intentions. The early part of the summer had been disrupted by domestic political uncertainty, and in the latter part the notables whose participation, as will be seen, was necessary to the successful launching of a corps, were absent on holiday. As Lord Elcho said in 1861, 'There was no denying the fact that when the Volunteer movement first began it met with little sympathy from the public and little encouragement from official men.'[30] There was apathy, and occasional opposition. But in the winter of 1859-60 the Volunteer movement spread widely; its rapid growth led to frequent discussion of its significance, and as will be shown in the next chapter that significance was seen to be as much social as military.

Notes

1. C.J. Bartlett, *Great Britain and Sea Power, 1815-53* (Oxford, 1963), pp. 155-74, 241.
2. ibid., pp. 189-90.
3. 'The Three Panics', *The Political Writings of Richard Cobden* (London, 1867), vol. II, pp. 230-4.

4. ibid., pp. 236-42.
5. J.P. Baxter, *The Introduction of the Ironclad Warship* (Cambridge, Mass., 1933), pp. 83-122; A. Temple Patterson, ' "Palmerston's Folly": The Portsdown and Spithead Forts', *The Portsmouth Papers*, No. 3, 1967, pp.3-6.
6. *3 Hansard 152*, cc. 902-913 (25 Feb. 1859).
7. I am indebted for this point to Peter Kent who is currently working on a thesis on fortifications in nineteenth-century Britain at the University of Kent.
8. C. Sebag-Montefiore, *A History of the Volunteer Forces* (London, 1908); J.R. Western, 'The Volunteer Movement as an Anti-Revolutionary Force 1793-1801', *English Historical Review*, vol. LXXI (1956), pp. 603-14.
9. W. Lamont, *Volunteer Memories* (Greenock, 1911), p.9; C.A.C. Keeson, *The History and Records of Queen Victoria's Rifles 1792-1922* (London, 1923), pp. 491-504.
10. E. Hargrave, 'The Leeds Volunteers, 1820', *Publications of the Thoresby Society*, vol. XXIV, pp. 451-68; W. Lamont, op. cit., p.12.
11. F.C. Mather, *Public Order in the Age of the Chartists* (Manchester, 1959), pp. 90-4.
12. HO 51/96-7.
13. HO 51/98.
14. HO 51/99.
15. HO 51/99.
16. H.A. Bruce (ed.), *Life of General Sir William Napier* (London, 1864), vol. II, p. 522; Palmerston, *3 Hansard 140*, c. 1578 (29 Feb. 1856), cited in H.S. Wilson, 'The British Army and Public Opinion from 1854 to the end of 1873' (Oxford Univ. unpublished B.Litt. thesis, 1954), p. 115.
17. HO 51/99; G. Pycroft, *The Origin of the Volunteer Movement of 1852, and History of the First Volunteer Rifle Corps showing by whom it was Raised in the Year 1852* (London, 1881); R. Hunter and I. Macalpine, *Three Hundred Years of Psychiatry* (London, 1963), pp. 1063-4; *The Times*, 26 Sept. 1857.
18. C.A.C. Keeson, op. cit., pp. 504-19.
19. *The Witness* (Edinburgh), 26 Mar. 1853; B. Rose, 'The Volunteers of 1859', *Journal of the Society for Army Historical Research*, vol. 37 (1959), p. 99; L.A. Vidler, *The Story of the Rye Volunteers* (Rye, 1954), p. 9; R.B. Rose, 'Liverpool Volunteers of 1859', *Liverpool Bulletin*, vol. VI (1956), p. 50; T.H. Hayhurst, *A History and Some Records of the Volunteer Movement in Bury, Heywood, Rossendale, and Ramsbottom* (Bury, 1887), p. 111.
20. B.L. Crapster, 'A.B. Richards (1820-76): Journalist in Defence of Britain', *Journal of the Society for Army Historical Research*, vol. 41 (1963), pp. 94-7; F.G., *The True History of the Origin of our Volunteer Army* (1867); *VSG*, 6 Oct. 1860; Sir Duncan MacDougall, *The History of the Volunteer Movement*, 2nd ed. (London, 1861). Cf. Brian Harrison, *Drink and the Victorians* (London, 1971), pp. 90, 120 for similar disputes about the origins of social movements.
21. *The Times*, 22 and 23 Sept. 1857; Sir G. Douglas and Sir G.D. Ramsay (eds.), *The Panmure Papers* (London, 1908), vol. II, pp. 439, 444.
22. *The Times,* 18 Apr. 1859.
23. But see Matthew Arnold to Miss Arnold, 21 Nov. 1859, G.W.E. Russell (ed.), *Letters of Matthew Arnold 1848-88* (London, 1901), vol. I, p. 126; and F.M.L. Thompson, *English Landed Society in the Nineteenth Century* (London, 1963), p. 271. I owe this latter reference to Richard Price.
24. This circular, and other official documents on the Force, are usefully reproduced in R.P. Berry, *A History of the Formation and Development of*

the Volunteer Infantry (London, 1903), pp. 490-1.

25. *3 Hansard 154*, c. 689 (5 July 1859).
26. Sir T. Martin, *The Life of His Royal Highness The Prince Consort*, 7th ed. (London, 1880), vol. IV, p. 437.
27. R.P. Berry, op. cit., pp. 125-8.
28. Lord Stanmore, *Sidney Herbert, Lord Herbert of Lea, a Memoir* (London, 1906), vol. II, pp. 202-93, 386-9.
29. R.D. Baxter, *The Volunteer Movement; its Progress and Wants* (London, 1860), pp. 3-14; *VSG*, 4 Feb. 1860; RC (1904), App. XCII.
30. R.D. Baxter, op. cit., p. 19; *3 Hansard 163*, c. 779 (7 June 1861).

2 THE VOLUNTEERS AND THE WORKING CLASS, 1860-1870

'What we want now,' said Sidney Herbert in 1859, 'is to get the middle classes imbued with an interest in our own means of defence, and I think the Volunteer Corps will be useful in doing that.'[1] His hopes were to be fulfilled for a few years, but within the first decade of the Volunteer Force's existence the middle class was losing interest and dropping out, and the majority of the Force was working-class. This chapter seeks to describe and explain this remarkable transformation. How were Volunteer Corps raised? On what terms did the working class enter? What significance was attached to their entry?

The Government's circular of 12 May 1859 left the raising of Volunteer corps to the initiative of each locality; its only proviso was that the formation of any corps must be recommended by the Lord Lieutenant. The latter, therefore, was in a position to affect the number and social composition of Volunteer corps in his county, but few Lords Lieutenant seem to have been keen to exercise this power. Some seemed to be apathetic, if not hostile, and the early lack of success in Somerset and Bedfordshire was blamed on this. Others took an initiative in recommending places where corps could usefully be formed, or in attempting to recruit through their Deputy Lieutenants. In general, however, Lords Lieutenant seem to have preserved a discreet neutrality. Lord Leigh of Warwickshire was exceptional in his declared willingness 'to shoulder his rifle by the side of a sweep', as was Lord Hardwicke of Cambridgeshire in his refusal to admit the enrolment of the working classes 'because I have always considered they had other duties to perform, and that there was a great difference between men who had property to lose and those who had none, and that if a weapon was given to a man who had no real property, his natural tendency would be to acquire a property which he had not.'[2]

In most instances, the initiative to form a corps came from someone other than the Lord Lieutenant. Occasionally the professions organised themselves in their different corps. Edinburgh must take pride of place here. Within three months there were founded companies of Advocates, Citizens, Writers to the Signet, Solicitors, Accountants, Bankers, Merchants, members of the University and of the Civil Service. In Glasgow the procurators, accountants, bankers and journalists were all separately organised.[3] London had its Inns of Court, Artists, and Civil Service Corps.

All these of course were exclusively middle-class corps. The same probably applies to a second group of corps which were offshoots of

18

existing organisations. In Somerset the first attempt to raise a corps
came from the members of the St. Decumen's Cricket Club in Williton;
a cricket club was also the first scene of activity in Birmingham. In
neighbouring Edgbaston Joseph Chamberlain, Secretary of the Debating
Society, unsuccessfully offered the services of that body to the Lord
Lieutenant. Edinburgh had a freemasons corps, Hereford an Oddfellows
one. Teetotal corps were formed in London (under George Cruikshank)
and in Edinburgh.[4] But examples of corps raised in this manner are
isolated, and the corps themselves rarely maintained their exclusive
character.

The most common way to raise a corps was to call a public meeting.
Normally a signed requisition would be made to the Mayor or Provost,
and the latter would take the chair. These public meetings were largely
set-piece affairs in the sense that their function was to legitimise the
activities of an existing *ad hoc* committee. They were organised by a
committee, and ended by electing the same one to carry out the
formation of the corps. The more local notables who could be
persuaded to sit on the platform the better. Watford, with the Earl of
Verulam, the Lord Lieutenant, in the chair, and the Earl of Clarendon,
Lord Ebury and Lord Rokeby among the speakers was more successful
than most. If aristocracy could not be prevailed upon to attend, the
Mayor, the Member of Parliament, and the Vicar were normally
sufficient. What could not be doubted was that the presence of *some*
local notables was a necessary though not a sufficient condition for
success. In Oldham there was little support for the Volunteers until
'some of the influential men in the district gave in their adhesion to
the movement', and in Scotland as late as 1867 the number of
Volunteers in any area was thought to be proportionate to the amount
of upper-class support.[5]

Some of these public meetings met with apathy. This was
particularly true in the early months of the Force's existence. In
Guildford, Henry Drummond, MP, and Martin Tupper, the poet, were
unable to raise the necessary enthusiasm to launch a local corps, and at
a public meeting in Chester there was no one willing to move or
second a resolution that a corps should be formed.[6]

More interesting than such apathy is the occasional opposition to the
Volunteers which manifested itself at these public meetings. This
opposition came partly from individual Quakers and members of the
Peace Society, moving amendments but never meeting with any kind of
success. It was the opposition which believed the Force to be class-based
which is more significant. It was claimed that the financial conditions
under which corps were established, which made it necessary for each
man to supply his own uniform, effectively excluded the working class
from the corps; and that, this being the case, government authorisation

of the Force was an attempt to divert the people from concern with social and political reform; further, that a class-based Force would inevitably in time come to be used to put down disturbances. These various arguments could be summed up in the cry 'No vote, no rifle.'

It was in the spinning area of Lancashire that this kind of opposition seems to have been particularly strong. In Rochdale in December 1859 at a meeting to form a corps, an amendment to defer the question was passed by 'a considerable majority'. Although part of the reason for this was dissatisfaction with the proposed officers, it was also true, as the *Rochdale Observer* noted, that intelligent working men looked on the movement as 'a Tory device to keep them out of their political rights'. At Oldham in the same month, with the Town Hall overflowing, there was considerable doubt whether the resolution to form a corps received a majority, though the Mayor eventually declared that it had. The proposers of the motion were clearly aware of the opposition with which they had to contend. Declaring it to be 'really and truly a working man's question', the proposer, J.G. Blackburne, argued that if the people did not join the Force the Government would increase the standing army and add to the burdens of the people. This did not prevent the moving of an amendment 'that in the opinion of this meeting, the agitation for volunteer rifle corps to repel an invasion, is uncalled for and useless, and is resorted to as a means of diverting the people from those great reforms of representation and taxation which the condition of the working classes so urgently demands at the present time.' The amendment was eloquently supported from the body of the hall, the theme of each speaker being that only when there was a vote to defend would working men shoulder a rifle in the defence of their country. 'The question that night', said one speaker, 'was the question of Parliamentary Reform, and if they decided by their vote that they would have no rifle-corps they would be a credit to the whole country.'[7]

There was other opposition of this kind to the formation of the Force, particularly in the North of England. In Huddersfield, for example, Joseph Woodhead, later Mayor and Member of Parliament, was in the lead, arguing that the Volunteer Force was a class movement, and that it would divert the attention of the people from domestic reform.[8] But such opposition was isolated and it rarely impeded the organisers in their aims of legitimising their authority, and raising both men and money.

The support of the wealthy was indeed essential, particularly if the working class was to join. Sometimes there was a public fund to which subscriptions were made, but most men of wealth preferred to see how their money was spent and exercise the influence which derived from largess. They began to organise their dependents or employees in corps, and it was generally by this means that working-class men entered the

Force. From the Queen downwards people of wealth raised companies of Volunteers. The Queen equipped her servants both at Osborne and at Windsor; in the latter place the corps was never officially accepted as the Queen thought there was too great risk in the gamekeepers, of whom it was largely composed, being liable to be called away from the preservation of game.[9] There were other personal corps of this kind. At Aske and Upleatham, Lord Zetland's seats in the North Riding, in December 1859, 'the whole of the male members of the household are daily turned out for drill.' The 1st Administrative Battalion in Dorset formed in May 1860 wore its Colonel's family crest as a badge. Similarly at the 1860 Royal Review in Edinburgh many of the Argyll Corps wore their Company Captain's crest on their bonnets and belts. In Kincardineshire an artillery battery consisted entirely of fishermen who were clothed and commanded by their landlord.[10]

Examples could be multiplied; nor were they confined to rural areas. In Lambeth, William Roupell, MP for the constituency, equipped some 250 men and commanded them. In neighbouring Southwark, Marcus Beresford raised and equipped at his own expense the first company of sixty men, and again, as was natural, took the command. In Lincoln, as the Minute Book records, John Swan offered to clothe thirty men 'provided the appointment of officers be left to him. Resolved that the offer be accepted.'[11] But in towns it was more usual for a corps to be raised and equipped, not from the population at large, but from a firm. Wylie and Lochhead in Glasgow claim the initiative for starting such a corps in November 1859. The firm subscribed £80 and bought the cloth for the uniform, the members undertaking to repay over a period of weeks. The officers were elected, but the results can hardly have been a surprise: a Wylie was Captain, a Wylie Lieutenant, and a Lochhead Ensign. If Wylie and Lochhead were in fact the first firm to raise a company from their men, there were many others who followed close on their heels. In West Ham, the manager of the Victoria Dock raised 300 men from the dock employees, Hugh Silver enrolled 200 men from the indiarubber works, and the Chairman of the Eastern Counties Railway promised outfits to railwaymen becoming Volunteers, and raised four companies. In Manchester, Alexander Henry equipped sixty of his employees.[12] All over the country working men were entering the Force in financial and organisational dependence on their employers.

It is rarely clear whether artisans were pressing to be admitted, or the employers were appealing to them to join. Sometimes it appears that the former was the case. In Lanarkshire a new leading partner 'was asked by some of the leading workmen' if he would assist in raising a corps in connection with the Gartness Iron Works, and in Birkenhead it was the men who wanted the corps, and the employers who provided some of the money and all the officers.[13] But wherever the initiative came from it was hard to hide the fact that the working men who joined were dependent on their employers. There are some examples of refusal to accept such charity; in Edinburgh the printers felt that 'if the present movement fail it will be from the way in which it is managed, and from the very old-fashioned notion that if the thing be patronised by the "maister" the men will of course "fall in" '. In Warrington a meeting under the auspices of the Workingmen's Local Improvement Society aiming to get workers to volunteer failed because of the expense of the uniform and a refusal on the part of many to accept a free one. In Monmouthshire the fact that the Rifle Corps at the Tredegar Ironworks was 'entirely independent of the works' was thought worthy of special note, so widespread and justified was the assumption that those working men who joined the Force were in one way or another beholden to their social superiors.[14]

Artisans thus entered the Force in large numbers through these corps raised by their employers. In 1860 they also began to enter those corps which had been formed at public meetings and which were finding difficulty in recruiting if they confined their attention to the middle class. The difficulties of admitting artisans to such corps were numerous, and many of them are illustrated by the well-documented case of the 8th Kent Volunteers at Sydenham. The corps came into being after a public meeting in June 1859, but initially there were very few recruits. In July 1860, when there were only 62 efficients, a sub-committee was set up to strengthen the corps by the admission of the 'Artisan Class'. By the end of the month, according to the Secretary in an appeal for donations, 'upwards of seventy of the most respectable members of this class . . . have already volunteered, and it is fully believed from the earnest manner in which the men have come forward that this movement will conduce to great social and physical benefit, as well as to blend them together with the middle class, and tend to strengthen our National Defences.' Defence, it will be noted, was put last; and it was the matter of blending them together with the middle class which was to prove problematic. It was only after considerable debate that the existing middle-class Volunteers agreed that the artisans should be allowed to join their corps, only indeed after they had changed their constitution to ensure that the middle class remained in the majority and had the dominant voice in the running of the corps. This secured, '53 respectable artisans whose references had been enquired into and found to be satisfactory', were allowed to join, paying for their uniforms by instalments of 6d. a week. This, however, was not the end of difficulties in Sydenham. In January 1861 the middle-class secretary of the artisan sub-committee was writing to his Captain that artisans were abusing their uniforms, 'some two or three

22

even working at the Bench in their Trousers . . .' When told this must
stop, some of the artisans resigned. Even more serious the artisans were
backward in paying their 6d. a week. The artisan sub-committee wished
to bring summonses against what it called 'refractory Artisans'. The
captain hesitated to take such a disciplinary step, and the artisan sub-
committee resigned in disgust at such weakness. Within a few months,
however, it had been decided to bring those artisans who were in
arrears with their payments before the civil courts. In face of this
evidence it is hard to believe that class relationships in Sydenham were
much improved by the existence of the Volunteer corps; if anything,
the opposite.[15]

Although more is known about Sydenham than about most other
corps, it is clear from other evidence that the problems it faced were
common ones. A crucial question was whether or not there should be
separate artisan corps. The official view was clear — there should be no
class corps, by which it was meant that there should be no working-class
corps; no one envisaged disbanding the Inns of Court Corps because they
recruited only from the middle class. In London this problem was
particularly acute because a large number of middle-class corps had
been founded in the early days and were finding difficulty in keeping
up their numbers. The obvious solution was for them to accept artisans
to fill up the ranks as Sydenham had done. But the usual difficulties
arose. In November 1859 Lord Ranelagh had told his South Middlesex
Regiment that 'From the first formation of the corps he had always
recognised them as men of position and education; and, with this
impression, the rules and regulations for the future guidance of the
corps have been drawn more in accordance with the organisation of a
club than the discipline of a regiment.'[16] Could such a structure survive
if artisans were admitted? Many thought not.

Aside from the social difficulty, there was a financial one. The
uniform in the exclusive corps tended to be expensive. Lord Elcho was
particularly concerned about this latter point, and was one of a number
of men who tried to found corps which would be attractive to working
men. Writing to *The Times,* Elcho referred to a letter he had received
from John R. Walmisley, who claimed to be forming a brigade of
artisans and the more respectable of the labouring classes, and solicited
a donation. Elcho declared his opposition to special artisan corps:

> It is not desirable because in this country the different classes of
> society have few opportunities of meeting, and because
> volunteering presents this opportunity, and enables them to meet
> together and unite shoulder to shoulder in defence of their
> common country. All, indeed, who have taken an active part in
> this movement will bear witness to the social good arising from
> it, and it is impossible to over-estimate the many social advantages

to which it may lead. If, however, special artisan corps be established, not only is this great good lost, but positive evil will arise from the strengthening and perpetuating of class distinctions, which none but the political agitator can wish to do. In Elcho's own London Scottish 150 artisans had been admitted paying weekly instalments of 1s. 3d. But as a more general solution Elcho suggested three possible measures: there might be a basic cheap uniform with those who wished having a more expensive second one; artisan companies with a less ornamental dress might be attached to existing companies; or there might be a cheap corps confined to no class or district. It was this latter solution which Elcho most favoured as he was himself going ahead with the formation of a Metropolitan Rifle Brigade with 55s. as the cost of the equipment, each man to pay on the instalment system. Elcho believed, as he put it to Lord Salisbury, who as Lord Lieutenant would have to sanction the corps, that its existence would 'cut the ground from under those who are endeavouring, I believe for political purposes, to get up what are called Artisan Corps — created and supported in a great measure by private subscriptions.' Salisbury, however, was opposed to class corps and refused to sanction the Metropolitan Rifle Brigade.[17]

The real organiser behind the Royal National Rifles, which had provoked Elcho's letter was J.V. Shelley, MP. Shelley rightly pointed out that artisans would be made to feel their inferiority under the first two of Elcho's proposed measures. Anxious to get his own corps accepted, he wrote to Palmerston who seemed to favour it; de Grey at the War Office thought its services ought to be accepted, if only from prudential reasons: 'it is possible that some mischief may arise from a positive refusal on the part of the authorities to allow it to exist at all, as public meetings on the subject are threatened at which the Working Classes may be told that the Volunteer Movement is a class affair from which they are excluded and which is really directed against them.' By March 1861 the services of the corps had been accepted.[18]

One other man was closely involved in the attempts to raise a corps in London which would have particular appeal to the working class. This was A.B. Richards, one of the more prominent claimants to the title of 'Father of the Force', who as Honorary Secretary to the Workmen's Volunteer Brigade strove hard to get workmen admitted. His 'Brigade' had been accepted as the 3rd City of London Rifle Volunteer Corps before the end of 1860.[19]

In London, then, there was much agonising but an eventual establishment of two specifically working-class corps, despite much feeling that such corps were undesirable. The truth was that the middle-class corps could not admit working men in large numbers without radically transforming their nature, and this many were unwilling to do.

Elsewhere there was probably less overt debate about what policy to adopt to artisans. A common practice was for one corps to remain self-supporting, while others admitted artisans, sometimes in exclusively artisan companies, sometimes in mixed ones. In Edinburgh, for example, there were five specifically 'artisan corps'.[20]

It will be as well at this point to document the social composition of the Force in 1862. The 1862 Royal Commission assembled evidence about the social composition of the Force which, while it does not lend itself to presentation in tabular form, leaves little doubt about the overall position. In rural areas roughly half the Volunteers seem to have been artisans. In Northern England the greater part of the corps was composed of artisans, in North-Eastern Scotland nearly half. In Haddington the corps consisted of 26 lawyers', bankers', and merchants' clerks, 94 merchants and tradesmen, 205 mechanics and artisans, and 89 labourers.[21] This kind of composition was probably common throughout the country except for south-east England where the proportion of working men was lower.[22] In towns the first company formed often remained a preserve of the middle class, as in Liverpool and Manchester, but overall the working class again probably formed something like half the total. In Durham most of the corps were composed of 'workpeople', in Oldham 'the great bulk were artisans', in Birkenhead there were four companies of the better classes and five others, mainly working men, labourers, and farm servants, while in London the 19th Middlesex Rifle Volunteers were half artisans, and half clerks, warehousemen, shopmen and the like.[23] But there were other corps where the working class was outnumbered or excluded, for example Westminster where clerks and small shopkeepers formed the backbone of the movement, and the 4th Lancashire Artillery Volunteers which was composed almost entirely of clerks with some fifty mechanics and artisans in the band.[24]

'Mechanics and artisans' were the words most commonly used to describe the working-class Volunteers. In Glasgow they accepted anyone of respectable character, but not 'mere labourers'; in the 19th Middlesex there were skilled engravers, pianoforte makers and other highly paid mechanics but only very few 'mere common labourers'. A Manchester corps had 347 artisans, principally mechanics in the foundries and men of that description, but only 21 labourers.[25] Witnesses were unanimously of the opinion that recruiting for Volunteers in no way interfered with recruiting for the Militia or Regular Army, for the former were of a quite different class from the latter.[26] The working-class Volunteers, therefore, forming over half the Force by 1862, seem to have been predominantly from the upper working class.

The Royal Commission of 1862, from which this evidence concerning the working-class composition of the Force has been taken, was called into being primarily because of the financial problems which were the consequence of working-class enrolment. Initially, as has been seen, one of the Government's major concerns was to limit its financial obligations to the Force, but it was not long before inroads began to be made on the concept of a self-sufficient Force. In a letter to Lords Lieutenant on 13 July 1859 Sidney Herbert, while stressing that 'the very essence of a Volunteer Force consists in their undertaking themselves to bear, without any cost to the public, the whole charges of their training and practice previous to being called out for actual service', authorised the issue of rifles at government expense to 25 per cent of the effectives. This issue was made on certain conditions — the possession of a suitable range, the willingness to submit to periodic inspections, and so on — and was the first of many such increases of government commitment to the Force. From January 1860 the Government was supplying all the rifles, from February it was paying for an adjutant to be attached to a corps, from August 1861 it was paying for a sergeant-instructor.[27]

These increases were in part the outcome of pressure in Parliament. In July 1859 two Conservative MPs raised a short debate to express the 'universal dismay and disappointment' which, they claimed, was felt at the inadequacy of the Government's support for the Volunteers. In July 1860 there was demand from the House of Lords for more government help, especially for rural corps. And in June 1861, Lord Elcho, the most prominent Parliamentary spokesman for the Volunteers in these years, brought to the attention of the Government the results of a questionnaire sent to Commanding Officers which revealed the considerable financial difficulties under which many of them were labouring.[28] It was not, however, until 1862 that the question of the Government paying for the Volunteer's uniforms was seriously raised, and it arose at that time because the first uniforms were by then wearing out, and Commanding Officers had little hope that any substantial proportion of their men would be willing to pay for a new one. There was a prospect, therefore, of a sharp drop in numbers. In response to this the Government set up a Royal Commission in May 1862 'to inquire into the present condition of Our Volunteer Force in Great Britain, and into the probability of its continuance at its existing strength, and to report whether any Measures should be adopted for the purpose of increasing its efficiency as an auxiliary Means of National Defence.' While reporting the condition of the Force to be 'generally speaking, satisfactory', the Commission went on to recommend substantial government aid to meet the cost of uniforms. Any man who attended thirty drills as a recruit and nine drills each year in subsequent years, and went through a course of musketry instruction, should earn a capitation grant of twenty shillings for his corps. If he fired a defined amount of ball cartridge he should receive an additional ten shillings. The Commission stressed the need for continued subscriptions from the public, but it was in effect calling upon the Government to meet the major costs of the Volunteer Force, costs which its members, because of their social class, were unable to meet themselves. The Government accepted the Royal Commission's Report and an Act giving effect to its recommendations was passed in 1863. Subsequently, although Volunteer Corps were often in financial difficulties, there was not such a strong financial barrier to the recruitment of the working class. By passing the 1863 Act without much discussion on the issue of the capitation grant, Parliament was accepting that the Volunteers had become and should remain largely working-class.

There were of course some who objected to the recruitment of the working class. A correspondent to the *Volunteer Service Gazette* was more explicit than most when he stated his dislike of drilling with men 'who from no misfortune of their own, but as a necessary result of their position in society, cannot dress in a cleanly way.' More common, perhaps, was the feeling expressed by Nathaniel Bousfield, the Liverpool pioneer, in his evidence before the 1862 Royal Commission. 'We wish to retain,' he said, 'our self-supporting and gentlemanly feeling.'[29]

Those, however, who welcomed the working class into the Force were much more vocal than their opponents. The articulate upper middle class of Victorian Britain quickly came to see benefits in the Volunteer Force which extended far beyond the defensive needs of the country. The first of these benefits was that the Force seemed to have brought about what the *Rochdale Pilot* called a 'commingling of classes'. No theme was more prominent in the speeches and writings about the Volunteer Force in its early days. Martin Tupper, trying to establish a Rifle Club in West Surrey, issued a broadsheet declaring that 'whether national perils be imminent or not, our Club, under efficient regulations, will be a manly and pleasant mingling of classes now too little socially united.' The Force seemed to be an institutional setting within which the post-Chartist harmony of class relationships could be expressed. Tom Hughes, founder of the Working Men's College Corps, was perhaps the chief exponent of this viewpoint, writing in 1860: 'The difficulty of finding a common standing-ground, anything in which we may all work together; where we can stand shoulder to shoulder, and man to man, each counting for what he is worth; the peer without condescending, and the peasant without cringing, is almost as great as ever. Here, in volunteering, we think we have found what may, when rightly handled, do much towards filling up this gap . . .'[30]

The Volunteer Force, indeed, came to be seen as more than

symptomatic of better class relationships; it was believed to have
helped bring about those relationships. Charles Kingsley, in the Preface
to *Alton Locke,* pointed to the Volunteer movement as 'one absolute
proof of the changed relation between the upper and the lower classes
. . . Already, by the performance of a common duty, and the
experience of a common humanity, these volunteer corps are becoming
centres of cordiality between class and class.' 'Brother Volunteers,'
enthused the Liverpool Volunteer, James Walter, on the coming of age
of the Force in 1881, 'it is joyous to feel and know that there is a
largely increasing sympathy between our various classes of society. This
is one of the best signs of our times, and Volunteers have done much
for it.'[31]

This enthusiasm for the meeting of class with class only becomes
intelligible when seen alongside some of the other benefits which were
thought to arise out of working-class participation in the Force. It was
hoped that volunteering would have a moderating effect on a man's
politics. Lord Elcho was constantly making this point. *The Economist*
could not believe that the Force would be 'other than anti-democratic
in its influence on politics.' John Bright, with anything but enthusiasm,
thought the same. William Mathews, a Volunteer Captain in Somerset,
spoke from personal experience of his corps as 'a through amalgamation
of class, without an approach to undue familiarity', and went on to
doubt 'if the political demagogue, the Chartist, and Dissenter will not
be shorn of his pernicious authority through the agency of a really
sensible development of the good which exists in this upmoving of
patriotic sympathy.' Appropriately enough it was a working-class man
who put the point most directly: John Pettie, Colour Sergeant in the
London Scottish (Elcho's Corps), told the 1862 Royal Commission
that the headquarters of Chartism in London, Fitzroy Square, now
produced a loyal company of Volunteers, and that volunteering made
men worth three shillings a week more to their employers, 'more
attached to the Government in every way, and less likely ever to
promote political agitation'.[32]

To these political benefits must be added social ones. John Macgregor,
a Captain in the London Scottish, made the most systematic attempt to
catalogue these, in his paper on 'The Moral, Social, and Hygienic Effects
of the Volunteer Movement', read before the National Association for
the Promotion of Social Science. After sending out a highly unscientific
questionnaire to Commanding Officers, Macgregor was able to
summarise the results for the Royal Commission saying that 'discipline,
cleanliness, order, punctuality, promptitude, and obedience have been
imparted to them [working-class Volunteers] in such a manner as
could not have been done by any other means whatever.' Volunteering,
he said, made men 'less idle and dissipated, and more respectful to

authority', and there were places where 'casinos, dancing saloons, skittle alleys, billiard rooms, and similar places have been closed by the absence of the custom of men who once frequented them, but who now give their days to shoot, and evenings to drill, and find pleasure in band music and chorus singing.'[33]

If volunteering was thought to have such effects it is hardly surprising that it was attractive to employers. In Birkenhead John Laird was convinced that volunteering had a 'beneficial effect', and 'has improved the men in the yard generally'. The granting of some government assistance would 'spread a very good feeling among the working classes in this country'. In Swansea the Volunteers in a factory were 'generally speaking, much better conducted and steadier men since they joined', and 'young men about town, who used to hang about billiard rooms and the bars at public houses . . . now go to drill and shoot at the rifle ranges.' In Glasgow the 'social tone' of artisans had been much improved by their becoming Volunteers and they had become more loyal and more regular. In Durham artisans who volunteered displayed a marked improvement 'in their health, in their habits, and in their demeanour to others.' In Liverpool a magistrate and Volunteer had 'observed that many young men who before were lounging and idling about and spending their evening in places of questionable resort are now quite changed. They come to drill, and they induce others to come, and the effect has been of a very beneficial character to the neighbourhood; and I think that the money would be exceedingly well spent if for no other purpose than that.'[34]

These, of course, are middle-class voices, showing a significant concern with the maintenance of authority and the ways of spending leisure. If relations between the classes were to be changed through the Volunteer movement, it would not be in the direction of greater familiarity between employer and employee, rather through greater obedience and an improved demeanour on the part of the latter. The point is made clear when it is realised that in companies where the employer was an officer there was evidently little compunction in using the former status as a means of maintaining discipline and extracting funds. Thus in Colonel McIver's regiment in Liverpool, where the employers were officers, 'if a man should be disobedient he might lose 30s. a week good pay.' In Glasgow it was difficult to get payment by instalment for uniforms 'without you have a hold upon them through the party who pays their wages.' Similarly in the well-disciplined 24th Middlesex (Post Office) Volunteers, 'every man knew that unless he behaved well in camp, his PO chief would come to know of his conduct.'[35] In many ways the Volunteer Force was seen as an adjunct to other means of maintaining work discipline. It was a movement for the improvement of the working class under close control and within strict limits.

This middle-class rhapsodising about the benefits of the admission of the working class to the Force indicates, then, a concern with social control. At the same time it expresses the immense confidence of the middle class that such control could be maintained. Ten years previously it would have been a rare employer indeed who would have been willing to see his workmen armed. Now, in 1860, hardly a voice is raised to suggest that there is any danger in such arming. Moreover rifles were frequently kept not in a locked armoury but in the Volunteer's home.[36] Without this confidence in the loyalty of the upper working class to the established authorities the Force could not have existed, for the early years had shown that middle-class enthusiasm was not sufficient to fill the ranks.

Confidence in working-class loyalty seems to have been justified. Working-class newspapers, for example *Reynolds' Newspaper* and the *Glasgow Sentinel*, though deeply critical of aristocratic influence and middle-class exclusiveness, were on balance in favour of the Force.[37] Opposition to the formation of the Force was, as has been seen, isolated. Working-class men joined, and as will be shown in the next chapter, formed an increasing proportion of the Force. Their motives in enrolling, and the consequences for them of such enrolment, remain to be explored. What has been shown is that in welcoming working-class recruits the middle class had reasons which were as much social as military. The upper working class now seemed respectable, and through volunteering might be made more respectable. Having offered working men a rifle in 1860 without disastrous consequences, there was some precedent for hope when it came to giving them a vote in 1867. Lloyd Jones, writing in 1867, encapsulates the social change which had taken place to make the Force possible: a Lanarkshire Volunteer in the 1860s, loyal to Her Majesty, he confessed to 'having had his sharpened pike by him in 1832, ready for a march on London if the Reform Bill had not passed.'[38]

Notes

1. *3 Hansard 154*, c. 695 (5 July 1859).
2. W.G. Fisher, *The History of Somerset Yeomanry, Volunteer and Territorial Units* (Taunton, 1924), pp. 100-1; F.A.M. Webster, *The History of the Fifth Battalion the Bedfordshire and Hertfordshire Regiment (TA)* (London, 1930), p.4; T.S. Cave, *History of the First Volunteer Battalion Hampshire Regiment 1859-1889* (London and Winchester, 1905), p.40; C.J. Hart, *The History of the 1st Volunteer Battalion The Royal Warwickshire Regiment* (Birmingham, 1906), p.101; *VSG*, 10 Dec. 1859, 14 July 1860; *The Times*,

15 Nov. 1859.
3. J.H.A. Macdonald, *Fifty Years of it: the Experiences and Struggles of a Volunteer of 1859* (Edinburgh and London, 1909), pp. 3-4; D. Howie, *History of the 1st Lanark Rifle Volunteers* (Glasgow and London, 1887), p.72.
4. W.G. Fisher, loc. cit.; C.J. Hart, op. cit., pp. 102-3; J.L. Garvin, *Life of Joseph Chamberlain*, vol. I (London, 1932), pp. 61-2; W. Stephen, *History of the Queen's City of Edinburgh Rifle Volunteer Brigade* (Edinburgh and London, 1881), pp.248-9, 272-6; G.A. Parfitt, *Radnorshire Volunteers* (Hay-on-Wye, 1968), p.79; Cruikshank Papers, Middlesex County Record Office, Acc. 534/1-14.
5. *VSG*, 14 Jan. 1860, 9 Nov. 1867; RC (1862), q.2674.
6. D. Hudson, *Martin Tupper, His Rise and Fall* (London, 1949) pp. 197-8; Victoria County History, *Surrey*, vol. II (London, 1905), pp.148-9; W. Crompton and G. Venn, *Warrington Volunteers 1798-1898* (Warrington, 1898), pp.64-8.
7. *Rochdale Observer*, 10 and 17 Dec. 1859; *Oldham Chronicle*, 3 Dec. 1859; see also RC (1862), qq. 2378, 2642-3.
8. R.P. Berry, *A History of the Formation and Development of the Volunteer Infantry*, pp.384-9; R.W.S. Norfolk, *Militia, Yeomanry and Volunteer Forces of the East Riding 1689-1908* (East Yorks. Local History Series, No. 19, 1965), p.35; T.W. Bush, *Records of the 5th Battalion the Durham Light Infantry 1796 to 1914* (Aldershot, 1914), p.13; *VSG*, 28 Jan. 1860 (on opposition in Newcastle), and 25 Feb. 1860 (on Ernest Jones' attitude).
9. Sir C. Phipps to Lugard, 9 Feb. 1861, Herbert Papers.
10. *VSG*, 24 Dec. 1859; C.T. Atkinson, *The Dorsetshire Regiment* (privately printed, Oxford, 1947), vol. II, p.15; G.I. Malcolm of Poltalloch, *Argyllshire Highlanders 1860-1960* (Glasgow, n.d), p.3; RC (1862), 2. 3059.
11. J.M.A. Tamplin, *The Lambeth and Southwark Volunteers* (London, 1965), pp.4-17; A. Larking, *History of the 4th V.B. East Surrey Regiment* (London, 1912), p.12; Minute Book of the 1st Lincolnshire Rifle Volunteers, 1 Sept. 1860, Lincolnshire Archives Office, Hill 12/1/1.
12. D. Howie, op. cit., pp.307-10; J.W. Burrows, *The Essex Regiment – Essex Territorial Infantry Brigade* (Southend-on-Sea, n.d), pp. 3-4; H.C. Evans, *Records of the 4th Volunteer Battalion Manchester Regiment* (Manchester, 1900), p.10.
13. J. Orr, *History of the Seventh Lanarkshire Rifle Volunteers* (Glasgow, 1884), p.396; RC (1862), qq. 2540-2575.
14. Edinburgh printers cited in R.Q. Gray, 'Styles of Life, the "Labour Aristocracy" and Class Relations in Later Nineteenth Century Edinburgh', *International Review of Social History*, vol. XVIII (1973), p.449; W. Crompton and G. Venn, op. cit., pp.78-9; *VSG*, 10 Dec. 1859.
15. Lewisham Archive Depository, A58/6/1-4.
16. *VSG*, 16 Nov. 1859.
17. *The Times*, 15 Aug. 1860; Elcho to Salisbury, 6 Oct. 1860, Salisbury to Elcho (draft), 8 Oct. 1860, Middlesex County Record Office, Clerk to Lieutenancy Records, L 40. For Elcho's political views, see C.J. Kauffman, 'Lord Elcho, Trade Unionism and Democracy' in K.D. Brown (ed.), *Essays in Anti-Labour History* (London, 1974), pp.183-207.
18. *The Times*, 17 Aug. 1860; de Grey to Herbert, 6 Sept. 1860, Herbert Papers.
19. *VSG,* 8 Sept. and 29 Dec. 1860.
20. W. Stephen, op. cit., pp.218-94.
21. RC (1862), qq. 4061, 2080, 1683.

22. ibid., qq. 2184, 2454-7, 2765, 3019, 3344.
23. ibid., qq. 2277, 2645, 2829, 2663, 2540, 1127, 1171.
24. ibid., qq. 2151, 3173, 3255-7.
25. ibid., qq. 1536-9, 1172-3, 3444.
26. ibid., qq. 1533-6, 1685, 1803, 2597, 2725, 3547-8, 4277-8.
27. R.P. Berry, op. cit., pp.491-2, 137, 140, 525-6.
28. *3 Hansard 154*, cc. 678-99 (5 July 1859), *160*, cc. 184-8 (26 July 1860), *163*, cc. 778-813 (7 June 1861).
29. *VSG*, 21 Jan. 1860; RC (1862), q. 2298.
30. *Rochdale Pilot* quoted in *VSG*, 28 July 1860; D. Hudson, op. cit., back endpaper; T. Hughes, 'The Volunteer's Catechism', *Macmillan's Magazine*, vol. II (July 1860), p.193.
31. C. Kingsley, *Alton Locke* (London, 1889 ed.), p.xxx; J. Walter, *The Volunteer Force* (London, 1881), p.5.
32. For Elcho, *3 Hansard 163*, c. 785 (7 June 1861); *The Economist*, 10 Mar. 1860; Bright quoted in B. Rose, 'The Volunteers of 1859', *Journal of the Society for Army Historical Research*, vol. 37 (1959), p.108; *VSG*, 15 Sept. 1860; RC (1862), qq.851, 857-8.
33. *Transactions of the National Association for the Promotion of Social Science*, London Meeting, 1862, pp. 768-73; RC (1862), qq. 2607-8.
34. RC (1862), qq. 2572, 2580, 4275-6, 4305, 1573-6, 2904, 3258.
35. ibid., qq. 2375, 4327; J.H.A. Macdonald, op. cit., p.299.
36. 'Report on Reserve Forces 1868-9' by Major-General Jas. Lindsay, p.21, WO 33/19.
37. *Reynolds' Newspaper*, 22 May, 17 July 1859, 29 Jan., 1 July 1860, 10 Feb. 1861; *Glasgow Sentinel*, 21 May, 12 and 26 Nov. 1859.
38. J.M. Ludlow and Lloyd Jones, *Progress of the Working Class 1832-67* (London, 1867), p.22.

3 THE COMPOSITION OF THE FORCE

In this chapter an attempt will be made to assemble certain vital statistics about the rank and file Volunteers: the occupations of the members of the Force, their age and length of service, and their geographical spread.

It will have been apparent already that issues of class and status were important from the very beginning in determining the structure of the Force. These influences continued to be important and to the historian concerned with the social significance of the Force they are obviously vital. We are fortunate in dealing with the Volunteers that the single most important determinant of class, occupation, is what we know most about. On the basis of an analysis of occupations it will be shown, first, that a high and increasing proportion of the Volunteer was working-class, and, second, that the working-class component of the Force became less exclusively upper working-class as time went on.

It must be admitted immediately that the evidence on which these assertions are based is not as comprehensive as could be wished. Only for 1904 are there any figures on a national scale giving occupations and, of course, without any previous figures it is not possible to deduce any trends. As so often is the historian's lot, it is necessary to make the most of what is available. This consists of a number of scattered occupational breakdowns of particular corps at various dates, for example, the 23rd Middlesex in 1887, and the Galloway Rifles Volunteers in 1897; a considerable amount of verbal evidence as to occupational trends, particularly that presented before various Commissions of Inquiry; some figures on Volunteer recruitment into the Regular Army or Militia; and finally, an analysis of three companies of Lincoln Volunteers from 1859 to 1891, and of the 36th Middlesex Rifle Volunteers from 1860 to 1908. This analysis is derived from a one in five systematic random sample of the former, and a one in ten of the latter, taken from the muster rolls of these corps.[1] All figures which appear below relating to the Lincoln and 36th Middlesex are taken from these samples.

We may start with the returns to the 1904 Royal Commission, which give a national breakdown by occupation (see Table 1). If we assume, as will be done throughout this chapter, that the division between middle and working class is one between non-manual and manual occupations, we may simplify this table by taking the professional men, clerks, shopmen and men in business on their own account as middle class, the men in government employ and other occupations as unknown, and the rest as working class. These figures show that at least 70 per cent of the rank and file was recruited from the working class in 1904.

33

TABLE 1

Occupations of Rank and File Volunteers, 1904

	Occupation	%
1.	Professional Men	1.6
2.	Clerks	9.2
3.	Shopmen	4.8
4.	Men in business on their own account	2.7
5.	Artisans	40.3
6.	Agricultural labourers	3.8
7.	Town labourers	8.6
8.	Miners	5.4
9.	Factory or manufacturing hands	10.9
10.	Men in private employ (gardeners etc.)	1.8
11.	Men in government employ	2.5
12.	Other occupations	8.4

TOTAL	100
TOTAL 1 - 4	18.3
TOTAL 5 - 10	70.8

Source: Calculated from RC (1904), App. Pt. IV.

There are no comparable figures for an earlier date, and it is necessary to go back a quarter of a century to 1878 to find a time when there is enough evidence again to attempt an overall assessment. A Committee under the chairmanship of Lord Bury, appointed in 1878 'to enquire into the Financial State and Internal Organisation of the Volunteer Force in Great Britain', assembled in its Minutes of Evidence a considerable amount of information about occupation and class. Thus in Edinburgh the men were stated to be nearly all artisans, in Liverpool there were one or two companies composed chiefly of superior clerks in offices and gentlemen, but the remaining eight companies were artisan. In Derbyshire, stated the Commanding Officer, 'I have a small number of agriculturists, that is one outlying corps; I have two strong companies from the Butterley Iron Works, and a company and a half from Lord Belper's cotton works; these are outlying companies. Then I have seven companies in Derby; the first is made up of bankers' clerks and the better class of shopmen, and clerks high up in office in the Railway Company, and all the other artisans.' In Glamorgan the artillery were stated to be almost exclusively artisan, in Worcestershire the Volunteers were 'mostly artisans and agriculturists', salt workers in Droitwich, but no miners, and 'not shopmen or that class'. Even in Sussex where formerly half the battalion had been 'farmers in a very good position', there were now only five or six per company: 'there are a good many agricultural labourers; there are a good many small tradesmen, and a good many tradesmen doing a fair business in the different towns, and there are a good many mechanics.' And in London, stated Sir Hector Hay in 1877, 'except in some half-dozen regiments, the bulk of the men belong to the working class.'[2]

This evidence points to a situation in which there might be one or two companies in a large town which were the preserve of the middle class, and the rest almost exclusively working-class, and in agricultural areas a greater mixture, but a distinct lowering in class since 1862. It may help to put some flesh on these rather bare bones if we simply list the occupations of two very different corps.

First, published in *The Nineteenth Century* in 1887 was an analysis of a Volunteer Battalion by Robert Routledge (see Table 2). Routledge was Commanding Officer of the 23rd Middlesex, and we may assume the battalion analysed to have been his own. Of the total of 452 only the clerks and draughtsmen are clearly not manual workers, and they form only 10 per cent of the total. The biggest single group, it is interesting to note, is the unskilled porters, but artisans clearly form the overall majority.

TABLE 2

Occupations of 23rd Middlesex Volunteers, 1887

Porters	56
Printers	45
Clerks	44
Compositors	39
Packers	26
Bookbinders	25
Tailors	24
Painters	19
Brass finishers	15
Carpenters	15
Plumbers	14

Blacksmiths	13
Engineers	13
Joiners	10
Fitters	9
Letter sorters & carriers	9
Machine managers	9
Carmen	8
French polishers	8
Gas fitters	7
Harness makers	7
Shoemakers	6
Machinists	5
Bricklayers	4
Brushmakers	4
Surgical instrument makers	4
Draymen	3
Stokers	3
Stone grinders	3
Clockmakers	2
Draughtsmen	2
Engine drivers	1
TOTAL	452

Source: R.W. Routledge, 'A Volunteer Battalion', *Nineteenth Century,* vol. XXI (May 1887), p. 744.

Second, looking to a very different type of Volunteer Battalion there is an analysis of the Galloway Rifles in 1897; of the seventy-one occupations occurring amongst the Volunteers in this scattered battalion of 811 members, only those which have six or more members are listed (see Table 3). The editor of the *Galloway Rifles Gazette* in which this list of occupations appeared, abstained, perhaps wisely, from further analysis. It should be pointed out that the list includes officers, which accounts, for example, for the solicitors. Although there is a fair number of non-manual occupations, both clerical and distributive, the overwhelming proportion is again working-class, with a significantly high number listed simply as labourers, and therefore presumably unskilled.

The value of this information from London and Galloway is restricted by two factors: we are dealing with corps which may be atypical (though there is nothing to suggest that they are), and our knowledge about them is confined to a particular date. The second, but not the first factor, is surmounted when we turn to the Lincoln and 36th

TABLE 3

Occupations of the Galloway Rifles, 1897

Masons	100
Labourers	99
Joiners	68
Tailors	64
Clerks	41
Weavers	32
Blacksmiths	28
Plumbers	24
Turners	23
Painters	22
Bakers	18
Cabinet makers	17
Farmers	16
Printers	16
Shoemakers	13
Clothiers	13
Coachbuilders	11
Saddlers	11
Millers	10
Merchants	10
Grocers	9
Teachers	8
Insurance agents	8
Watchmakers	8
Solicitors	7
Engineers	7
Gardeners	7
Polishers	6
Foresters	6
Cloggers	6
Letter carriers	6
TOTAL	**714**

Source: Galloway Rifles Regimental Gazette, vol. I (Jan. 1897), pp. 11-115.

Middlesex Volunteers. In the analysis occupations were divided into seven categories: Professional (1), clerical and white collar (2), distributive (3), skilled manual (4), unskilled manual (5), other (6), and not given (7). There are inevitably difficult cases; for example, a baker might be either category 3 or 4; in such cases I have given a man the benefit of the doubt, and put him in the higher category; one reason for so doing is that it will tend to bias the results against rather than in favour of the conclusions which I shall draw. The categories I have adopted divide occupations by type of work, not class.[3] But by adopting the distinction made earlier between non-manual and manual work, it is clear that categories 4 and 5 between them compose the working classes (see Table 4). With the exception of the 1900-8 figures for Middlesex, there is here a consistent trend, with the proportion of both corps which was working-class rising from decade to decade. Moreover, an increasing percentage of the working-class Volunteers are in unskilled occupations. There are of course particular rather than general factors which may account for this, for example a decline in the social respectability of the area within which the corps recruited. These factors are difficult to assess, and impossible to exclude. The most that can be said on the basis of this analysis is that it gives some support to the proposition for which there is much verbal evidence, that not only was the proportion of the Force which was working-class high, but that it was increasing, and becoming much less exclusively artisan.

These figures find consistent support from the verbal evidence. Since most of this evidence comes from military men, it is not surprising that the class position of the Volunteer is often defined by comparing it with other potential recruits for the Army, in particular the Militiaman. We have seen that the chief function of the Militia was to provide recruits for the Regular Army; men often joined it because they were under age or under size for the regular Army, or because they wanted a taste of military life before committing themselves to the Regulars. Thus the social position of the Militiaman was similar to that of a private in the Regular Army. Bearing this in mind an assessment may be made of the evidence produced which compares the Volunteers with the Militiamen and Regulars.

In 1862 no one was in any doubt that the Volunteer Force and the Militia were recruiting from quite different sections of the community. There was a unanimous opinion expressed that the Volunteers in no way interfered with recruiting for the Line or the Militia; 'These men would have nothing to do with the Militia,' said John Laird of his Birkenhead Volunteers.[4]

By 1878, our next benchmark, although it was still generally agreed that the class of man who went into the Volunteers was different from the Militia or Line recruit, it was admitted that there was some interchange. Lord Elcho knew of Volunteers who had joined the Regular Army, Lieutenant-Colonel Wilmot in Derbyshire thought some of his artisans might join the Line, and in Glamorgan some fifty Volunteers joined the Regular Army at the time of the war scare in spring 1878.

38

TABLE 4

DISTRIBUTION OF LINCOLN AND 36th MIDDLESEX VOLUNTEERS BY OCCUPATION CATEGORIES (in percentages)

Corps	Date of Enrolment	Occupation Categories (%)							Total	Sample Size
		1	2	3	4	5	6	7		
Lincoln	1859 - 69	8.0	19.6	13.0	48.6	3.6	0.7	6.5	100.0	(138)
	1870 - 79	2.9	8.0	8.8	69.3	8.8	2.2	0.0	100.0	(137)
	1880 - 91	0.0	5.6	2.2	70.0	20.0	1.7	0.6	100.1	(180)
36th Middlesex	1860 - 69	5.2	28.9	13.4	39.2	7.2	0.0	6.2	100.1	(97)
	1870 - 79	2.8	28.7	12.5	45.4	10.2	0.5	0.0	100.1	(216)
	1880 - 89	1.5	13.9	11.3	50.5	18.6	3.6	0.5	99.9	(194)
	1890 - 99	0.7	11.8	9.7	52.8	20.1	4.2	0.7	100.0	(144)
	1900 - 08	3.7	18.3	9.2	34.9	25.7	5.5	2.8	100.1	(109)

Note: The trend over time from categories 1 - 3 to categories 4 - 5, and from category 4 to category 5 is statistically very significant (i.e. at 1% level).

John Holms MP claimed that 3-4 per cent of the Volunteers annually entered the Army. In the 1880s in Routledge's London battalion of over 450, some 20 a year would join the Regulars.[5] By the 1870s and 1880s, therefore, it is justifiable to assume that the Volunteers and the Regular Army have converged in the class of recruits they attract.

It might be argued that this was in fact a case of the Army rising in social respectability rather than the Volunteers falling. But in 1904 most witnesses were clear in their minds that there was a distinction between the Militia or Line recruit and the Volunteer. 'The Militiaman', said Colonel Cave of the 1st Volunteer Battalion, Hants Regiment, 'is a man of casual employment, and the Volunteer is a man of regular employment; of course there are exceptions in both cases, but that is the general line of division.' 'In Yorkshire', said an officer with experience of both Volunteers and Militia, 'the men of the Militia come from a lower stratum of the working class than those of the Volunteers. The Volunteer in Yorkshire is usually a workman in regular employment — the Militiaman a workman in intermittent employment. The Volunteer is far more intelligent and better educated.' There is evidence that this distinction was accepted by the rank and file, for when in Monmouthshire in 1900 many tradesmen joined the Militia, they declared themselves to be labourers; when asked why, they replied, 'Because it is not the correct thing for an artisan to enlist in the Militia.'[6]

This general distinction in type of employment, and hence in class position, between the Volunteer and the Militia or Line recruit, was therefore still maintained in 1904, as in 1878, and is well documented. In East Surrey, a few casual labourers occasionally joined the Volunteers, but they rarely stayed long; 'the majority of the men', it was said, 'are in good employment, earning about 35s. a week on the average.' In Sheffield, in the artillery, the men were 'fitters, turners, forgemen, smiths, and that class of man — men that could really turn their hands to anything — an intelligent body of men,' earning £1 — £3 a week, and of 'a very much higher class' than the ordinary recruit for the Army. In Birmingham 'our Volunteers are men who are in continuous employment, while the men who go into the Militia are casual labourers, who have no continuous employment.' In Glasgow the Volunteers were in a superior class to those who go into the Militia — they were ' in steady employment'. Amongst the Engineers in that town, the men being mostly fitters in iron works and shipbuilding yards, the Commanding Officer did 'not think any of the class of men that are in my corps would go into the Militia', though some joined the Regulars.[7]

It is the exceptions to this rule, however, that are interesting. They come from both rural and urban areas. On Tyneside Lord Algernon Percy, commanding the Militia, thought the Volunteers were 'largely composed of the same class as the Militiamen', while admitting that in his Militia regiment he had more 'of the artisan class' than most. In Salford, where the Volunteers were nearly all mechanics in the cotton trade, and 40-50 joined the Militia every year, the Commanding Officer thought that his men were 'very much of the same class' as the Militiamen; he had 'a large sprinkling' of casual labourers.[8] In Devon, 'the Volunteer is sometimes a little superior to the man who goes into the Militia, but, on the other hand, in some of the country regiments the rank and file of the battalion are very much of the class of men you will find in the Militia, and they go into the Militia.' In Hampshire, the Earl of Selborne, commanding the Militia, was 'perfectly certain that there are a great many men in the county Volunteers that when I joined the Militia would have been in the Militia.' And in Wales 'a great many of the men now in the Volunteers are very closely related,brothers, to those in the Militia.'[9]

Figures for Volunteer recruitment into the Regular Army, Militia, or from 1908 Special Reserve, which are available from the end of the century give support to the view that there was a progressive convergence in the social composition of the various sections of the armed forced (see Table 5). There is, then, evidence to suggest that the Volunteers were recruiting lower down the social scale as time progressed. Shifting boundaries between the upper working class and others, and a possible rise in the class of those joining the Regular Army or Militia, make firm conclusions difficult. Nevertheless it would seem reasonable to suppose that by the early twentieth century about one-quarter of the Force may have been unskilled workers.

TABLE 5

Volunteers Joining the Regular Army, Militia, or Special Reserve

Years	Average Number Joining Regular Army	Average Number Joining Militia or Special Reserve
1895 - 9	2,446	No figures
1902 - 7	3,085	1,103
1908 - 13	3,222	2,297

Source: Calculated from Annual Returns of the Volunteer and Territorial Forces, 1895 - 1913.

On the other side there can be no doubt that the Force became less and less middle-class. This middle-class disaffection is reflected in the chronic shortage of officers, and the difficulties of exclusive middle-class corps. In Edinburgh, claimed J.H.A. Macdonald, 'with a few laudable exceptions, the leisured class and well-to-do business people disappeared from the ranks, and if it had not been for the zeal and energy of the working classes the Volunteer Force might have dwindled and possibly perished altogether.' In 1868 the Advocates' and Writers' to the Signet companies in Edinburgh were dissolved, having for some time led a merely nominal existence, and in London too, 'the supply of the higher middle-class men was unequal to the demand.'[10] In the late 1870s some were to claim that the middle class had been 'elbowed out' of the Force by what were thought of as the lower standards of conduct of the artisan Volunteers; in Bristol in 1877 the swearing at the march-past was 'simply horrible', and gentlemen, it was said, were kept from joining the corps from the knowledge that 'as soon as their names become a little known among the men, they are liable to be addressed at any time by half-a-dozen ill-mannered fellows with the words "Well, Johnson", "Well, Smith" . . .' But the authoritative voice of the *Volunteer Service Gazette* argued that the middle-class had simply 'melted away' and that 'the gradual reduction in numbers of the regiments composed of the highest class men was owing entirely to the spontaneous extinction of the enthusiasm which had led those men to join.'[11] Whether elbowed out or melting away, however, there was no denying that the middle-class proportion of the Force decreased as the working-class increased. The exclusive companies found they must recruit lower down the social scale or dissolve.

The Volunteer Force, then, is more properly thought of as the workers rather than the shopkeepers in arms. It can also be thought of as youth in arms. It will be shown that the Force was a young one, and became younger as time went on, and further that length of service was often short.

In the first few years of the Force's existence there was in most corps a wide range of ages, with many enrolling in their twenties, thirties and not infrequently forties and fifties. Thus the average age of the twenty-seven men who enrolled in the 7th Cumberland Rifle Volunteers in June 1864 was 25, five of them being in their teens and six in their thirties. In the Weald of Kent amongst 87 recruits between 1860 and 1870 the average age was 28.5[12] But it is to the Lincoln and 36th Middlesex that we must turn again, for only here are there figures to show the trend (see Table 6). The figures for these two corps are very similar and the trend towards youth is marked. Moreover, the majority of Volunteers served in the Force for only a few years (see Table 7). These are figures for completed service and since the muster book for the 36th Middlesex was not always completed after 1890 it is not

TABLE 6

DISTRIBUTION OF LINCOLN AND 36th MIDDLESEX VOLUNTEERS BY AGE AT ENROLMENT (in percentages)

Corps	Date of Enrolment	% aged 18 or under	% aged 19	% aged 20 or over	% not known	Total	Sample Size
Lincoln	1859-69	21.0	4.3	71.7	2.9	99.9	(138)
	1970-79	38.0	18.2	43.1	0.7	100.0	(137)
	1880-91	51.7	11.1	37.2	0.0	100.0	(180)
36th Middlesex	1860-69	21.6	6.2	63.9	8.2	99.9	(97)
	1870-79	38.9	15.7	45.4	0.0	100.0	(216)
	1880-89	46.3	16.0	37.6	0.0	99.9	(194)
	1890-99	54.1	13.2	32.6	0.0	99.9	(144)
	1900-08	55.0	11.0	33.9	0.0	99.9	(109)

Note: The trend over time from older to younger age groups is statistically very significant (i.e. at <1% level).

TABLE 7

DISTRIBUTION OF LINCOLN AND 36th MIDDLESEX VOLUNTEERS BY LENGTH OF SERVICE (in percentages)

Corps	Date of Enrolment	3 years & under	4 or 5 years	6 years or more	not known	TOTAL	Sample Size
Lincoln	1859-69	60.1	15.9	23.9	0.0	99.9	(138)
	1870-79	68.6	18.2	13.1	0.0	99.9	(137)
	1880-91	61.7	16.1	16.7	5.6	100.1	(180)
36th Middlesex	1860-69	38.1	20.6	38.1	3.1	99.9	(97)
	1870-79	53.3	17.6	26.9	2.3	100.1	(216)
	1880-89	56.7	25.3	14.4	3.6	100.0	(194)

Note: The trend over time from long service (6 years or more) to shorter service is statistically very significant for the 36th Middlesex (i.e. at 1% level), but not for Lincoln where the unknowns in 1880-91 complicate matters.

possible to carry the table further. Although there are no such clear trends here as with ages, it is noteworthy that with the exception of the 36th Middlesex in 1860-9, over half the Volunteers for each decade in both corps served three years or less.

The evidence from Lincoln and Middlesex receives confirmation on a national scale when we look at figures which exist from 1895 onwards giving the ages and amount of time served of all enrolled Volunteers at the beginning of November in each year (see Table 8). The figures are not strictly comparable with those for Lincoln and Middlesex since they give the age and amount of time served at that particular date rather than on enrolment or in total. Nevertheless the conclusions to be drawn are the same. The figures for age show that at four- or five-year intervals (1900, 1904, and 1909) the Force suddenly became younger. The trend towards youth is confirmed. Most Volunteers were in their late teens or early twenties. The figures for length of service are less consistent, but by the end of the period a considerably higher proportion than at the beginning had served three years or under.

TABLE 8

The Ages and Length of Service of Volunteers, 1895-1913

Year	% Aged 20 and under	% Aged 25 and under	% Who have Served 3 Years and under
1895	32	64	47
1896	31	62	46
1897	30	61	45
1898	31	62	46
1899	32	62	46
1900	38	66	56
1901	37	67	56
1902	35	66	53
1903	36	67	48
1904	40	70	51
1905	41	70	52
1906	41	71	51
1907	40	70	48
1908	43	70	57
1909	48	76	69
1910	45	76	70
1911	40	75	61
1912	40	76	48
1913	45	76	59

Source: Calculated from the Annual Returns of the Volunteer and Territorial Forces, 1895-1913.

The youth of the Volunteers sheds light on the occupational structure of the Force. We may suspect that many of those who have been listed as skilled workers were in fact teenage apprentices. An eighteen-year-old carpenter is less obviously a member of the upper working class than a thirty-year-old one. Many of the members of the Force were men who precisely during their period of service as Volunteers were in their occupations acquiring the skills which would ensure them a place in the upper working class. The implications of this we shall explore later.

We may turn finally to the geographical spread of the Volunteers (see Table 9). Too much significance should not be placed on the apparent overall decline in the percentage of the available population which was at any point in time enrolled in the Volunteers. 1899 was not a good year, and numbers were to increase dramatically with the Boer War, and more important, remain at a higher level. In 1903 2.7 per cent of all males aged between 15 and 49 were Volunteers. While most regions remained relatively constant over the years in the proportion of the available population enrolled, the decline of London and the south-east from a position of leadership within England is notable. The are most vulnerable to a French invasion seems to have been least able to maintain the enthusiasm of the early years. Nevertheless, looking at the changes over time, what is most remarkable is how stable the Force was in the areas from which it recruited, and how early the geographical pattern was set.

Within that pattern the figures for Scotland are those most in need of explanation. In Scotland, compared to the rest of Great Britain, a markedly higher percentage of the available population enrolled in the Volunteers. Why should this have been so? There is no obvious answer. Possibly in Scotland there was more acceptance of military values and of the Regular Army; the Scottish Volunteers, as we shall see, were much more willing than their English counterparts to adopt the scarlet of the Regulars.[13] It also seemed possible that Volunteers in general recruited best in the least densely populated areas, and that, because of this, rural Scotland had an advantage over the rest of Great Britain. In Scotland itself the more rural areas did indeed recruit better than the rest (see Table 10). Nevertheless, as the table also shows, the northern areas of Scotland were those with the highest percentage of the available population enrolled in the Force. The two more densely populated northern counties (Aberdeen and Forfar) had a better enrolment record than the southern rural ones. It was in the Highlands of Scotland, an area surely relatively secure from the danger of French invasion, that the British people most enthusiastically enrolled themselves in the Volunteer Force. And even in urban areas the Scots were much keener to join the Volunteers than the English or Welsh. The

46

correlation between high enrolment and low density of population may partly explain the regional distribution of Volunteers within Scotland, but it cannot account for the much greater number of Volunteers in relation to the available population in Scotland compared to the rest of Great Britain. Only one English county, Westmorland with 5.0 per cent of its available population in the Volunteer Force, had a better record than Ayrshire, the Scottish county with the lowest percentage of its available population in the Force (3.8 per cent). Scotland's superiority was overwhelming, and to this historian at least it remains something of a mystery.

TABLE 9

Regional Distribution of Volunteers as a Percentage of the Male Population aged 15-49

Region	1862 %	1881 %	1899 %
London and South-East	3.6	2.6	2.1
Eastern	2.6	2.3	2.1
Southern	2.4	2.6	2.6
South-West	2.8	3.0	2.9
West Midlands	1.8	1.9	1.6
North Midlands	1.8	1.7	1.4
Yorkshire	2.0	1.9	1.6
North-West	2.9	2.9	2.4
North	2.7	2.8	2.5
Wales	3.0	2.6	2.0
Scotland	5.0	5.5	4.3
TOTAL	3.0	2.8	2.4

Notes: 1. Regions: *London and South-East:* London, Middlesex, Surrey, Kent, Sussex.
Eastern: Norfolk, Suffolk, Cambridge, Huntingdon, Bedford, Hertfordshire and Essex.
Southern: Hampshire, Berkshire, Oxfordshire and Buckinghamshire.
South-West: Cornwall, Devon, Somerset, Dorset, Wiltshire and Gloucestershire.
West Midlands: Shropshire, Stafford, Hereford, Worcestershire and Warwickshire.
North Midlands: Lincolnshire, Nottinghamshire,

Derbyshire, Leicestershire, Rutland and
Northamptonshire.
North-West: Lancashire and Cheshire.
North: Westmorland, Cumberland, Durham, and
Northumberland.

2. The years chosen for analysis are as close as possible to a
census year. 1862 rather than 1861 because by 1862 the
Force had had time to settle down; and 1899 rather than
1901 in order to avoid the abnormal enrolment during the
Boer War.

Source: Population calculated from the 1861, 1881 and 1901 Censuses.
Numbers of Volunteers from RC (1862) App. 2, pp. 206-24, and from
Annual Returns of the Volunteer Corps, PP 1882 (C. 3146), XXXVIII,
pp. 789-90; PP 1900 (Cd. 199), XLIX, pp. 396-9.

TABLE 10

Volunteers and Density of Population, Scotland 1881

Persons per sq. mile per Country	No. of Counties	Male Popu- lation, 15-49	No. of Volunteers	Volunteers as % of male population, 15-49
Less than 100				
(a) Northern	11	131,887	9,566	7.3
(b) Southern	8	62,820	3,657	5.8
Total (a) & (b)	19	194,707	13,223	6.8
Over 100				
(a) Northern	2	113,386	6,892	6.1
(b) Southern	10	547,368	26,962	4.9
Total (a) & (b)	12	660,754	33,854	5.1

Source: Persons per square mile per county from PP 1882 (C. 3320),
LXXVI, p. xxvii; population from PP 1883 (C. 3657), LXXXI, pp. 4-5.
Volunteers from PP 1882 (C. 3146), XXXVIII, pp. 789-90.

In England there appears to have been no correlation between density
of population and the percentage of the available population in the

Force (see Table 11). In England, indeed, the distribution of Volunteers was remarkably even, the weakest areas being the inland counties in the Midlands. Given that the Force's purpose was to stop invasion, there was, of course, logic in this.

TABLE 11

Volunteers and Density of Population, England 1881

Persons per sq. mile per county	No. of counties	Male Popu-lation, 15-49	No. of Volunteers	Volunteers as % of male population 15 - 49
Less than 200	9	410,993	9,420	2.3
200 – 300	13	917,709	24,578	2.7
300 – 400	6	568,409	13,014	2.3
Over 400 a. Metropolitan & South East	3	1,310,826	34,474	2.6
b. Midlands & North	10	2,568,992	60,844	2.4
Total		5,776,929	142,330	2.5

Source: Persons per square mile per county from PP 1883 (C. 3797), LXXX, p.114; population from PP 1883 (C. 3722), LXXX, pp.3, 31, 81, 125, 165, 215, 277, 319, 375, 425. Volunteers from PP 1882 (C. 3146), XXXVIII, pp. 789-90.

One further point should be made about the distribution of Volunteers. The large majority of Volunteers came from the densely populated areas. In England 67 per cent of the total lived in counties with more than four hundred people per square mile, and in Scotland 72 per cent of the total lived in counties with more than one hundred people per square mile. The Force was dominantly urban.

Figures showing the Volunteers as a percentage of the male population aged between 15 and 49 may give a misleading impression of the number of men who joined the Volunteers at some point in their lifetime. Since the Volunteers were concentrated in the lower age ranges and served a short time only, they attracted into their ranks many more men than the figures might suggest. Probably about one man in twelve served in the Volunteers at some point in his lifetime.[14]

Certain salient facts emerge from this study of the composition of the Force. The working-class members, already the majority in 1862, came to form something like three-quarters of the Force by the early twentieth century. An increasing proportion of that working-class membership, eventually about a quarter of the whole Force, was composed of unskilled workers. Quite contrary to the expectations of the founders of the Force, the middle class drifted away from it, while the working class consolidated its numerical preponderance. At the same time the average age at enrolment declined, as, less dramatically, did length of service. Most Volunteers, by 1913 three-quarters of them, were aged between seventeen and twenty-five. Most of them, too, lived in the industrial areas or the crowded south-east, though it was in Scotland, and in particular the Highlands that the highest proportion of the available population was in the Volunteers. These young working-class men, then, were numerically the dominant element in the Force. Without them it would have been an ephemeral patriotic upsurge, instead of the enduring institution it became.

Notes

1. A B and C Companies, 1st Lincoln Rifle Volunteers, Muster Roll Book, Lincolnshire Archives Office, Hill 12/3; 36th Middlesex Rifle Volunteers, Muster Roll Books, WO 70/1-4.
2. Committee (1878-9), qq. 717, 2684-5, 866, 1577, 3582-4, 1356-8; *VSG*, 2 June 1877.
3. This system of categorisation, by no means wholly satisfactory, was to a large degree dictated by the quality of the material I was working on. In the vast majority of cases the occupations fell naturally into one of the categories. In difficult cases I have made use of the *Classification of Occupations 1950* (HMSO, 1951), following W.A. Armstrong, 'The use of about occupation' in E.A. Wrigley (ed.), *Nineteenth-Century Society* (London, 1972), pp. 203-14.
4. R.C. (1862), q. 2597, and other references in Chapter II, n. 26.
5. Committee (1878-9), qq. 529, 868, 930 1664-8; R.W. Routledge, 'A Volunteer Battalion', *Nineteenth-Century*, vol. XXI (May 1887), p.745.
6. RC (1904), qq. 5701, 7681, 16803.
7. ibid., qq. 8242, 9310-3, 10357, 10941, 11632, 11781-2.
8. ibid., qq. 4869, 5130, 11833-4, 11867-8, 11926.
9. ibid., qq. 14827, 17668, 18546.
10. J.H.A. Macdonald, *Fifty Years of it*, pp. 91-2; J.M. Grierson, *Records of the Scottish Volunteer Force 1859-1908* (Edinburgh and London, 1908), p. 181; Col. C.H. Lindsay in *VSG*, 16 June 1877.
11. *VSG*, 9 and 16 June 1877; *Daily Bristol Times and Mirror*, 4 Jan. 1878.
12. 7th Cumberland Rifle Volunteers, Minute Book 1868-74, Carlisle Record Office, D/Cu/1/44; 15th Kent Rifle Volunteer Corps, Muster Roll Book, Kent County Archives, U 120. 07.

13. J.M. Grierson, op. cit., p. 57; but Scots were under-represented in the late Victorian Regular Army – see H.J. Hanham, 'Religion and Nationality in the mid-Victorian Army', in M.R.D. Foot (ed.), *War and Society* (London, 1973), p. 163.

14. This figure has been calculated in the following way. In the late nineteenth century Volunteers aged 19 were more numerous than those in any other single year age group. From 1895 (when the figures are first available) to 1899 there were on average 21,945 Volunteers aged 19 in each year. In 1901, the nearest census date, the male population of England, Wales and Scotland aged 19 was 358,136. Thus, dividing the population figure by the number of Volunteers aged 19, we find that in any one year 1 man in 16.3 of those aged 19 was a Volunteer. But this leaves out of account those who either joined and left the Force before they were 19, or joined after they were 19. There was no obvious way of knowing what allowance to make for this except by returning to the Lincoln and 36th Middlesex samples. Remarkably similar results emerged. 44.4 per cent of Lincoln Volunteers between 1880 and 1891, and 44.6 per cent of 36th Middlesex Volunteers between 1890 and 1899 either joined and left before they were 19 or joined after they were 19. It may be of course that there was some rejoining on the part of those who had left before they were 19, but it seemed reasonable to add 40 per cent to the average number of Volunteers aged 19 in 1895-9. 40 per cent of 21,945 is 8,778. Dividing this new total, 30,773, by the population figure, we find that 1 man in 11.7 joined the Volunteer Force at some point in his lifetime.

4 AN OFFICER – AND A GENTLEMAN?

The Volunteer Force was only under martial law when on active service,
or after 1871 when training with the Militia or Regular Forces. Normally
discipline rested on the authority which derived from the social status
of the officer. Although rules were drawn up instituting fines which
were recoverable in the courts for such offences as non-attendance, or
loading contrary to orders, and although an officer could dismiss a
disobedient man, essentially authority stemmed from the officer's
personality or social status. Any Volunteer who was disgruntled could
resign on giving fourteen days' notice. It is not surprising that it was a
constant complaint that the Volunteer Force lacked the discipline
necessary for warfare, and as we shall see there was a laxity in the Force
which could not have been tolerated in the Regular Army. In part at
least this was because the Volunteers found it difficult to attract
gentlemen of sufficiently high social status. Any difficulties there may
have been in recruiting the rank and file were as nothing to the chronic
problem of finding enough officers.

The appointment of officers was vested by Parliament in the Lord
Lieutenant, subject to the Queen's approval. In a sense, therefore, the
problem was one for the Lords Lieutenant: whose advice should they
take, what criteria for selection or rejection should they adopt? But of
course Lords Lieutenant needed advice. That there were early difficulties
was apparent from Sidney Herbert's circular letter of 13 July 1859:

> Misconceptions having apparently arisen with regard to the
> selection of individuals to fill the position of Officers in the
> Volunteer Force and of their responsibilities, I can only
> repeat, that while I shall not be disposed to question the
> grounds upon which a Lord Lieutenant may recommend any
> person for a Commission for Her Majesty's approval, I
> cannot recognize the principle of the election of their Officers
> by any body possessing, in any sense, a military organisation.

This carefully worded statement in effect allowed a corps to choose its
own officers provided it did not blatantly hold an election. As Herbert
himself put it in a later letter, 'It is desirable that officers should be
appointed to volunteer corps who are agreeable to those whom they are
to command. There is no objection, therefore, to steps being taken to
ascertain who would, as officers, be most acceptable to the corps.'[1]

Herbert gave recognition to what he could not abolish – some
say by the rank and file in the choice of their officers. Most Lords
Lieutenant were content that this should be so, but as with the
formation of corps, so with appointments to commissions, some were

reluctant that their authority should go by default. It was the Lord Lieutenant of Kent, Lord Sydney, who earned himself the most unenviable reputation for discrimination in appointments:

Who is the Lord Lieutenant of Kent,
Whose business seems to be to prevent
    The muster of Riflemen plucky?
Mr Punch would be very content
If that ass of a Lord Lieutenant of Kent
    Were kicked from Kent to Kentucky.[2]

'We ignore all Clubs and Election of officers, neither of which the Government recognise,' wrote Sydney in August 1859, and adhering to this principle and to the belief that an officer should be a gentleman, he was in constant conflict with the Volunteers in early days. From Woolwich he was presented with a list of officers nominated at a ballot meeting, but as it consisted 'of an indiscriminate amalgamation of the names of some of the superior officers of the departments and the mechanics, without due regard to their classification,' he rejected it; later this dispute was resolved, and Sydney agreed to commissions being given to the head foremen in the laboratory. But in Chatham he withheld a commission from the keeper of the garrison canteen on the grounds that, if appointed, he would be in command of those to whom in his employment he was subordinate. In Sheerness he objected to a solicitor, in Gillingham to a licensed victualler.[3] Lord Sydney was perhaps exceptional, though there is evidence from elsewhere to indicate that Lords Lieutenant refused to give commissions to those in trade.[4]

The objections of Lords Lieutenant, in fact, seem to have been more to the status of the proposed officer than the process by which his name had emerged. Elections continued more or less overtly for some years, and were even considered a right. In Tower Hamlets in 1860 where a working man's corps was in process of formation, the Captain declared that he had 'heard that it was the intention of the Lord Lieutenant to nominate the officers of the regiment, but if that was to be insisted upon they would not submit to it.' And in Glasgow at the 1861 Annual General Meeting of the 77th Company, 1st Lanarkshire Rifle Volunteers, 'the Meeting expressed a desire and wished it to be an understanding for future guidance, in regard to any vacancies occurring in the Military Officers of the Company, that such might be filled up by a vote of the Company, upon any member, irrespective of seniority or promotion.'[5] Contested elections were not uncommon, and could lead to problems: in Birmingham, 'the subaltern officers were at first elected by the men, and in those companies where freedom of election was most favoured and most freely exercised there was generally a split which ended in a suspension of the constitution for a while.'

In Birmingham elections were brought to an end, after some struggle, in 1862.[6] In most corps, however, elections simply faded away, almost unnoticed, in the 1860s and early 1870s. The election itself might never have been more than a formality, and there was not much to choose between an uncontested election and a nomination. Thus in Edinburgh the 3rd Artisans seem to have elected their last officers in August 1861 — thereafter they were appointed; in the 4th Artisans, however, elections continued till 1865, in the 5th to 1867, and in No. 20 Company to 1873. The *Volunteer Service Gazette* was still fulminating against election in that latter year, so presumably the Edinburgh company was not alone in continuing elections.[7]

Usually, however, election gave way to some process of consultation whereby the wishes of the members were considered and the appropriate social status in the officer required. Thus in the 77th Company, 1st Lanarkshire, when Captain Neilson resigned in 1868 he suggested that a Committee be appointed to look out for a replacement; the Committee consisting of one lieutenant, three sergeants, one corporal, one lance-corporal, and three privates, was instructed to look for someone of some social position. It produced four names, of which two were proposed and seconded at a meeting of the company, and an election held to decide between these two. A Committee continued to make recommendations until 1871, but after 1868 seems to have only produced one name for each vacancy, and this was always approved by the Company.[8]

The decline of elections was part of a process whereby the Volunteers became more military and less club-like in atmosphere. In Highgate the last officers were elected in June 1868, and 'with the demise of that custom', writes their historian, 'the principal mark of the civil as against the military character of the Volunteers disappeared.'[9] In 1871 Lords Lieutenant lost any say in appointments to commissions except to lieutenancies. Regular officers inherited their rights, but it was the Volunteer Commanding Officer in whose hands real power was concentrating. Annual general meetings and committees which had maintained at least a semblance of democratic control were gradually abandoned. Meetings of corps, where they continued, were in general perfunctory. In Workington the only business transacted at the annual meeting was the election of three members to the Finance Committee, and if the Minute Book can be trusted, there was no hint of dispute.[10] By 1894 most Commanding Officers believed that general meetings were unnecessary and an impediment to discipline.[11] The Commanding Officer in effect appointed his own junior officers, and together the officers controlled the affairs of the corps.

What sort of men, then, became officers? The general popularity of the Force in the early years ensured that officers were forthcoming in sufficient numbers and quality. Election, though a dangerous principle, proved safe in practice. As the *Volunteer Service Gazette* pointed out in 1861, 'the Volunteers have shown a tendency (natural probably to Englishmen) to select caeteris paribus, those who stood comparatively high in social station for their officers.'[12] No instance has come to light of a working man seeking a commission. If entrusted with a vote employees would dutifully elect their employers. There were of course strong financial as well as social reasons why they should do so. A working man might aspire to non-commissioned but not to commissioned rank.

In the early years, particularly in London, there was much competition to secure noblemen as Commanding Officers. The Duke of Wellington, Earl Grosvenor, the Marquis of Donegal, and Lords Bury, Elcho, Enfield, Radstock, Ranelagh, and Truro all commanded London corps. The fact that they did so makes it exceedingly difficult to regard the Force as an expression of middle-class anti-aristocratic feeling. Matthew Arnold fulminated against 'the hideous English toadyism with which lords and great people are invested with the commands in the corps they join, quite without respect of any considerations of their efficiency. This proceeds from our national bane − the immense vulgar-mindedness, and, so far, real inferiority of the English middle classes.'[13]

London was exceptional. Normally rural areas had the advantage over towns in the search for officers of high social status. Thus in north-east Scotland in the early years the officers commanding rural corps were chiefly gentlemen in the county, several being retired officers, whereas in the towns they were mainly the leading tradesmen. Country gentlemen were often reluctant to identify themselves with town corps; in Girvan, for example, the 'gentry and landed proprietors' displayed 'utter indifference'. In the counties they could normally be relied upon to come forward to take the command. Thus in Berkshire in Loyd-Lindsay's time the officers 'were chosen from leading squires and country gentlemen'.[14]

In towns there was much dispute as to whether a commission could properly be granted to a man in trade. Lords Lieutenant, as we have seen, were inclined to demur, but often disagreements were settled at a lower level. Thus in Southampton, in No. 4 Company, the Captain, an attorney, refused the men's request that a senior sergeant who was a draper's son be promoted ensign, on the grounds that he could not associate with tradesmen or ask them to his table; the company eventually broke up. To be in trade, in fact, was still thought to be incompatible with the status of officer, and it was on these grounds that in Lyncombe in Somerset the Captain refused to accede to the petition of 67 members that he appoint a Mr. Milsom Lieutenant − Milsom was in trade. Association with trade, and possibly urban-rural disagreement about the status of an officer seem to have been at the

55

bottom of a dispute in Evesham a decade later, which rated a short debate in Parliament. Two Volunteers with ten years service, both town councillors and both tradesmen, failed to get commissions despite the unanimous approval of the corps. The objection came from the officers of a neighbouring company of the same corps. F.W. Knight, MP, the pioneer Volunteer in Worcestershire, explained that 'the course adopted in most of the towns of Worcestershire had been to appoint for officers the natural leaders of the men – namely, the merchants, manufacturers, and professional men . . . It was contrary to the principle that regulated Volunteer Corps that persons who stood behind the counter should be appointed officers.' As a Surrey Captain put it, 'Society demands consistency. It cannot assimilate the social rank of an officer in Her Majesty's service with one who serves beer over a public-house counter, or measures you for a suit of clothes in his shirt sleeves.'[15]

Given the doubts about trade, urban corps turned chiefly to professional men to fill the commissioned ranks. In the smaller towns of Kent solicitors were prominent. In Beccles in Suffolk a young doctor, W.M. Crowfoot, soon took command of the corps – he was a leading citizen, himself twice serving as Mayor, and his family providing four Mayors in the course of the century.[16] Even in London, despite the gilding of aristocracy, it was the professional men who dominated as an analysis of the occupations of 605 London Volunteer officers indicates (Table 1).

TABLE 1

Occupations of London Volunteer Officers, 1860-72

Occupation	No.	%
Professional	174	28.8
Clerks	86	14.2
Merchants	73	12.1
Manufacturers	71	11.7
Financial	51	8.4
Gentlemen	41	6.8
Other	78	12.9
None	31	5.1
TOTAL	605	100.0

Note:
Professional: Surgeons, doctors, lawyers, architects, surveyors, civil

engineers, veterinary surgeons, civil servants, authors, clergymen and students.

Clerks: Anyone so styled.
Merchants: Merchants, wharfingers and importers.
*Manufacturers:*Many so styled, and anyone engaged in production.
Financial: Stock and bullion brokers, accountants, bankers.
Gentlemen: Anyone so styled.
Other: Anyone who did not fit into the above categories, including 23 men working for HM Customs.

Source: Clerk to Lieutenancy Records, L56b, 60, 61, 63, 66, 73, 78, 85, Middlesex County Record Office.

As time went on it became less and less common for a man to rise through the ranks to a commission. In the early years some of the professional corps, particularly in Edinburgh and London, found that it was one of their functions to provide men from their ranks to take commissions in less favoured corps. Thus the Advocates' Corps in Edinburgh, before it faded into decline, was in effect a training institution for Volunteer officers. There were those, too, in corps which were less exclusively middle-class, who believed in the value of service in the ranks before taking a commission. Lieutenant-Colonel Warner in 1884 'laid great stress upon the advantage of having a leaven of the middle classes in the ranks and expressed his opinion that the best volunteer officers were those who had thus served.' In his Battalion, of 41 officers between 1859 and 1885, 22 did service in the ranks of the 3rd Middlesex or its predecessors before taking a commission, 13 did no service, and 6 did service in another battalion. For those who did do service the average length of time in the ranks was 5.1 years, no easy apprenticeship.[17] Of the 605 London Volunteer officers whose occupations were analysed above at least 31 per cent had seen some service in the ranks before being commissioned (see Table 2) With increasing emphasis on discipline, however, the maintenance of social distance between officers and other ranks became more important. The man with local prestige was preferred to the recruit who had served his time in the ranks. Official blessing was given to this in May 1872 when the Auxiliary and Reserve Forces Circular recognised it as desirable that local corps should be commanded by 'gentlemen who had local influence' who had 'not served in the lower ranks.'[18]

It is not until 1904 that we again have anything like comprehensive information on the occupations of officers (see Table 3). Professional men and businessmen dominate the officer corps. The intriguing category is employees; if more was known about what kind of employees they were it would be possible to say how low the authorities were stooping in their search for officers. The concern was certainly to keep the status high, and no less than 59 per cent of the 1904 officers had been to public schools or University. In Buckinghamshire, 19 of the 29 officers were public school men, no less than 12 of them Old Etonians. This was probably exceptional. In Yorkshire the country gentlemen tended to go into the Militia or Yeomanry, in Northumberland 'there are two battalions where the officers are solicitors, lawyers, merchants, and people of that sort, and then there are two battalions where there is a lower class altogether.' And in Sussex, according to A.M. Brookfield, the squirearchy was reluctant to be engaged in anything of a military nature.[19]

TABLE 2

Previous Service of London Volunteer Officers, 1860-72

	No.	%
No previous service recorded	262	43.3
Previous service in ranks: same corps	102	16.9
: different corps	84	13.9
Previous service as officer: same corps	12	2.0
: different corps	41	6.8
Previous service as Volunteer, no rank given	45	7.4
Previous service in Militia or Regular Army	59	9.8
TOTAL	605	100.1

Source: Clerk to Lieutenancy Records, L56b, 60, 61, 63, 66, 73, 78, 85, Middlesex County Record Office.

TABLE 3

Occupations of Volunteer Officers, 1904

Occupation	%
Gentlemen of independent means	6.1
Professional men	29.8
Men in business on their own account	34.4
Employees	21.3
Students	3.5
Other	4.9
TOTAL	100.0

Source: RC (1904), App. Pt. IV.

Increasingly it was the public schools and Universities and their cadet corps which were seen as the most promising source for officers. Highgate School, where a cadet corps was founded in 1892, was providing nearly half the officers of the local battalion by 1914. Tonbridge School had a close link with the 1st Middlesex Volunteer Engineers. But although cadet corps had existed from early years, they were few and weak until schools were encouraged to form corps after 1886, and it was not until the institution of the Territorial Force that a determined effort was made to channel youth via the cadet corps and other youth organisations into the Force.[20] In the Universities volunteering never held the attraction of cricket, football or rowing. When Spencer Wilkinson was up at Oxford in the 1870s, the University Corps 'was rather a bye-word among the undergraduates.' It would seem that matters had improved somewhat by the early twentieth century, for in 1904 one in four undergraduates at Cambridge and one in five at Oxford were Volunteers. Here and in the cadet corps the 1904 Royal Commission and later Haldane saw the possibility of overcoming the chronic shortage of officers, and at the same time tapping a source of sufficient social respectability.[21]

These new sources of supply, however, were insufficient to lay to rest the continuing anxiety about both the quantity and quality of officers. The vacancies in the commissioned list were considerable. By 1873 there were 2,233 vacancies, between 1895 and 1899 an average of 1,606, between 1904 and 1907 an average of 2,427, and in the years of the Territorial Force from 1908-13 a slight improvement with the average number of vacancies being 1,898.[22] Not infrequently corps simply ceased to exist because of lack of officers, as in Lanarkshire in the 1870s. Commanding Officers, asked a composite question by the 1878-9 Committee of Inquiry, expressed their nagging concern about filling the commissioned ranks: 178 answered in the negative, only 111 in the affirmative to the questions, 'Do you get a sufficient supply of officers without difficulty? Are they generally of such a social position as you would desire?'[23]

Contemporaries were in almost unanimous agreement that there were two chief reasons for the shortage of officers. The first and most straightforward was the cost. An officer had to buy his uniform, and in addition normally paid a subscription according to rank to meet band expenses, prize money, entertainment costs, and so on. The cost, of course, might vary considerably from corps to corps, but there is ample evidence that it was a price which many found too high to bear. In corps where there was a subscription it was by no means certain that that would cover all expenses — there might be special calls for camp or for a new drill hall. Accurate figures are therefore hard to come by, but a few examples will show the kind of expenses which an officer might have to meet. In Lancashire it was reckoned in 1862 that an officer would need £50 per annum excluding his uniform. In Lambeth and Southwark officers' subscriptions in 1873 were: Lieutenant-Colonel £20, Major £10, Captain £3, and Lieutenant £2. In the 1st Middlesex Volunteer Engineers at the end of the nineteenth century the subscriptions to the officers' mess were: Colonel 25 gns; Major 18 gns; Captain 13 gns; Subaltern 10 gns. In 1894 it was reckoned in Sussex that a Captain's expenses would be £20 per annum, a Subaltern's £10 per annum including uniform but excluding camp, and in Glamorgan that an officer would have to pay £40 for his uniform and £10 to cover expenses in a year in a well-regulated regiment. In Liverpool by 1904 an officer's expenses were at least £25 per annum and in nearly every corps in the country the officers were out of pocket in camp.[24]

In spite of an outfit allowance introduced in the 1890s, and schemes of deferred payment for uniform introduced in some corps.[25] there can be little doubt that anyone seeking a commission in the Volunteers was rendering himself liable to the kind of expenditure which might otherwise have met his subscription to his Club.

Moreover if he became Commanding Officer, he incurred a further liability, and became responsible in law for the debts of the whole corps. This put a premium on wealth as a qualification for high office, as a financially insecure man would be unwilling to run the risks involved. And it was only too easy for a Volunteer Corps to mount large debts. When the Commanding Officer of the 1st Herts Light Horse Volunteer Corps fled the country in 1878, his fellow officers and men had to meet claims totalling some £2,000 against the corps.[26]

The second reason given for the shortage of officers was the low status of Volunteer officers in society. Those who argued against the admission of tradesmen to the commissioned ranks were recognising that the Volunteer officer would only enjoy high status in society if he was, and was seen to be, a gentleman. But this, alas, was not the case. Few bodies of men can have met with such bitter criticism on account of their social origins. 'In the *personnel* of many of the Volunteer officers in the counties of England, in Wales and in Scotland,' wrote the wisely anonymous N. Taillefer, 'are men of intensely vulgar, conceited and ignorant manners, men who still drop their h's, and are among the uneducated *nouveau rich* in local society, men wealthy and stingy, arrogant and fawning, men incorrigibly addicted to money-grubbing. . .' There were other more temperate attacks: 'I know battalions myself where the officers are really of the class which ought to be the sergeants . . .' declared one witness before the 1904 Royal Commission.[27]

Some would have preferred going without officers rather than lower the class from which they were recruited.[28] The consequence of offering

60

commissions to those who were not clearly gentlemen was to reduce the status of the whole Force, and to give occasion for many gibes from the well-heeled. The 'grocer colonels' as they were known in early twentieth-century Scotland[29] did not enjoy great prestige in their communities. Nor was this condition of disrespect new. In Edinburgh some of the officers were 'of but small estimation in what is called society,' but, in the 1870s, for the young clerks in the civil service who were getting commissions 'it was the only ladder which they had to a little distinction in the town, and they took a great interest in their companies . . .'[30] Upwardly mobile socially, and using the Volunteer Force as a ladder, it is not difficult to understand why so many of them must have been hurt at the lack of respect according to them. By 1873 the *Volunteer Service Gazette* was sadly recognising that 'in ordinary middle-class society − particularly in towns − it is a distinct disadvantage to a young gentleman to be known as a subaltern or captain of Volunteers.' Being an officer, the 1878-9 Committee of Inquiry was told, was not 'a passport to society'. 'It is not considered quite the thing to be an officer in a volunteer corps', reported a Manchester Colonel to the 1894 Committee. And it was the belief of the experienced C.B. Brackenbury in 1889 that the main reason for the shortage of Volunteer officers was 'the uncertain, and therefore unsatisfactory, standing of the Volunteer officer. Give what titles you will, they are discounted by society . . .'[31]

The Volunteers tried to overcome their lack of prestige in the eyes of society by devising schemes which would enhance their status. An early and recurring plan was that they should be relieved of jury service.[32] In 1865 a Committee was formed in Manchester to bring the question of the military and legal rank and status of Volunteer officers before the Government. Earl de Grey told them that Volunteer officers were entitled to recognition of their rank, promised them that if admitted to Court they would have their rank recognised by the Lord Chamberlain, and said he would consider further the question of exemption from jury service.[33] But by the 1890s at any rate the status the Volunteer officer aspired to − and it is an interesting indication of the new popularity of the Army − was that of an officer of the line. There would be no more shortages of officers 'if you could make it as much desired to be an officer in a volunteer battalion as it is in a line battalion,' declared a witness before the 1894 Select Committee.[34] The way to achieve this status, it was believed, was to put the Volunteers under the Army Act − that is, make them liable to full military discipline; no mean sacrifice to make for the sake of status.

Despite all the discussion not much was done to raise the status; the introduction of a long service medal in the 1890s, the Volunteer Decoration, was hardly sufficient inducement for men to come forward for commissions, though it may have persuaded a few of the older officers to serve a few more years in order to receive the decoration. The shortages, however, remained.

Furthermore it was the constant complaint of commentators that the weak point of the Volunteer Force was its officers; not only, it was said, were their numbers short and their social status low, but also their military qualities and disciplinary powers left much to be desired. It was a vicious circle. The number of vacancies forced Commanding Officers to look for their subalterns lower down the social scale than they would have wished; discipline then suffered as it rested not on the Mutiny Act but on the authority which came from status. Thus the vacancies, the lack of status, and the low quality were connected. The Government's response was to introduce proficiency tests to improve the quality,[35] but this immediately ran up against the complaint that a Volunteer was after all a Volunteer, and not too much should be asked of him. It was perhaps fair that something should be asked of him: W.E. Forster, setting up a corps in his mill, described his 'total and ludicrous ignorance. To make the men take to it, I shall have to be one of their awkward squad myself; and awkward enough I shall be, for I never could keep step with any-one, and never handled a gun in my life.' But at least he was willing to learn, and underwent a course at Hythe. How many were there, one may wonder, like George Melly, who at a field day in Sefton Park, had to call on no less a person than the Duke of Cambridge to assist him as he was unable to give an order for moving twelve paces to the right?[36]

Those who criticised the qualities of the Volunteer officers – and they ranged from Engels to *The Times*[37] – sometimes saw the solution to lie in placing the Volunteers under Regulars. There were always a number of retired Regulars who took commissions in the Force, as also a number who held commands in both the Volunteers and the Militia, and in some areas it was thought that the rank and file responded better to a military man. Others, however, objected to this injection of military men, either, like J.H.A. Macdonald, because they found that the retired officers appointed to commissions were 'absolutely useless', or because they wanted the Volunteers to be an Army in itself, separate from and independent of the Regulars.[38] The appointment of an ex-Regular could certainly have a marked impact on a corps; for instance, in the 7th Middlesex the appointment of an ex-Regular to the command in 1891 led to much closer links with the regiment being formed;[39] in general, corps with Regulars as officers were likely to have a more military bearing, though there were of course exceptions, and if the Regular were too much of a martinet he would find his ranks diminished.

This argument about the impact of Regular officers on Volunteer corps was part of the ongoing debate about discipline. It was an axiom that the maintenance of social distance was essential if there was to be any pretence of discipline. Deficiencies in discipline, said Sir Howard Vincent, arose from the 'great familiarity which often exists between officers and NCO's and men; officers do not maintain their position sufficiently; they hobnob with the men constantly after parade.' This kind of familiarity was seen as the cause of trouble in Airdrie where discipline reached such a low ebb that the corps had to be disbanded, leading to a debate in Parliament in 1897. In Airdrie, it was revealed, three of the officers were publicans whose customers were the privates, and another was a plumber who was paid by the corps for work done on the range. Christian names were used by both officers and men on parade, blank cartridges were fired in the streets and at stations, and men appeared to drill in slippers.[40]

Airdrie was doubtless exceptionally bad, but, for example, firing in the streets or in railway carriages was not uncommon.[41] And there are other almost incidental remarks which lead one to doubt how far the Volunteers can be considered as a militarily disciplined body. The Acting Adjutant of a Sheffield corps, for example, wrote that 'the talking in the ranks is I fear a general failing with Volunteers, but I always try to stop it as they cannot attend to words of command or instruction.' 'One of the marked peculiarities of the Volunteer service,' remarked George Melly, 'is the "colloquial intercourse" which is always going on in the ranks.' Even more astonishing, the *Volunteer Service Gazette* in 1874 'thought that the practice of smoking in the ranks, while marching in the full gaze of the public, had been as prevalent as it could be; but we are sorry to say that it appears to be on the increase. We now hear of regiments of Volunteers marching in broad daylight through the Royal Parks with pipes in full blaze.'[42]

This kind of behaviour was anathema to the majority of Commanding Officers. And just as they wished to be drawn closer to the Regular Army so that they could share the prestige of a Regular's commission, many of them also wanted the military discipline of the Volunteers to approximate more closely to that of the Regulars. Certainly it seems that discipline improved as time went on. In part this was due to the eradication of the club-like atmosphere of the early days and the concentration of power in the hands of the officers; but it probably owed something too to the increase in social distance between officer and rank and file. Without the Mutiny Act, and with every Volunteer having the right to resign at fourteen days' notice, it was still on the social prestige of the officer that discipline rested; essentially, that is, on authority which derived from civilian life.

This point is driven home by an examination of the social origins of non-commissioned officers, the intermediates in the chain of authority.

63

NCOs, like their officers, were often elected in the early days, but men showed a distinct tendency to choose those who were naturally in authority over them. Thus in Birkenhead in the 1860s the sergeants were 'generally the foremen and the better class of the workmen,' and at Gartness in Lanarkshire 'the foremen of departments became sergeants and corporals, occupying pretty much the like relative positions in the Volunteer Corps that they held over their men at their daily labour.' The world of the factory was reproduced on the parade ground. The position was unchanged in the early 1900s. In Edinburgh the NCOs 'are older men generally, and men who are perhaps foremen in business, and that sort of thing, so that they have a good deal of command naturally.' The same was true in Durham, and in Birmingham where the NCOs 'as a rule are superior men to the ordinary rank and file; they naturally do get their stripes. They are mostly small trades-men and clerks in offices, men with education superior to the rank and file.' If the NCO was socially on the same level as the privates his authority was thereby diminished. In socially homogeneous communities it was difficult to find suitable NCOs; in the Welsh mining area, it was said, 'the NCO is really useless because the private will punch his head when he gets him down below.'[43]

From a disciplinary point of view, the ideal corps was one in which the officers derived their authority from their civilian position and were socially as far as possible removed from the rank and file. Working men, it was commonly agreed, submitted better to the rigours of drill than those socially superior to them. As a Midlands Adjutant put it in 1862, 'the best volunteer is by far an artisan; he is a man that you can drill, a man that will work, and who understands you; but if you get hold of tradesmen, very fine gentlemen, they are so thin-skinned that you cannot do it; but you can order an artisan to do a thing, and he will do it like a man.'[44] The employer, of course, was, as officer, in an exceptionally good position to maintain discipline. In the 2nd Cheshire Railway Engineer Volunteers 'generally speaking, the men . . . serve, directly or indirectly, under their officers in their civilian or home occupations, whereby a good understanding amongst all ranks exists, and a good state of discipline is maintained.'[45]

This was the ideal, and was all too rarely attained. The generally low status of the officer deprived him of authority, and discipline suffered. The lack of discipline laid the Force wide open to the objection that militarily it was unreliable. Improvements were made, but they were never sufficient to meet the complaints. Officers were never forth-coming in sufficient quality or quantity, and those who did hold a commission must often have wondered whether it was not more of an embarrassment than an honour. A social ambiguity hovered over the Volunteer officer who could not with confidence be known to be a gentleman. A spokesman for the Force stressed that the deficiencies of the officers should not be blamed on the Volunteers themselves, but rather on society as a whole, or as the *Volunteer Service Gazette* put it in a moment of exasperation in 1873, 'on the utter lukewarmness and apathy of the nation towards the Force.'[46]

Notes

1. R.P. Berry, *A History of the Formation and Development of the Volunteer Infantry*, p. 493; *VSG*, 3 Mar. 1860.
2. *Punch*, 26 Nov. 1859.
3. Sydney to William Deedes, 27 Aug. 1859, Deedes Papers, vol. 3; *VSG*, 4, 11, and 25 Feb., 3 and 17 Mar., 14 Apr. 1860.
4. Cruikshank to Ensign Worthy, 25 July 1863, Cruikshank Papers, Middlesex County Record Office, Acc.534/5.
5. *VSG*, 7 Apr. 1860; Minute and Cash Book of Volunteer Corps projected by members of the City Drill Class, 'City Rifle Guard', 7 Mar. 1861, SUSM, 6323B.
6. C.J. Hart, *The History of the 1st Volunteer Battalion The Royal Warwickshire Regiment*, pp. 118-23.
7. W. Stephen, *History of the Queen's City of Edinburgh Rifle Volunteer Brigade*, pp. 245, 254-5, 293, 297-8; *VSG*, 29 Mar. 1873.
8. Minute Book No. 2, 1st Lanarkshire Rifle Volunteers, 77th Company, 5 and 26 Mar.,2 Apr. 1868, 8 Nov. 1870, 10, 14 and 21 Apr. 1871. SUSM, 6323H.
9. E.T. Evans, *Records of the Third Middlesex Rifle Volunteers* (London, 1885), pp. 127-8.
10. Minute Book, 7th Cumberland Rifle Volunteers, 1868-74, Carlisle Record Office, D/Cu/1/44.
11. SC (1894), qq. 610-20, 634-80, 1582-9, 1720-5, Report, pp. iv-v.
12. *VSG*, 18 May 1861.
13. [Charles] Rudd, *The Early History of the 17th (North) Middlesex Volunteer Rifles (formerly the 29th), 1859-89* (London, 1895), p. 25; G.W.E. Russell (ed.), *Letters of Matthew Arnold*, vol. I, pp. 126-7.
14. *Army and Navy Gazette*, quoted in *VSG*, 7 Nov. 1863; RC (1862), App. 3; *VSG*, 7 Jan. 1860; Harriet S. Wantage, *Lord Wantage, VC, KCB* (London, 1907), p. 151.
15. A Temple Patterson, *A History of Southampton 1700-1914*, vol. II (Southampton, 1971), pp. 138-9; W.G. Fisher, *The History of Somerset Yeomanry, Volunteer and Territorial Units*, pp. 104-5; *3 Hansard 202*, cc. 1088-9 (28 June 1870), *203*, cc. 785-92 (22 July 1870); Charles Harding, *The Volunteer Service as a Branch of the Army of Reserve* (London, 1870), p.4.
16. C. Igglesden, *History of the East Kent Volunteers* (Ashford, 1899), pp. 81-2, 87, 96-9, 125, 172-5; E.A. Goodwyn, *A Suffolk Town in Mid-Victorian England: Beccles in the 1860s* (Beccles, 1965), pp. 55-6, 67-8.
17. W. Stephen, op. cit., p. 167; E.T. Evans, op. cit., pp. 273, 318-23.
18. R.P. Berry, op. cit., p. 190.
19. RC (1904), App. Pt. IV, qq. 12141, 8865, 4945; A.M. Brookfield, *Annals of a Chequered Life* (London, 1930), p. 248.
20. E.J. King, *The History of the 7th Battalion Middlesex Regiment* (London,

1927), pp. 87-8; D.K. Edwards, *A History of 1st Middlesex Volunteer Engineers 1860-1967* (1967), p. 24; J.D. Sainsbury, *Hertfordshire Soldiers* (Hitchin, 1969), p. 80.

21. H.S. Wilkinson, *Thirty-five Years 1874-1909* (London, 1933), p. 7; RC (1904), qq. 17846, 11259, Report, p. 19; *4 Hansard 176*, cc. 248-9 (17 June 1907); see also J.O. Springhall, 'The Boy Scouts, Class and Militarism in Relation to British Youth Movements 1908-1930', *International Review of Social History*, vol. XVI (1971), esp. pp. 144-7.

22. 'Return of the Number of Commissions Vacant in the Volunteer Force', PP. 1873 (118), XL, p. 615; 1895-1913 figures taken from Annual Returns of the Volunteer and Territorial Forces, 1895-1913.

23. J. Orr, *History of the Seventh Lanarkshire Rifle Volunteers*, p. 141; Committee (1878-9), App. XIX.

24. RC (1862), q. 2707; J.M.A. Tamplin, *The Lambeth and Southwark Volunteers*, pp. 36, 49, 60; D.K. Edwards, op. cit., p. 14; SC (1894), qq. 365-6, 1764; RC (1904), q. 13233, App. Pt. IV.

25. RC (1904), App. XCII; Minute Book of Regimental Committee, 1st Lanark Rifles, 9 Nov. 1891, SUSM, 6323J.

26. J.D. Sainsbury, op. cit., p. 30.

27. N. Taillefer, *Rondeaus of the Auxiliary Forces, Militia and Volunteers*, 8th ed. (London, 1882), p. 88, n. 5; RC (1904), q. 7695.

28. RC (1904), q. 9153.

29. I owe this information to Ian Shiell.

30. J.H.A. Macdonald, *Fifty Years of it*, p. 91; Committee (1878-9), q. 693.

31. *VSG*, 5 Apr. 1873; Committee (1878-9), qq. 2130-1; SC (1894), q. 750; C.B. Brackenbury, 'A Real Volunteer Army', *Contemporary Review*, vol. 55 (June 1889), p. 937.

32. Adam Gladstone to Boyle, Oct. 1859, Correspondence of the Advocates Volunteer Rifles, National Library of Scotland, Adv. MS 81.2.12, ff. 35-6; *4 Hansard 1-5, 8*, (1892-3) for unsuccessful attempts to pass Volunteer Forces (Jury Exemption) Bill. The matter was further considered by SC (1894).

33. *VSG*, 18 Feb., 4 and 18 Mar. 1865.

34. SC (1894), q. 772.

35. Proficiency tests were first introduced in 1872.

36. T. Wemyss Reid, *Life of the Right Honourable William Edward Forster* (London, 1889), p. 178; G. Melly, *Recollections of Sixty Years* (Coventry, 1893), p. 106.

37. W.H. Chaloner and W.O. Henderson (eds.), *Engels as Military Critic* (Manchester, 1959), pp. 7-8, 40-3; *The Times*, 16 Nov. 1860, 2 Apr. 1866, 24. Sept. 1870.

38. RC (1862), qq. 859, 3283; *VSG*, 23 Jan. 1867, quoting *Daily Telegraph*; J.H.A. Macdonald, op. cit., p. 116; for those who wanted an independent Volunteer army, see below, pp. 84-60.

39. E.J. King, op. cit., pp. 82-3.

40. Committee (1878-9), qq. 1105-6; *4 Hansard 46*, cc. 1595-7, *47*, cc. 769-82, *51*, cc. 953-68 (4 and 16 Mar., 23 July 1897).

41. C. Igglesden, op. cit., p. 8; E.E. Dyer, *The History of the Volunteers of Clackmannan and Kinross* (Alva, 1907), p. 123.

42. H. Kennedy to Wharncliffe, n.d. [1864], Wharncliffe Muniments, Wh. M. 459, Sheffield City Library; G. Melly, op. cit., p. 119; *VSG*, 28 Mar. 1874.

43. RC (1862), q. 2540; J. Orr, op. cit., p. 397; RC (1904), qq. 8069, 9575, 10022-6, 10275.

44. RC (1862), q. 3774; see also *VSG*, 30 June, 1877.

45. RC (1904), q. 6051.
46. VSG, 18 Jan. 1873.

5 CITIZENS AND SOLDIERS

'Volunteers live and move under the very sceptre of opinion,' wrote
The Times on 13 June 1863. Unlike the Regulars, most of whose
service was overseas, and who when at home were concentrated in
barracks, the Volunteers were both local and visible. The public having
in some sense at least called the Force into being was continually
reminded of its existence. A march-out, a church parade, or a rifle
contest would bring the citizen-soldiers prominently before the public
eye; bazaars and theatrical shows would remind the public of the
Force's need for funds; and a glance through any newspaper, local or
national, would tell the reader of the Volunteers' activities. The public,
in turn, was in a position to praise or criticise, flatter or denigrate. A
Volunteer could not but be conscious that certain sections of society
gave general support to the Force, while others were disinterested or
hostile. And it was not only the attitudes of his fellow-citizens of
which he was aware. The regular soldier, too, kept a watchful and
critical eye on these part-time newcomers to military life. It was under
the sceptre of military as well as of civilian opinion that the Volunteers
lived and moved.

The Volunteers, however, were not simply the plaything of opinion.
They were capable themselves of moulding opinion and of acting as a
pressure group. And they formed something of a bridge between the
Regular Army and the people, so that in the opinion of many it was the
Volunteers whom the Regulars had to thank for the improved image
of the Army in later nineteenth-century Britain. Nevertheless to a large
degree the Volunteers were at the mercy of opinion. A shift in the
prevailing view of the nature of warfare or of the value of volunteer
troops could make all the difference between outspoken praise and
niggling criticism. Suppliants to Parliament for public funds, the
Volunteers could not turn a blind eye to the public's opinion of their
worth. Thus if we are to understand what it meant to be a Volunteer,
and what the Volunteer Force meant to the country, it is vital to look
at the status of the Force in both civilian and military society. How well
integrated were the Volunteers in local society? Which groups in society
supported and which opposed them? What military role was assigned
to them, and how effectively was it thought that they could perform it?
In a word, what was their status?

Volunteer corps, as has been seen, frequently came into being at
formally requisitioned public meetings. In so far as such meetings were
unopposed, and this was normally the case, the citizen-soldier started
out with the backing and often the enthusiasm of the local community.

Indeed, what must strike the historian is the extent to which the Volunteers were fired not so much by love of Britain as by pride in and a sense of belonging to their local community. The Volunteer movement became so quickly part of the established social scene that by about mid-1860 any sizeable town without a flourishing local corps felt itself disadvantaged in comparison with its neighbours (and vice versa). More important, the local corps did not stem from some fringe element in the community, but were from the beginning associated with the local elite. They thus quickly came to play a part in local functions, and their success or failure was seen as a commentary on the civic or village leaders, and on the community as a whole.

Bury, for example, was quick off the mark, with a corps embracing 'large numbers of every branch of local society; there were the gentry and the manufacturers, men with large families, and men with no family at all, skilled workmen of high standing in their calling, clerks and labourers . . . The corps', wrote the local historian, 'gave us a certain indefinable status among the towns of East Lancashire which were hastening in the same direction.' And, to show the opposite case, the threatened disbandment by the War Office of the Weston-super-Mare Volunteer Artillery led to the local magistrates heading a public meeting in the Town Hall, summoned by a notice calling on the public to attend to help prevent 'that disgrace falling on the town which must necessarily follow the disbandment of a Volunteer Corps.'[1]

This concern with the fortunes of the local corps was lasting. Whenever a corps came into disfavour with the War Office the local community would be quick to come to the defence of their criticised Volunteers. Thus in 1880 when the War Office demanded the resignation of some officers in Hull, the Town Council, at a special meeting, called upon the Secretary of State to institute a searching inquiry. And when the Airdrie Volunteers were disbanded after a series of irregularities in 1897, local Members of Parliament pressed hard for a reversal of the decision. The Provost, magistrates, Town Council, and over one thousand members of the public were present at a meeting to demand a rescinding of the order or an inquiry. There would be 'a lasting stigma upon these men and upon the district from which they came', claimed one Member of Parliament. And even Sir Henry Campbell-Bannerman harped on the indignity which would be done to the locality if the corps was disbanded.[2]

A crisis was not necessary, however, for the blossoming of local patriotism. The first parade of the local corps in uniform was frequently a civic occasion with a church service, a dinner given by the Mayor, and often a holiday. At Kidderminster the corps made its first public appearance in full uniform on a Sunday; the day started with mulled wine and biscuits provided by the man who lent them a drill room, followed by a march to church for a special service. The corps was then dismissed, but was enthusiastic enough to reassemble in the evening for another church service where 'they had again the advantage of listening to an appropriate and excellent sermon.' In Carlisle the first public appearance in uniform of the 1st Cumberland Rifle Volunteers, on a Monday, 'was observed throughout the town as a whole holyday.' In Bristol, on the occasion of the arrival in the town of the guns and ammunition for the artillery corps (a Thursday), 'The streets and shipping were gaily dressed with flags, and throughout the day merry peals issued from several church belfries, and cannon were discharged at various points . . . Throughout the whole line of procession the shops were closed, and, the weather being remarkably fine, the occasion was made a general holiday.'[3]

It was not only these first parades which were the occasion for public attention. In three different ways the Volunteers made an impact on their localities. In the first place their purely military activities attracted attention and spectators. Volunteering may be considered the spectator sport of mid-Victorian Britain. At the 1860 review at Knowsley, the Earl of Derby's seat in Lancashire, there were thought to be between 150,000 and 200,000 'holiday-makers' watching 11,000 Volunteers. 'Tens of thousands habitually attend every muster of Volunteers as spectators,' said the first Inspector-General of the Force. They came to watch and to enjoy themselves. County rifle meetings, said Lord Lyttelton, were 'a great feast day and amusement for the whole county.' In Beccles in the 1860s, 'Inspections were popular local spectacles,were often made the occasion for public half-holidays, and sometimes followed by a dinner.'[4] Spectators indeed threatened to dominate the Force as they pushed their way on to parade grounds, or unintentionally intervened between opposing armies at sham fights.[5]

It was at the Easter Monday review, most popularly held at Brighton, that the public's presence was most noticeable. It was as much a holiday as a military occasion. As *The Times* wrote of the 1870 review at Brighton, 'everybody came to be pleased and was pleased, and from the holyday point of view the thing was a complete success.' And when the abolition of the Easter Review was being mooted in 1871 the *Daily Telegraph* was aghast; the Easter Review, it thought,

> has taken so firm a hold on the popular feeling, and it has come to be recognised as an event so thoroughly national, that the bitterest disappointment and discontent would be excited were an Easter Monday to pass over without the familiar gathering. We could almost as soon spare the Derby . . . . It is idle to say that a Volunteer Review is simply a matter of business, and that the sightseers have nothing to

do with it. So long as it is held on Easter Monday the celebration is a holiday as well as a parade, and the holiday-makers have their right to enjoy it in the fullest degree compatible with the perfect freedom of military operations.[6]
Aside from their purely military activities, the Volunteers were useful in lending dignity to civic occasions. Thus in Beccles they paraded on the occasion of the funeral of the Prince Consort, they formed a procession and fired a *feu de joie* at the celebrations marking the marriage of the Prince of Wales, and their band played at a dinner in honour of the Mayor. The Volunteer Force came into being at a time when the brass band had just established itself as a popular form of music, and their own bands did much to spread that popularity. In the second half of the nineteenth century public music was frequently Volunteer music. By providing music and a show of military formality, the Volunteers were an essential part of any public function.[7]

Finally, in their search for funds Volunteers organised fêtes, bazaars, and theatrical entertainments. Sometimes in doing so they were providing entertainment where previously there had been none. Thus when the Lincoln Volunteers announced a fund-raising theatrical performance in 1861 the local press noted: 'An amateur play will be a novelty in Lincoln, and will, therefore, no doubt, be well patronised by the *elite* of the city, as well as by numerous visitors.' Sometimes amateurism was perhaps carried too far; witness Kilvert's Diary entry for 27 February 1871: 'I hear the Rifle Volunteer Corps Concert at Hay last Wednesday was moderately successful. In the middle of the performance the Rifle Corps band played "Vital Spark", and a man named Clement skated round the platform upon wheel skates, and fell off into the front row of ladies. Everyone rose, the ladies were very much frightened, and one lady's dress was irretrievably damaged. Can anyone conceive a more senseless piece of buffoonery?' Perhaps not, but still it was worth mention in the Diary, the good ladies of Hay were there in the front row, and Kilvert himself in the following year met his Daisy for the first time for three months at the Volunteer Rifle Concert.[8] In rural areas in particular the Volunteers contributed to the social life of the community.

In all these ways the Volunteers were before the public eye. They were the local military Force *par excellence*, much larger than the Yeomanry, and much more local than the Militia or the Regulars. When an elephant escaped from Wombwell's Menagerie at Bursley Wakes it was the Volunteers who were at hand to fire a volley at a distance of five yards, then to be 'borne off as heroes to different inns'. And in late nineteenth-century Cambridge it was 'the beautiful scarlet Volunteers, marching by in all their glory', who cast in a young girl's mind 'a kind of shadow image of what war might be'.[9] No one could be totally unaware of the Volunteers. Drill halls were erected for them, and pubs named after them. If you did not actually see them drilling, marching out, firing, or receiving prizes, you could read about it in the newspaper. The Volunteers were part of the community.

It was one sign of the involvement of the community in the Volunteers that women played an important part in the movement — not, of course, as riflewomen, though there were ladies' rifle matches — but as supporters and fund-raisers. Few corps survived the early years without a succession of bazaars and fêtes to replenish their funds, and these were occasions when women played the important role. It was women, too, who presented prizes, or, commonly in the early years, silver bugles; there would be a special parade, a few words spoken by some lady of note, or the wife of the local captain, and the corps would receive its bugle. Stated thus it may seem a banal kind of event, hardly worth mentioning. But it could be a significant event in a local context. When the Hon. Mrs. Richard Cavendish Boyle presented the Frome Volunteers with a silver bugle on behalf of their womenfolk 'as a proof of the deep interest we take in their success', about two thousand people attended, many of the 'elite of the neighbourhood' were present, and all businesses were closed. It was a day to be remembered, the presentation itself a symbol of union between men and women, class and class; 'never have we seen our townspeople so strong in union', reported the press.[10]

The *Volunteer Service Gazette* was fully alive to the importance of women in the movement.

> As our system of protection is by a combination of all classes
> for the great work of public defence, so let our chivalry be
> exhibited in the heartiness of our union with those of the
> weaker sex in carrying forward the greater work of civilisation
> and happiness to mankind. It is to preserve this blessed union
> that we shoulder our rifles and practise at the butts; and we
> accept the encouragement of lady prize-givers, not only from
> being the willing slaves of their beauty, but as the protectors
> and champions of their rights and liberties. If the Volunteer
> ponders well on these relations, with a pure heart, as he trudges
> to parade, we believe that, after all, he will find some poetry
> in drill, and something as noble as knight-errantry in an
> advance in line and file-firing from the right of companies.

Such elevated ideas perhaps had a limited appeal, though they played a full, if self-conscious, part in the middle-class ideology of the movement. At a time when many associated anything to do with soldiery as liable to lead to immorality, the Volunteers set themselves up as the protectors of 'Our Hearths and Homes': '. . . the safety, the purity, the sanctity of English homes, are the root-ideas out of which [the Volunteer movement] has sprung.'[11] Men were being asked to spend their evenings and Saturday afternoons, time which they might otherwise have spent with their families, drilling and shooting; in the context of a society which placed high value on the family it was necessary to stress the moral excellence of volunteering, and at the same time encourage women to attend Volunteer events.

And attend they did. At the first inspection of the Edinburgh Volunteers in February 1860, 'it was an encouraging sight to witness so many elegantly dressed ladies on the ground, who, in spite of mud and strong easterly wind, bravely stood out the inspection to the end, and evinced the keenest interest in the first official field day of the Edinburgh Volunteers.' At Eye in Suffolk when the local corps first appeared in uniform in May 1860 'to the immense pride and satisfaction of not only the Volunteers themselves, but of the whole town besides . . . the ladies . . . were not backward to show their appreciation of the manly and patriotic zeal which induces men to undergo the ordeal of drill.'[12] And so on — women attended, applauded, organised bazaars, even enrolled themselves as honorary members. Their encouragement must have given confidence to many recruits who felt uncomfortable in their new uniforms; it may even have helped to propagate the belief from which the Volunteers had nothing to lose, that the donning of a uniform was the road to a lady's heart[13] (see Plate 4).

Be that as it may, there is no doubting the aura of romanticism under which the Volunteers set about their duty. How far it was a form of Dutch courage, a means of boosting morale on cold winter nights in dour drill halls, it is difficult to know. All that one can say is that the sight of the Volunteers was enough to stir some men to the most purple of passages. Witness a journalist reporting the administration of the oath of allegiance to the Bath Volunteers by the Mayor in April 1860 — the kind of event which was happening all over Britain at that time:

It was a grand sight, and went deep into the heart of England's fair daughters, to see the healthy, handsome muscular men come voluntarily forward to defend them in the hour of danger; what a beautiful picture the imagination may depict, the mother bending over her cradled babe, bidding the beloved infant to lie still and slumber, for God and the Volunteers were keeping guard; many a prayer will ascend to heaven to draw down blessings on the brave noble-hearted fellows who sacrifice time, and at pecuniary loss, to shield the old, the helpless, and all that is dear to an Englishman; what a holy spirit has been infused into the breasts of the male population of this great, glorious, and free country.[14]

It would be foolish, of course, to suppose that female support was universal. It was to a large degree middle or upper-class and essentially patronising. Lower down the social scale women might actually be hostile as they were initially in working-class Durham where 'the female part of the population was very much against the movement; they thought that all the men were going to be drafted off to India or to China.' And in the twentieth century the *Territorial Year Book* for 1909 believed that the objections of relatives, especially female ones, was an important cause of difficulty in getting recruits. 'This could be cured', it believed, 'by persuading the women first, and using them as recruiting agents, a very proper function.'[15]

The Church was another important supporter — at least the Church of England which provided the corps with their chaplains. Anglican parsons were frequently to be found in the vanguard of support for the movement. Bishops subscribed, vicars chaired meetings, curates joined; in Dunmow sixteen clergymen belonged as subscribers, honorary or effective members.[16] The support of the Established Church was general and sustained. The Nonconformists were more doubtful. A more pacifist tradition was inclined to see only a potentially riotous soldiery and a glorification of war in the burgeoning rifle movement. A placard announcing 'Twelve reasons why thoughtful and serious-minded persons should not join a Rifle Corps' was primarily Christian in inspiration. Quakers in particular were to be found opposing the movement. But undoubtedly some Nonconformist ministers gave support. At the July 1860 meeting of the 29th Middlesex Rifle Volunteers 'The Rev. W.C. Williams MA, said the great beauty of the Volunteer movement was its unsectarian character . . . Mr. North, a dissenting minister, seconded the resolution and expressed his approval of the movement.' At Cumbernauld in Scotland the meeting to form the Volunteers was actually held in the United Presbyterian Church, and the Ministers of the Free Church, the United Presbyterian Church and the established Church all moved resolutions in favour.[17]

In general, however, the Nonconformist churches dissociated themselves from the Force, providing neither support nor opposition. Such an attitude was probably wise in view of their members' divisions of opinion on the Volunteers. These divisions were rarely aired, but when they were, as in the *Methodist Recorder* in 1870, the correspondence was long and bitter. It opened with 'A Wesleyan Volunteer' claiming that 'in avoiding too much mention of these 200,000 men you but too truly represent Methodist opinion on the subject.' 'Peace' replied, claiming that the Volunteers had a 'baneful influence upon the minds of many of our youth.' Others enlisted in the verbal fray, revealing if nothing else that Methodists were divided in their opinion about the Force.[18]

Organised labour was as hesitant about the Volunteers as were the

74

Nonconformists. In 1913 the 'very rigid neutrality' of the trade unions and the Free Churches was said to make the work of the Territorial Force difficult. In both cases the neutrality probably stemmed from the fact that trade unionists and Nonconformists belonged to a Force which was too much part of the Establishment to be thoroughly welcomed. To have criticised, however, would have antagonised the members. A deafening silence, relieved only by criticisms of detail rather than substance, was the natural response. The Social Democratic Federation's more open and radical critique of Haldane's proposals laid it open to the charge that it was an ally of the National Service League. The safer course was to object to the influence of Lords Lieutenant or to the encouragement of the cadets rather than propose any alternative form of defence for the country.[19]

Employers were much less reluctant to express their opinion of the Force; and they, it was universally and increasingly recognised, held the key to the size and role of the Force. If employers were in favour of the Force there would be some inducement for, perhaps even pressure on the employee to enrol, and time might be allowed off work for rifle practice or even camp. But if employers came, as many of them did, to 'look upon volunteering as only an amusement and recreation, in which men join for their own pleasure'[20], then there would be no pressure to enrol, and considerable difficulties for the Volunteer in meeting his military obligations without endangering his job. There was in fact a significant change over time in the attitudes of employers towards the Force.

Employers, as we have seen, were in the forefront of those who in the early 1860s raised corps, and clothed, armed and officered their employees.[21] They were thereby contributing to the nation's defence, and also, as they were the first to admit, improving their workmen. It was an axiom of those days that becoming a Volunteer made a man a better workman. This theory was never entirely abandoned. Thus Sir Howard Vincent in 1886 declared in Parliament that there was 'hardly a place of business in the country whose best hands have not been, or are not, Volunteers', and two years later J.T. Brunner 'confessed that he was not fond of a Militiaman, but he might say that he had a number of Volunteers in his employ, and he recognized them as amongst the smartest, most upright and most trustworthy men he had.' Even more strikingly, in 1907 Lt -Col. E.H. Carlile, MP for the St. Albans division of Hertfordshire, claimed that

> men who were selected for positions as heads of departments in business concerns were frequently appointed because they were in the Volunteer Force. He remembered when it was his good fortune to be in command of a Volunteer battalion in

an industrial district, a man at the head of a large industry,
who was not himself a Volunteer, was asked by him why he
selected men from the Volunteer Force as heads of his
different departments, and his reply was that he did so
because they were accustomed to receive words of
command and to see that they were carried out. He found
that that was a great advantage to both employers and
employees.[22]

Although some employers were sympathetic to the Volunteers, there is
mounting evidence as time went on that the duties which a Volunteer
was obliged to carry out were such as to interfere with his work, and
thus set his employer against him. In 1878 the editor of the *Volunteer
Service Gazette* told the Committee of Inquiry into the Force that
some employers were opposed to the Force because of the obligations
which volunteering involved. And in 1888 while Brunner was declaring
his faith in the Volunteer as a model employee, there was considerable
stress on the fact that any increase in the Volunteer's duties would
meet with the opposition of the employers; in face of this, the
Government withdrew from an attempt to assimilate the conditions
under which Volunteers might be called out to those of the Militia. In
spite of this government sensitivity to the attitudes of employers, the
latter were often hostile; as Lieutenant-Colonel Thorne of the Council
of Midland Volunteer Officers Association told the 1894 Select
Committee, 'at present there is some difficulty in getting employers of
labour to allow men to join the Volunteer force.'[23]

By the turn of the century, then, the employer was recognised to be
the key figure whose support must be won if enrolment was to increase.
The obligations which were imposed, however, were hardly calculated
to please the employers. When new camp regulations were introduced
in 1902, 'the attitude of employers was generally half-hearted and often
positively hostile.' From evidence given before the 1904 Royal
Commission it is clear that large employers were more inclined than
small to be favourable to the Force, and that it was the banks and
insurance companies employing white-collar labour who were most
favourable of all.[24] Some employers refused to let their men join. John
Ward, Labour MP for Stoke on Trent, claimed in 1907 that 'he had
known instances where employers had laid it down as a condition that
they would not engage Volunteers. He had seen advertisements to that
effect.' Worse still, a Volunteer might lose his job because he had
fulfilled his obligations; the chairman of Vickers, Sons and Maxim Ltd.
of Sheffield reported that 'I have heard of a large number of men who
have been dismissed for going to camp.'[25] By the early twentieth
century then a Volunteer might well be at a disadvantage in the
employment market; moreover by this time even employers who

allowed concessions to those of their employees who were Volunteers
were clearly baffled by the idea put to them in 1904 that a Volunteer
might be a better workman.[26]

With the establishment of the Territorial Force the question of
recruitment became a matter of annual Parliamentary debate, and
always the attitude of the employer was recognised to be crucial.
Haldane, desperate for recruits, was foolish enough to give public
support to the Alliance Assurance Company which had issued a notice
to the effect that men entering their employment would be required to
join the Territorial Force. A shower of Parliamentary protest forced
him to backtrack, but no one disputed the importance of the employer,
only the wisdom of asking him to put direct pressure on his employees.[27]
By 1912 one MP had suggested a bounty for employers of Territorials,
while another favoured a fine for those who refused to employ them.[28]
Similar suggestions were coming from the County Territorial Force
Associations, and the Government took into consideration the question
of compensating employers. On the one side the Government wanted to
extend the obligations of the Force, while on the other employers
resisted. The critical difficulty was camp. In December 1913 Bethune,
the Director-General of the Territorial Force, wrote that he had
'interviewed hundreds of Commanding Officers and others interested
during the last six months, and the majority say that if we could overcome the business difficulties which are raised by employers and
foremen we should get more me to stay out for fifteen days.'[29]

Confirmation of the importance of the employer in the life of the
Force comes from an examination of the minute books of the City of
London Territorial and Auxiliary Forces Association. In the first month
of the Territorial Force's existence, April 1908, the Recruiting
Committee felt that the principal reason for poor recruiting 'is the
uncertainty as to facilities for serving which will be given by employers. . .
The Committee's efforts were therefore directed at employers. A
resolution expressing willingness to give all reasonable facilities to men
of the Territorial Force to comply with the Regulations was drawn up,
and many employers signed it. Recruitment, however, was still
unsatisfactory, and it was decided to call a conference of employers at
the Mansion House 'to come to some arrangement as to the holidays to
be given to Territorial Soldiers. It was reported that the Recruiting
Committee thought it was essential to get the ear of the Employer first,
and having engaged their friendly assistance it might be possible to do
some good work among the heads of the departments.' At the Mansion
House meeting textile employers agreed to spread the camp load and
to 'promote and encourage recruiting amongst the men in their
employ.' By January 1909 many employers were exhibiting recruiting
posters in their warehouses, but attempts to get employers other than

those in the textile trades to come to some agreement were in vain. And although some firms allowed recruiting to be done at the works, most employers put a quota on the number of men in their employ whom they would allow to join the Force.[30]

Employers, therefore, at first enthusiastic about the Force, became critical as the demands of time on the Volunteer increased. Their own personal commitment to the Force declined; corps recruiting from a business sometimes found the employers reluctant to take the natural position of officer. After about a decade the Volunteer Force lost its place as the key to improved industrial relations. Employers no longer had faith that the drill and shooting improved their men, but were instead conscious of the time off that the Volunteer in their employ demanded. That demand, it was clear to authority, must be tailored to the wishes of employers, for the latter could affect the ebb and flow of enrolment. At first a friend to the Force, the employer became known as the chief stumbling block to any increase in military proficiency.

Another, and very different social group was critical of the Force: there was no better target than a Volunteer, self-conscious in his uniform, for the 'rough' or the 'street Arab'. The cry 'Who shot the dog?' was liable to greet any Volunteer at large in the street, as notoriety attached to the case of an over-enthusiastic Volunteer who had fired his rifle at a dog in Wandsworth Park (see Plate 6). The news spread fast and far, and when the Bury Volunteers marched out to Heywood, Ramsbottom and Radcliffe 'they were hailed with cries of "The awkward squad;" "Who shot the dog?" ' London was probably worst. Two Bury Volunteers in London for the 1860 Hyde Park review found that 'some of the gamin made fun at their expense, and rather impolitely inquired which of them had shot "the dog?" A sort of hue and cry on the point was raised by the youthful cockneys, to the intense disgust of Shaw J.H., who returned to his hotel, and resumed the character of a civilian.' According to the historian of a Middlesex corps, 'it was almost impossible for an officer to appear in the streets without being subjected to some form of insult by the more uneducated and less intelligent of his fellow countrymen.' The 29th Middlesex in 1863 thought to escape the attentions of the urchins by parading at 7.00 a.m., but 'even at that early hour, many young street gamins were to be found bellowing and shouting around the Battalion while at work, disporting themselves freely and airing their lungs in the fresh morning breeze.' As A.R. Bennett remembered, the Volunteers 'were born into an atmosphere of popular, or rather lower-class, ridicule.'[31]

Occasionally there was more than harmless if persistent chaff; indications indeed of real hostility to the Volunteers. At such a prestigious event as the inspection of the London Rifle Brigade by the Duke of Cambridge in St James's Park, 'a considerable portion of the mob of spectators seemed . . . anxious to "improve the occasion" by volleys of low abuse at the expense of the members of the rifle corps, who bore their sneers, though oftentimes accompanied by gross insult and personal violence, with great good humour and equanimity.' Mounted Life Guards had to be brought in to control the spectators. In the following year at another inspection in Regent's Park, 'The crowd was exceedingly riotous and troublesome, and some of the horses of a mounted volunteer corps, which was present, were severely injured with knives, and the riders with sticks and stones.'[32]

Nor was this hostility confined to London. The Canterbury Volunteers parading on the cricket ground found themselves attacked by 'a motley crowd of roughs' who threw turnips 'and missiles of a harder and more varied description' at them. The Volunteers were with difficulty restrained from breaking rank. Similarly the Grantham Volunteers, marching out to the drum and fifes of the Band of Hope, were set on by a gang of youths who 'began a series of howls and jeers accompanied with insults of the grossest description to the Volunteers. Three of the gang armed themselves with stakes, and by the time the company had come half a mile on their return march, they were attacked with stones, and were charged in rear with the stakes.' Discipline was clearly not so strong as in Canterbury – one of the attackers was 'lynchlawed'.[33]

The examples cited so far have all been from the early years of the Force, and it was undoubtedly then that overt antagonism to the Force was strongest. By 1861 *The Times* could declare that 'in passing through the streets a Volunteer excites no more notice than a policeman' – a significant comparison. Certainly the Volunteers remained a symbol of authority and respectability which it was tempting to insult. In 1864 the prosecution in a case of assault on a Volunteer by a pianoforte maker claimed that 'there was a growing practice among persons of the prisoner's class to insult and assault Volunteers.' Sometimes the Volunteers retaliated. Indeed in 1872 two Volunteers found themselves in Southwark Police Court for assault on one James Wicks. Wicks, they claimed, had called out at them, 'Who shot the cat?' (an interesting variation!); 'it was a common thing, they said, 'to insult Volunteers in the street when in uniform.'[34]

This kind of ridicule continued right up to 1914. In 1893 George Melly, writing his *Reminiscences,* noted that 'All Volunteers are more or less exposed to the ridicule of the general public, and have always to face a fire of chaff from the "gamins" of the "pave" . . .' In London in 1897 it was said to be 'one of the great difficulties of Metropolitan Corps to find accessible ground where the mob will not interfere with the operations.' And in Newbury shortly before the First World War Territorials marching down to the meadows to drill passed the night shift at the local engineering works, and were regularly met with derisive whistles; but on 4 August 1914 the same night shift cheered.[35]

One possible reason for this lower-class resentment of the Volunteers is that the latter were seen as representatives of law and order, and as likely to use their discipline and rifles to put down riot at home as to defend their country against a foreign invader. Historical precedent pointed to the former as the key role for Volunteers. The Yeomanry continued to play an important part in the preservation of law and order,[36] and doubtless to the uninitiated there was little to distinguish between a Yeoman and a Volunteer. On the Volunteer side the fact of being entrusted with a rifle, and of having some role, if an indeterminate one, in the control of public disturbances, placed him firmly on the side of authority, and therefore of respectability.

The actual responsibilities of the Volunteer in the event of disturbances were by no means clear. In June 1861 Lord Herbert as Secretary of State for War issued a circular containing the passage, 'I have . . . learnt that in some cases Volunteer Corps have been called out in aid of the Civil power on the occurrence of local disturbances, and I have therefore to point out to you, that as the Volunteer Force is not intended to be employed in this manner, it is inexpedient to assemble it on any such occasion.'[37] This, it will be noted, declared it not unlawful, but merely inexpedient to assemble Volunteers on such occasions. The truth was that since the Volunteers had rifles and at least an element of military discipline, they could not be ignored in any discussion of riot control. Their rifles might be a target for the rioters, and it was therefore argued that Volunteers must be allowed to organise, and if necessary to fight, to prevent this. And since the Volunteers had organisation, it seemed to many absurd not to make use of it, even if the Volunteers were acting officially as special constables. In the 1863 Volunteer Bill the Government tried to rationalise the situation by giving a more positive role to the Volunteers. Under Clause 19 they would have been allowed to respond voluntarily to a call from the Lord Lieutenant to act for the suppression of riots or tumults, provided the call was approved by the Government; and if they did so come out, they would be deemed to be under military discipline. There was much opposition to this clause, chiefly on the grounds that the popularity of the Volunteers depended on their not being involved in such disturbances. The Government therefore withdrew the clause, but this left the state of the law as uncertain as it had been before.[38]

In 1866-7, with the Fenian crisis, there was renewed discussion. The Government was alerted to danger by evidence from Liverpool that the majority of the 64th Liverpool Volunteers was composed of Fenians. In September the Liverpool Police found a cache of rifles which, it turned out, belonged to members of London rifle corps. Many Irishmen, they claimed, joined the Volunteers in order to acquire knowledge of drill to use in the Fenian cause. The lack of control over Volunteer arms, and the fact that many Volunteers kept their rifles at home, and not in an armoury, caused the Mayor of Liverpool to write to the Home Secretary expressing apprehension about Fenian infiltration 'but quite irrespective altogether of this it has long been felt that some precautions for the safe custody of the arms were necessary during the winter months when from a long prevalence of Frost or other circumstances the Labouring Classes are more or less thrown out of employment and disturbances are consequently more likely to prevail.'[39]

The main fear in 1866-7, however, was not Volunteer disloyalty, nor the riots of the unemployed, but a concerted rebellion by the Fenians. As General Peel told Spencer Walpole, 'numerous applications have been received from Lords Lieutenant of Counties, and officers commanding Volunteer Corps, for instructions for their guidance in cases of civil commotion; and as to the liability or the competence of the Volunteers to act as a Military Body under Arms in aid of the Civil Power.' The Home Office was frankly as uncertain as anyone else.[40] Parliamentary debate and demands for clarification were sparked off by the action of the Chester Volunteers who were sworn in as special constables and assembled in Volunteer uniform to defend the Castle against the threatened Fenian attack. The outcome of Parliamentary debate and discussion amongst the legal experts was a circular laid before Parliament in June 1867. This laid down the duty of every citizen to help in quelling a disturbance, but still left a considerable amount of discretion to be used in deciding what role the Volunteers could play. As W.E. Forster stated in criticism, the circular was more the expression of a legal opinion than the definite instructions which were wanted, and it was withdrawn to be reissued in October.[41] In this amended form it appeared that the only occasion on which Volunteers might be called upon to act differently from other citizens was when their armouries were attacked.[42] Even so, as practice was to show, Volunteers were too useful a body not to be employed in the control of disturbances.

In 1860 Volunteers had actually been called out to help quell a mutiny of Regulars in Hamilton barracks in Lanarkshire. More usually, however, their efforts were directed against the civilian populace. Thus in Chesterfield in 1862 when Irish Roman Catholics objected to a proposed Protestant lecturer in the town, Volunteers were ordered under arms by the Mayor, and then themselves took the initiative in offering to protect the lecturer, and in clearing the streets. In the same year in Birkenhead, Volunteers acting as special constables played a leading part in putting down a disturbance between Roman Catholics and Garibaldians.[43] But it was during the Fenian scare that the services of the Volunteers were most in demand. In Birmingham some 650 of the 2,000 special constables enrolled were Volunteers. In Edinburgh 4,000 special constables were enrolled, and were placed under the command of J.H.A. Macdonald, a leading Edinburgh Volunteer; as he himself wrote, 'The whole drilling was done by Volunteers . . .' Similarly in a Middlesex battalion 'practically the whole battalion was sworn in as special constables, with Lt-Col. Wilkinson as their superintendent.' From Caithness to southern England Volunteers were sworn in as special constables, and clearly made use of their drill to guard against the danger of Fenian attack.[44] Manchester Volunteers acted as special constables during the trial of the Fenians, and Salford Volunteers kept the peace at the time of their execution. At a Sadler's Wells performance for the benefit of the Clerkenwell sufferers armed Tower Hamlets Volunteers kept guard.[45]

The Fenian scare over, Volunteers were less frequently called upon to keep the peace. What had been made quite clear, however, was that, despite the misgivings of some Commanding Officers, Volunteers were only too willing to enrol as special constables, and that their services were welcomed by local authorities. Their actions in this respect help to place them in context. Composed as they were largely of working men, they were yet, with the single exception of Fenian infiltration of the Liverpool Volunteers, implicitly relied on by authority as a force which could be used in cases of public disturbance. Moreover they responded to these opportunities. The Volunteers were firmly on the side of authority. As *The Times* noted in 1878, 'the man who enters a Volunteer regiment cannot, even if he would, escape the influence which is called *esprit de corps*. He is enlisted at once on the side of "order"; he may have been inclined to disorder, or even to sedition, but when once he becomes a soldier, a citizen soldier, he feels that he has ranged himself on the opposite side to all disturbers of society, from the highest to the lowest.'[46] This enlistment of the working classes on the side of order could not but win support for the Force from all those who feared disorder.

It was indeed easy for anyone in authority to find something good to say about the Force. The continuing and increasing financial support for the Force owed much to the fact that different people could see quite different purposes in its existence. The Earl of Derby in the 1880s gave a good description of these differences:

> The Volunteer system has had the curious feature of securing the good word of persons and classes who agree, perhaps, in little else. Sanitarists tell you what are the advantages of healthy bodily exercise, combined with interest and excitement, for men living in dismal cities, and engaged in sedentary pursuits; philanthropists tell you of the social advantage of bringing different classes together in a natural and healthy

way; the others dwell, reasonably enough from their point of
view, on the benefit which each individual Volunteer derives
from some personal experience of order and discipline.
Others, again, remember that a man's attachment to his
country depends much more on what he does for it than what
it has done for him, and they see in Volunteering a powerful
stimulus to that sentiment of patriotism without which no
community can hold together. Nay, more than that, those
who hold the most opposite views as to national policy,
by a singular chance, agree in their desire for the continuance
and development of the Volunteer system. Those who believe
that it is the destiny and the duty of England often to be
engaged in military adventures on a great scale, are naturally
well pleased that the national forces should be increased by
150,000 intelligent and willing soldiers. Those, on the other
hand, who believe that English dangers are rather financial
than military, and that the policy of peace is that which
suits our position best, are equally gratified by an
arrangement which obviates the necessity of a vast and costly
increase in the regular army; and, lastly, men of every party,
who believe that the establishment in England of a
conscription on the Continental model would be a distinctly
retrograde step in civilisation, accept with pleasure a
system which gives most of the advantages of conscription
without any of its drawbacks. Thus, animated by various
motives, and starting from different points of view,
representatives of all classes and of all shades of opinion agree in
sympathy for and support to the Volunteer cause.[47]
The almost universal chorus of support from the elite in society should
not disguise the fact that that support was essentially patronising.
Members of Parliament, aristocrats and other notables could be
prevailed upon to present prizes and make suitable speeches to men
who were the embodiment of so many of the qualities valued in their
society. But a relationship of patronage carries with it some
uncertainty as to the patron's real view of the patronised. To volunteer
was respectable, but not obviously respected. In rural areas this kind of
patronage was so much part of everyday relationships that it probably
did not arouse much notice. But in towns the Volunteer may have had
the uneasy feeling that the gleeful shrieks of the urchins met with some
echo in the drawing-rooms of the patrons. Indeed they met with some
sympathy in himself. For there was no disguising the fact that there
was something absurd and comic in this serious playing at soldiers by
men whose daily avocations were thoroughly civilian. Volunteer artists
and authors — and there seem to have been many of them — copied

Punch, a staunch supporter of the Force, in pointing up the absurd, the fat man in his gaudy uniform, or the civilian struggling with the finer points of military drill and etiquette[48] (See Plates 2 and 7). Uncertain of their own status, and conscious of a gap between their patrons' public and private opinion of the Force, the Volunteers in self-protection and escape from reality, laughed at themselves. But it was often a somewhat bitter laugh.

This ambiguity of status did not stem solely from civilian opinion of the Force. There was also considerable and genuine doubt about the military role which the Volunteers might be capable of fulfilling, and about their proper relationship with the Regular Army. The Volunteers themselves were inclined to suspect that their military role was non-existent and their organisation a sham, and that Inspecting Officers who flattered on the parade-ground were more critical in the mess. Once again it was a relationship of subordination, in this case to the Regular Army, the War Office, and military opinion which made the Volunteers uncertain where they stood.

In 1859 and 1860 few of those who hailed the formation of the Volunteer Force with such enthusiasm gave much thought to the military role which the citizen-soldiers might perform. There was, however, a body of opinion which believed that the Volunteers should be the nucleus of a future citizen army, which would eventually replace the Regular Forces, and would in the meantime act as an entirely independent army with its own command structure and auxiliary services. The motivation of such men was hostility to the Horse Guards, and it is not surprising to find that the latter reciprocated the opposition and quickly won the battle. The advocates of an independent Volunteer army were never very many, but their leader, Viscount Ranelagh, was a man with enough force of personality to ensure that his ideas were at least discussed. As Commanding Officer of the South Middlesex he was able to use the meetings of the Metropolitan Commanding Officers as a forum. In April 1860 he secured the passing of a resolution by the Metropolitan Commanding Officers 'That upon divisional field-days the command shall be taken in roster by the Commanding Officers of regiments holding the rank of Lt-Col. commanding commencing with the senior officer present.'[49] This resolution effectively excluded any Regular from command of the Volunteers. In early 1861 Ranelagh was planning a Volunteer camp, and it was now that the voice of authority, in the person of the Commander-in-Chief, the Duke of Cambridge, spoke out in anger and alarm:

> I object in the strongest manner to the formation of a
> Volunteer Camp. This is by far the most objectionable
> proceeding on the part of the Volunteers I have yet heard of,
> and as usual it emanates, as all these objectionable proposals ever

have done, since the formation of the Volunteer Force, from *Lord Ranelagh*. If Volunteer Camps are once admitted by authority, they will be the severest blow which can possibly be struck by the Volunteer movement as against the Army. The Army is the natural and legitimate force for the defence of the Empire. The Volunteer Force is merely an *auxiliary* body in the event of Invasion. Keep up the force with this view, and no harm is done to the Army, but let it once be found that the Volunteer force can do the *duties* of the Army, and the latter must be sensibly and most seriously affected in point of numerical force, for it is very clear that the Army is a far more expensive establishment than the Volunteer Force. But I go further and contend that the Volunteer Force instituted as it ought to be, and as it is intended to be, must be a purely local and auxiliary force, and the members comprising it, cannot, and ought not to have time to devote to their duties away from their homes, and for more than an hour or two a day.

A month later Cambridge was again writing to Herbert trusting that the latter would not allow Ranelagh to hold a field day at Brighton on Easter Monday as rumour had it he was planning.[50] Rumour was correct and Ranelagh held his field day in opposition to an official field day at Wimbledon under Lord Bury. Whether it was the attractions of Brighton or Ranelagh, there were more Volunteers on the south coast than at Wimbledon. As Engels noted, Londoners at any rate appeared not to want to be under the command of Regular officers.[51]

The Volunteer Commanding Officers, however, were now alive to Ranelagh's ways, and keen to disclaim his irresponsibility. In April 1861 they rescinded the resolution of the previous year, and now agreed that field manoeuvres above brigade level should be organised by the War Office, and directed by military authority, the command being entrusted to some military officer specially appointed for the purpose. An attempt by Ranelagh in February 1862 to confirm the earlier resolution was defeated by 20 votes to 6.[52] Ranelagh had established the right of Volunteers to manoeuvre in large numbers, and his choice of Brighton as a venue was soon to be copied by officialdom. But he had failed in his attempt, crucial to any idea of an independent Volunteer army, to exclude serving Regular officers from command.

Ranelagh, however, had his allies in the Press, allies with whom he must otherwise have had little sympathy, for he was a keen Conservative, and they chiefly Liberal. Their support, indeed, stemmed from a traditional radical dislike of the Regular Army, and a belief that a successful Volunteer Force offered the best hope of securing a reduction of the Estimates. The Duke of Cambridge's fears that the Volunteers might be thought of as in some sense a replacement for the Regular Army were echoed from more respectable mouths than that of Lord Ranelagh. Thus Sir Joseph Paxton, in the House of Commons, supported the movement on national grounds, but he also supported it because he believed that it would ultimately tend to economy in their Army Estimates, and Tom Hughes was another who thought that one aim in establishing the Force should be the lowering of the Army Estimates.[53] In February 1862 when Ranelagh's campaign was at its most bitter, he had the support of the *Morning Herald*, the *Observer*, and the *Daily Telegraph*, all of whom, according to the *Volunteer Service Gazette*, had as their object 'to make the gap between the Regular troops and the Volunteers as wide as possible.'[54] In July the *Morning Star*, which after initial discountenance had become a staunch advocate of the Volunteers, supported Ranelagh's action at Panshanger in refusing to recognise the authority of the Government-appointed Assistant Inspector of Volunteers. 'The permanent existence of the Volunteer force,' it declared, 'depends upon its independence. It cannot survive if it is converted into a mere slave and tool of the Regular Army. It is essential to the self-respect of its members that their independence should be established on a substantial basis.' It advised a few corps to assemble without permission from the Horse Guards, and see what the Government would do: nothing, it believed.[55] This, from the journal of Cobden and Bright, was simply seizing an opportunity to attack the Regular Army.

Ranelagh continued his campaign for an independent Volunteer army after 1862, but without any further success. In December 1867 he excited much attention by referring to the Volunteers as a 'sham Army'. Attention naturally focused on the word 'sham', but for Ranelagh the crucial one was 'Army'. Considered as an independent Army, the Volunteers were indeed a sham, without mobilisation plans, transport and other auxiliary services, and lacking either a General Staff or a Commander-in-Chief. But the truth was that very few people within the armed services, and even very few Volunteers, ever thought that the Volunteers should be an Army. Even the Press gave little support to Ranelagh in 1867, for by then there was much less readiness to accept that Volunteer troops were the answer to any nation's military needs.

Public opinion as expressed in the newspapers was inclined to favour the Volunteers in the early years, up to the mid-1860s, whence they underwent a gradual decline reaching a trough at about the time of the Franco-Prussian War, and remaining in comparatively ill repute until the early twentieth century when there was in some quarters a revival of belief in their value. These changes in attitude were to some extent associated with technical changes in the conduct of war. The coincidence of the widespread introduction of the rifle with the formation of the Volunteer Force, and the latter's adoption of that weapon as its own, made the Force seem abreast of modern developments in warfare and a harbinger of the future as compared with the Regular Army. Some saw future war as skirmishing and sharpshooting, and were thus inclined to accord high value to the Volunteers. But the Prussian victories from 1864 onwards, and the debatable performance of Volunteer troops in the American Civil War cast considerable doubt on this romantic conception of warfare. Discipline, it appeared, might be an old-fashioned virtue, but it was one no army could afford to do without, and there could be little doubt that the discipline and training of the Volunteers were inferior to those of the Continental troops they were likely to meet in battle.[56] For the next thirty years officials and publicists struggled with this problem; while aware of the inadequacy of the Volunteers they were yet hampered in attempts at reform by the fact that Volunteers were what their name implied, and could resign at fourteen days' notice. The Force, therefore, had to be fitted into general mobilisation schemes in such a way as to make the Volunteers feel that they were useful without risking them as front-line troops. The Boer War in which Volunteers served in a manner which was generally thought creditable did something to revive people's opinions of their value, but bringing with it as it did a general scare about the adequacy of the nation's military forces, it also led to attempts to increase the workload demanded of the Volunteers. This was a perennial and insurmountable problem. More hopefully for the Volunteers, the introduction of smokeless powder and the repeating rifle in the 1890s revived the belief that a force of irregular sharpshooters could play a crucial role in modern warfare, an opinion which the performance of the Boers did everything to enhance. Thus by the opening of the twentieth century the time was ripe for a discussion of the value of Volunteers to be an important part of the general debate on the nation's defences. With this debate we shall deal in another chapter.

The Times illustrates well the general trend of military opinion in the first decade of the Force's existence. Its initial enthusiasm for the Volunteer cause was sustained for five years; as late as September 1864 it found it 'exceedingly satisfactory . . . that the establishment of our Volunteer force has not only provided the country with an army of reserve, but has called into existence exactly such a body of troops as the tactics of modern warfare appear especially to demand.' In October 1866 the Volunteer seemed to *The Times* 'a well-trained soldier, fit for any service in any battlefield.' When Garibaldi's defeat at Mentana in 1867 called forth adverse comments on Volunteer troops,

The Times came to their defence, believing that 'military men are generally apt to make too light of the capabilities of Volunteers.'[57] But the Volunteers' renewed demand from 1867 onwards for a higher government grant forced public attention on to them in a more critical manner than before, and although *The Times* was by no means in the forefront of the critics (that position was held by the *Pall Mall Gazette*), its course changed with the prevailing wind. A leading article on Christmas Day 1869 had a new sound about it:

> It is ten years since the Volunteer Force was established, and every one will admit that it is now time that the true principles of its administration were discovered and applied. It cannot be said that there has been any lack of opportunity, for Volunteering, with all its adjuncts, has probably engaged the attention of more energetic people than any subject of public interest in our time. Yet there has been a very slow advance towards the constitution of the Force on principles clearly recognized and definitively determined upon. The chief change is towards the more efficient direction of the Force by the War Office.[58]

The tone was as yet not hostile, rather indicative of a willingness to take a new look at the Force.

The Franco-Prussian War enforced a more urgent approach. Sir John Garvock, a regular officer inspecting Volunteers at Chester, sparked off the debate by daring to cast doubt on the value of Volunteers. In a subsequent letter to *The Times* he wrote that '. . . as matters now stand, the Volunteers, as a body, are not fit to stand in line with the regular troops against an enemy; . . . constituted and officered as they, in a great majority of cases, are, it is not their place at all, and . . . those who say the reverse are simply throwing dust in the eyes of the country, however unwittingly, and talking nonsense.' *The Times* supported Garvock, and two days later launched a campaign for military service for all. 'The Militia as it is, and still more the Volunteers as they are, would be of very little use against such an invasion as the Emperor of the French has thought fit to invite across his frontier.' And increasingly it was the Militia in which *The Times* came to put its faith. The Volunteer Force 'can hardly be said to be composed of soldiers and it certainly has no trained officers.' 'We confess we cannot see how men who, like our Volunteers, never pass a night away from home can be formed into steady troops of the Line even by monthly classes, or the occasional loan of camp equipage as now proposed; but there is no reason whatever why a regiment of the Militia should not in all respects be as good as a regiment of the Line.'[59] The 1871 Easter Monday Review was a further occasion to criticise the Volunteers: 'If England were about to be invaded, no wise man would think of putting the Volunteers in the first line of the defending Army.

Dorchester Volunteers, 1863. A typical photograph of a corps in the early days, the members deliberately casual, the uniforms by no means identical.

Scottish Volunteers, Royal Review, 1881. A humorous depiction. Note the ubiquitous urchins, and the pipe-smokers.

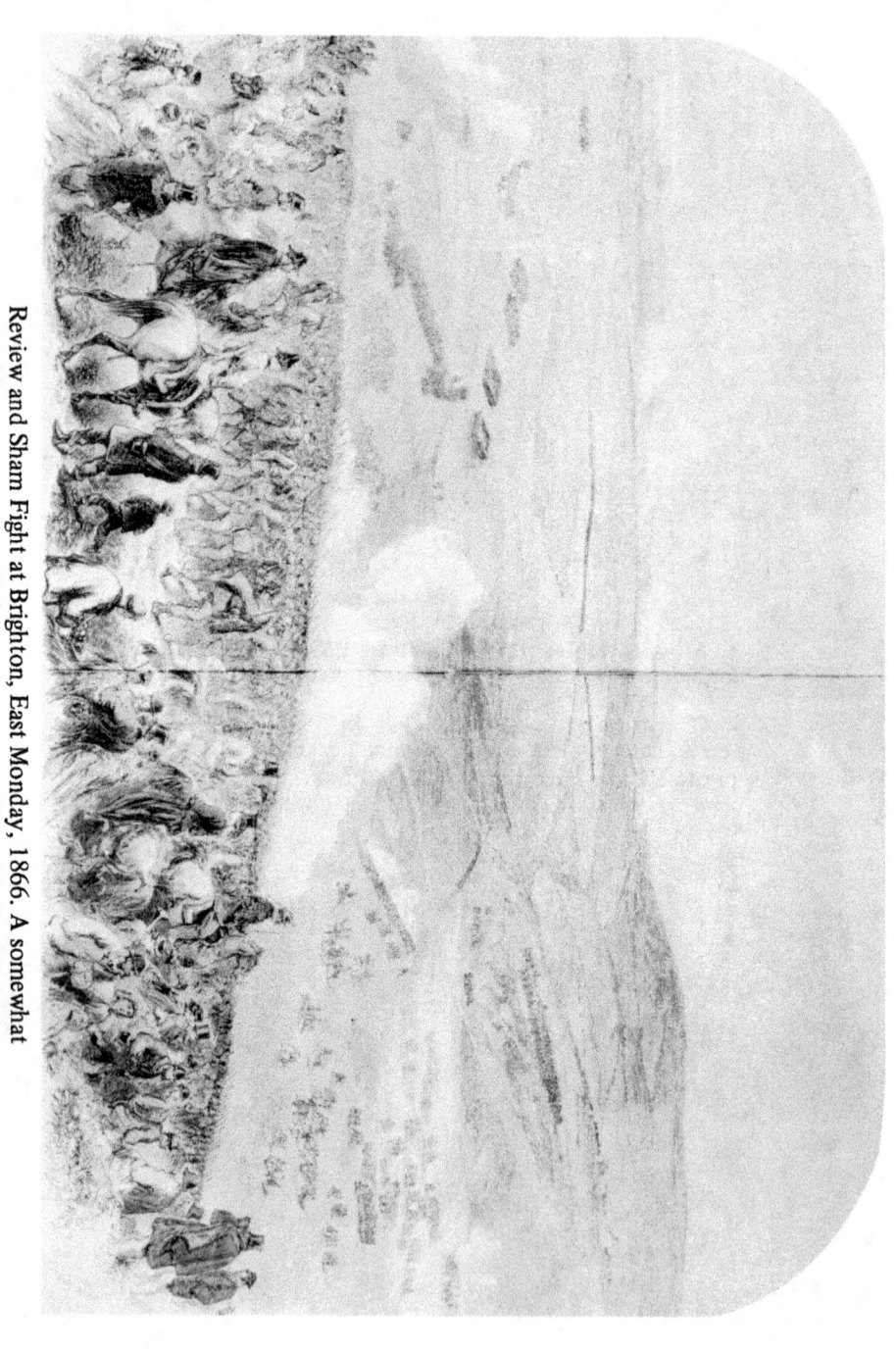

Review and Sham Fight at Brighton, East Monday, 1866. A somewhat romanticised view of the Volunteers in action. Note the spectators on

A HINT TO THE "ENGAGED ONES" OF ENGLAND.

ALICE (TO RODOLPH, OR RATHER WE SHOULD SAY, JONES). "NOW MIND, SIR! YOU ARE A VOLUNTEER RIFLEMAN, AND IT ENTIRELY DEPENDS UPON YOUR ATTENTION TO DRILL, WHETHER I GIVE YOU THAT LOCK OF HAIR, OR NOT!"

Female pressure.

MAJOR W. C. KNIGHT CLOWES AND SURVIVORS OF HIS COMPANY, 1912

Patriotic employees.

STREET BOY (*fortissimo*). "*Who Shot the Dog!*"

'Who shot the dog?' In 1860 an over-enthusiastic Volunteers fired his rifle at a dog in Wandsworth Park, and the incident was used to mock the Volunteers all over the country.

Volunteer humour. A typical example of Volunteer self-mockery.

VISCOUNT RANELAGH, LIEUT.-COL. COMMANDANT
OF THE 2ND SOUTH MIDDLESEX V.R.C.
DRAWN FROM LIFE BY H. FLEUSS

The Volunteer as hero: Lord Ranelagh. An alternative style of art,
depicting, suitably enough, the chief advocate of an independent and
strong Volunteer Army.

Volunteer Festival at Grimston Park, 1864

Still less could they be trusted to work independently in loose order. To attempt it would be ruin.' The Volunteers should simply be asked to hold fortified positions. 'They must be assigned a definite place and limited duties as a part of the whole National Force.'[60]

By Easter 1872 *The Times* was moving back to a more moderate stance. '. . . the truth is,' it admitted, 'that the Volunteers have some ground to recover in popular estimation.' After the issue of General Ellice's balanced report on the last Brighton field-day, it concluded

> that the more closely the Force is identified in appearance as well as discipline with the Regular Forces, the more serviceable it will become . . . The notion that a second Army, homogeneous in itself and complete in all its branches, but differing entirely in composition and stamp from the Regular Army, is to be forthcoming from this Force must at once be given up. It was a chimerical idea at the best, though it conduced probably to the success of the movement in its early days. But we have now learnt that soldiering is no mere game of play. It is hard work, and in some of its branches necessarily professional work.

Henceforth *The Times* pursued an unchanged course: made more efficient, the Volunteers would be useful auxiliary troops, capable of performing minor tasks in support of the Regular Army in the event of invasion.[61] As such, they should take every opportunity of training with the Regulars. Given such a limited role, they were of course far less worthy of the attention of leader writers than in the early days, and the amount of attention paid to them correspondingly dropped.

In the course of this continuing debate about the value of the Volunteers the War Office had been step by step increasing its control over the Force. The pattern was a simple and perhaps inevitable one: the more public money was spent on the Volunteers, the more they became accountable to Whitehall, and the greater the efficiency which was required of them. Thus in the circular of 13 July 1859 under which the Government was willing to supply a rifle corps with 25 per cent of its rifles, it did so on the conditions that there was a sufficient and safe range, a secure place for custody of the arms and a competent person to take charge of them; that the Rules and Regulations had been approved by the Secretary of State, and on the understanding that the corps was subject to periodic inspection by an officer appointed by the War Office.[62] In a sense this was reasonable enough: public money was being spent, and must be accounted for. But many Volunteers came to resent the pattern as it established itself. In 1869 Elcho was protesting 'against the language so freely used of late to the effect that any increase of the capitation grant must be accompanied by conditions of increased efficiency. Such language implies that an increased grant would be a favour conferred by Government and the nation on the Volunteers, whereas the favour would, in fact, only be conferred by the nation on itself.'[63]

Despite these protests, the Government was not likely to abandon its most useful control over the Volunteers – the provision of their finances. Thus as the Volunteers became more and more dependent on public money, so government control became more rigorous. It would be both tedious and unnecessary to chronicle in detail the bargaining that went on, and the solutions that were arrived at. Suffice it to say that the life of a Volunteer corps could be deeply affected by such matters as the size of the transport allowance, the pay of adjutants and drill sergeants, the regulations as to class firing, the non-issue of great-coats, and so on. It is issues such as these which are debated in the correspondence columns of Volunteer newspapers, which form the content of questions in the House of Commons, and which doubtless occupied Volunteer officers in their spare time. Could they afford to go to camp? What was the cheapest form of transport to brigade drill? Should they pay the drill sergeant anything above the government rate? Could a uniform be made to last more than three years?

It was during one of these periodic exchanges between the War Office and the Volunteers as to the expenses which were properly chargeable to the Government that Cardwell came into office. His plans for the reform of the British Army reached far beyond the Volunteers and their detailed if urgent requests for more money and equipment. Of the three main aspects of his reforms, that is control of the Horse Guards by the War Office, abolition of Purchase, and territorialisation combined with short service, only the latter concerns us here. The Army Enlistment Act of 1870 introduced twelve-year enlistment, six with the Colours and six with the Reserve. The aim was to build up a Reserve of 80,000. In addition Cardwell set up sixty-six military Districts, mainly corresponding to counties, within each of which would be localised two line battalions, and the local Militia and Volunteers. The line battalions would take it in turn to serve abroad. This reform, together with the Regulation of the Forces Act 1871 which removed control over Militia and Volunteers from the Lords Lieutenant to the Crown, clearly placed the Volunteers in much closer contact with a particular line regiment, and further laid the ground for giving them a recognised place in the country's defence.[64]

Cardwell was by no means a convinced admirer of the Volunteer Force. He wanted to weed out the more inefficient corps and made it plain that a higher grant was dependent on greater efficiency.[65] His detailed proposals with regard to the claim for a greater grant were by no means to the liking of Volunteer officers. Accepting the larger proposals of examinations for Volunteer officers, the Volunteers quibbled over what to the uninitiated must have seemed trifling – the abolition of the distinction between 20s. and 30s. efficients (whose effect was to call for greater shooting ability), and the imposition of a minimum number to be present if a drill was to qualify towards efficiency. The debate lasted from December 1869 to the late summer of 1870,[66] and it is obvious that one consequence of it was that the Volunteers were in no mood to receive with rapture Cardwell's proposals for closer ties with the Regular Army. A key part of those proposals was Cardwell's intention to place the Volunteers under the Mutiny Act when they were brigaded with the Regulars and Militia. It is true that some Volunteer Commanding Officers were happy to accept this, and said their men would be too, but the *Volunteer Service Gazette* was opposed, as were a number of speakers in Parliament. Colonel C.H. Lindsay led the attack on the Regulations in a strong speech, claiming that if they were enforced, 'there would not be half-a-dozen regiments in London, or many more than that in the country, in a creditable existence by the end of the year.' Colonel Beresford declared that 'in his judgment the whole tendency of the Army Bill was to annihilate the Volunteer Force, or, at all events, to exalt the Militia at the expense of the Volunteers.'[67]

The Volunteers, therefore, entered the new era of closer association with the Regulars with mixed feelings. Their role was now clearly that of auxiliary force, not independent army. Their increased training with the Regulars was gained at the expense of submission to the Mutiny Act, and an impending end to their beloved Easter Monday Review. A marginal increase in the government grant had been won only at the cost of the requirement of greater efficiency. Like the schools of the time, the Volunteers were under the payment by results system, and there were as many objections to such a system in a military as in an educational context.

With the completion of the Cardwell reforms, the Volunteer Force entered a more settled phase of its existence. After the heady early years when praise had been heaped on their heads, the Volunteers had undergone a period of criticism and reform which visibly affected morale. From 1868 to 1873 the numbers enrolled in the Force dropped year by year, men being unwilling to join or remain in a Force which was the target of so much public criticism. After the early 1870s the public lost interest, and the Volunteers commenced a renewed period of growth, together with increasing definition of their military role.

The Cardwell reforms had brought the Volunteers into closer contact with the Regulars, but they had not of themselves assigned them any definite role in the event of war. No one, least of all the Volunteers, knew what the Force should do if invasion threatened.

Many, like the author of *The Battle of Dorking* believed that the Volunteers would be liable to cause more confusion to their friends than their enemies.[68] Some advance, it is true, had been made since the Prince Consort's circular of 25 May 1859 which envisaged them as small independent units. Groups of one hundred Volunteers, totally independent of each other, attempting to defend London or any large city, would simply have been a danger to each other. By July 1859, therefore, we find the Government allowing the formation of battalions of eight companies or of a force of not less than 500. In towns battalions were a manifest advantage, in scattered rural areas their formation was much more problematical since meeting for battalion drill involved considerable travelling. The Government, therefore, in March 1860 issued regulations for two kinds of battalion, consolidated for urban areas, and administrative for rural.[69] Within months of the formation of the Force, therefore, the idea of independent bodies of sharpshooters had been abandoned in favour of a battalion organisation, though of an admittedly rudimentary form in rural areas.

It was not the Volunteers' fault that organisation for war progressed only slowly beyond that. It is one of the more extraordinary features of the British Army in the nineteenth century that there was no mobilisation scheme until 1875 when one began to be drawn up by Colonel Robert Home of the Intelligence Department. Home envisaged the Volunteers having a place in the Garrison Army and assigned places for the various Volunteer units for the defence of the United Kingdom; for example, Volunteer infantry detachments from Derby were detailed for the defence of Plymouth. But Home clearly thought that the Volunteers would be of use only in garrisons -- unlike the Yeomanry and Militia they do not appear in the eight localised Army Corps.

After Home's death in 1879 there seems to have been a decline in concern with mobilisation.[70] The *Army List* for July 1881 is the last to publish the mobilisation scheme. In 1886, however, with the appointment of Henry Brackenbury to the Intelligence Department, mobilisation was once again taken seriously. Volunteer corps were allotted to garrisons on the principle that they should not travel more than two hours by rail from their Headquarters. The remaining 112 battalions unallotted should be used to throw up earthworks for the defence of London, and man those works when constructed. It was admitted that the number of infantry Volunteers was in excess of the need, but it was felt that to reduce the numbers would cause discontent and not save much money. This scheme was finalised by J.C. Ardagh in 1888; stressing that the danger was an attack on London, Ardagh drew up a scheme whereby the Regular troops were to be stationed at railway junctions between London and the coast in order to give them maximum mobility to meet the invasion threat wherever it might appear. Between the Regulars and London were to be stationed the whole of the Volunteers except those units detailed for garrison work. They were to assemble and practise in six entrenched camps surrounding London. This allotment of Volunteer troops was approved by the Commander-in-Chief in May 1889.[71] In 1888 all Volunteer corps had been made part of a Brigade. Thus by the end of the 1880s the Volunteers had a definite place in the defence plans of the nation. It was, no one could help noting, a humble place. A.M. Brookfield, commanding the 1st Cinque Ports Rifles at the end of the century, believed 'the true official view of the Force . . . to have been that, while it represented a popular national movement which it might be a pity to discourage, it was still essential that it should never be regarded as an asset that could be turned to any useful purpose in actual warfare.'[72]

In their training, however, there could be no doubt that the Volunteers were brought into greater contact with the Regulars as time progressed. In general in the first decade contacts were infrequent. Each Volunteer Battalion had its adjutant and drill sergeant seconded from the Regulars, and it was of course a Regular officer who carried out the annual inspection. But other than this there was only rarely contact between Regulars and Volunteers. This did not stop generally hostile opinions being formed. The Regulars, in their own journals, as became professionals, were not a little contemptuous of the efforts of the amateur Volunteers, and the Volunteers were inclined to find the annual inspection a farce, and the drill book of the Regular Army both tedious and useless. But while the Regulars were rarely as alarmed as the Duke of Cambridge had shown himself to be over Ranelagh's antics in 1861, the Volunteers displayed a continuing sensitivity to criticism from the Regulars.[73]

From the 1870s there was more likelihood that opinions could be tested by face-to-face contact. This did not happen to quite the extent hoped for because of the difficulties that line battalions had in adjusting to localisation. The problem was not ill will, but the perpetual headache of the Army in the later nineteenth century, lack of recruits. The calls for overseas service continued heavy, and inevitably were only found at the expense of the home battalions. In 1872 there were 70 battalions at home, and 71 abroad, by 1879 59 at home and 82 abroad. Few if any of the home battalions were fit for active service without substitution of Reservists. It was with these battalions, often absent, and never up to strength that the Volunteers were brought into association in the 1870s.[74] In the circumstances the chances of the District military Depot becoming a focus for the military enthusiasm of enlisters and Volunteers were slim. The Depot system failed because of the inadequacies of the Line battalions which were stationed there.

Nevertheless contacts between Regulars and Volunteers were increasing. Already in 1868 the *Volunteer Service Gazette* was noting the extension of the fashion of rifle matches between Regulars and Volunteers. These occurred both locally, and at the Mecca of rifle shooting, Wimbledon. Elcho, on resigning the chairmanship of the National Rifle Association in 1867, declared, 'If there is one thing more than another which is good in this meeting, it is that the officers and men of the army and the officers and men of the Volunteer force are brought together, learn to appreciate each other, and are bound together, I believe, in indissoluble bonds of friendship.' By 1875 the Volunteers were reported to be receiving a cordial reception from Regulars at the Autumn Manoeuvres.[75] Camps at which Volunteers were brigaded with Regulars became a fruitful occasion for fraternisation. In 1892 the Birmingham Volunteers, particularly the sergeants, struck up a good relationship with their Regular opposite numbers. In 1895 when the Artists' Rifles were quartered in the same barracks as the 2nd Life Guards, 'The two Regiments became the greatest friends, and most cordial and enthusiastic meetings took place between the Officers, Sergeants, and men of both Regiments in their various messes and barrack-rooms.' At a Whitsun Camp in 1897 the Hampshire Volunteers were associated with the Royal Artillery, and 'of the *camaraderie* established between the gunners and the Volunteers there were many evidences . . .'[76]

Such evidence is of course no more than anecdotal, and may indeed have only merited insertion in the histories of the Volunteer corps as a case to disprove what we may suspect to have been the general opinion, that the Regular Army held the Volunteers in some contempt. Volunteer sensitivity to this belief is noticeable, and nothing is more marked towards the end of the century than the Volunteer desire to draw closer to the Regulars. It pervades the Evidence and Report of the 1894 Select Committee, and it took outward manifestation in the matter of uniform. The early Volunteer uniforms had been a medley of different styles and colours, having perhaps only one thing in common – that no one could have mistaken a Volunteer for a Regular. 'There seems to be strong objection on the part of Volunteers to be dressed in scarlet,' wrote Luard, Assistant Inspector of Volunteers for South-East England in 1862. This objection to scarlet was undoubtedly stronger in the South of England than in the North, and more especially Scotland. The Scottish artillery and engineers adopted the uniform of their regular branches in 1863-4, and about one-third of the Scottish battalions adopted scarlet at the same time.[77] It was not until the 1870s that there was much movement towards scarlet in England. General Ellice in his report on the 1872 Brighton Field Day wrote that 'the more closely the Force is identified in appearance as well as

discipline with the Regular Forces, the more serviceable it will become.'
Before then, it is true, some regiments had adopted scarlet, for
instance the 1st Lincoln, and the City of London. But of most it must
have been true, as the historian of the Hampshire Volunteers records,
'that had the red uniform been ordered by the authorities in 1859,
many corps that then sprang into existence would never have been
formed. Even with the grey unsoldierly cut that was exhibited to early
recruits, there was a distinct shyness to enrol, because they were afraid
of being entrapped, as it were, into enlistment, and made real soldiers
of. By 1877, when the change took place, nothing could have been
more popular than the national colour, and assimilation to the regular
soldier.'[78] There was a nationwide move to scarlet, so that by 1878-9,
91 regiments wore scarlet, 66 green, and 57 grey of various shades. In
Lanarkshire the change to scarlet in 1879 is said to have helped fill up
the ranks.[79]

It must be emphasised that although the authorities were
encouraging the change to scarlet, they were not enforcing it. The
change came about essentially because the Volunteers wanted it. By the
1870s voting on uniform was by no means common, but the men could
vote with their feet if not their hands, and simply resign if they did not
like the change. No Commanding Officer could afford to make the
change if he thought it would be unpopular, for the change itself
involved the expense of replacing in one year the uniforms of the
entire corps. There was a second wave of 'scarlet fever' in the 1890s,[80]
the laggards being forced to assimilate to the Regular's uniform in
1908.

Uniform, therefore, is a good guide to the Volunteers' attitude to
the Regulars; there was an increasing desire to be assimilated, which
probably cannot be disassociated from an equal desire that their
value should be recognised, and an acceptance that this could only
come about through close ties with the Regulars. This move towards
the Regulars on the part of the Volunteers is of course also an indication
that the Regular Army itself was more popular than it had been in
mid-century. The origins of that popularity have been traced to a
period predating the formation of the Volunteer Force, in effect to the
Crimean War.[81] In fact the British maintained an ambiguous attitude
towards their soldiers — they were both heroes and outcasts, praised for
their courage, and excluded from places of public entertainment. On
distant battlefields a hero was a hero whatever his social origins; in
Britain he might too obviously bear the birthmarks of the slum to be
recognisable as other than lower-class. This ambivalence was never
fully resolved until the First World War when men of all classes joined
the rank and file. But in so far as it was resolved before then, and the
individual soldier seen in the street became an object of acceptance

rather than avoidance, contemporary opinion was strongly inclined to place the reward with the Volunteers. There were of course other factors at work, in particular the frequent fighting of extensively reported colonial wars, but it is at least probable that the Volunteers' discovery that the soldier was little different from himself may have percolated through the Volunteer world into society at large. 'The South African war has done much to remove the prejudice against the soldier,' wrote Colonel Lamont; 'but even more than that the existence and fraternising of the Volunteer has brought the soldier nearer the heart of the nation, and given him a standing which he did not previously occupy.'[82]

This was a typical theme for after-dinner speeches and prizegivings; here, for example, is Sir Evelyn Wood at the Council Dinner of the National Artillery Association in 1899: 'Ever since the Volunteer movement took root, some thirty-five years ago, the Volunteers have done more for the Army than the Army has been able to do for itself. This is a fact that has been fully borne out and acknowledged for many years past . . . I am expressing as well as I can the feeling that I have in my heart, that we owe to the Association and the Volunteer movement generally a very deep debt of gratitude for the great efforts made in trying to uphold the interest of English men and women in the Army.' The 1904 Royal Commission echoed the same theme: 'The Volunteer force has had a great effect in educating the people of Great Britain to think of the Army as a national institution, and at the same time it has enlarged the ideas of professional soldiers on the subject of the means and methods of military training.'[83]

A more impressive opinion, however, in that it was unsolicited and confidential, came from Wolseley, formerly Inspector-General of the Reserve Forces, in 1878. He wrote to Lord Bury, and wished it to be considered part of the evidence before Bury's Committee, then sitting. It is worth quoting at some length:

> The Volunteer movement has been a great national success;
> its direct value to the country may be estimated by the number
> of effective riflemen it furnishes, but its indirect value cannot
> be counted in figures, although it is felt and appreciated by
> all who have studied the military strength of our kingdom.
> In a few words, it may be described as having given a
> military impulse to the people unknown before; it has
> turned the attention of all classes, more or less, to military
> matters; men of all professions and of all trades have
> devoted much time and thought to drill, to efficient rifle
> shooting, and to the numerous details of a soldier's work;
> public thought may be said to have been given a military
> bent, to have been turned into military grooves. Formerly

96

the army had to depend upon its own members for reformation and improvement in drill and equipment, now it has taken the nation, through the Volunteer movement, into its confidence. Fresh, unprejudiced, and unbiased minds have been brought to bear upon subjects which had been previously considered only by the officers of our Regular Army over whom the disciplined education of the regiment had frequently exercised so powerful an influence that their minds were incapable of receiving or were at least unconsciously antagonistic to the consideration of new ideas. The result has already been most advantageous to the Regular Army, for as soldiers we have already learnt much from the Volunteers. Commonsense is making itself felt more and more every day in the clothing, equipment, armament, and drill of our soldiers, and the pipe-clay prejudices of our old-fashioned leaders which formerly hedged us round, forbidding admission to all reforms, are daily being broken down by the force of the practical commonsense directed to military subjects by the Volunteers of England.

The stigma formerly attached to the man who enlisted is quickly disappearing, and must disappear altogether if the Volunteer movement goes on prospering as it has hitherto done. When you have the large proportion of our male population, which is now either in the Volunteer ranks or has passed through them, all taught to look up to the Regular Soldier as their model of excellence, and who by contact with our men in schools of instruction or with our non-commissioned officers or their drill-master, have learnt to appreciate the many good sides of the British soldier's character; when such a condition of things exists, it is quite certain that the old prejudice against the soldier must soon die out altogether. In fact, the Volunteer movement has popularised the Army, and the soldier is now looked upon as one from whom much is to be learnt, as a model to be copied, rather than as the pariah to be despised, which he was before our citizen army sprang into existence.[84]

This is strongly stated, and coming from one who was reputed to be critical of the Volunteers, and who was himself to owe his fame in no small part to the increased popularity of the Army, it is hard to discount as simple flattery.

The Times in 1857, in its campaign for the formation of a Volunteer Force, declared, 'We must popularize the army, and martialize the population. The gulf must be narrowed between the soldier and the citizen.'[85] The Volunteer Force as the intermediary between the people and the Regular Army certainly played a key role in achieving that task. Nevertheless as an intermediary, its position was fraught with difficulty, for it was negotiating from weakness, not strength. It was dependent on both parties, financially on the people, and militarily on the Regular Army who were the appointed judges of the Volunteers' military capacity. As 'the child of the people',[86] visible to the people, the Volunteers were alternately liable to the felt injustice of parental criticism and the excessive praise accorded to a favourite son. Regular officers, too, could be scornful in their clubs, while all smooth flattery on the parade-ground. The Volunteers were aware of the ambiguity of their status, but they could not escape it. It derived from their dual role as both citizens and soldiers. They could neither retreat into the isolation of professionalism, nor pretend with conviction that professional skills were unimportant. Some tried to acquire those skills with an eagerness which embarrassed and bored the professionals.[87] Others were content to be ignorant, and were thus open to the criticism that they were useless. Most just carried on with the day-to-day tasks of volunteering, perhaps sometimes wondering why their patriotic endeavours met with formal praise and private sneers. The Volunteer Force was the embodiment of many of the canonised values of Victorian Britain. Patriotism, self-help, local initiative, discipline, order, health-giving recreation, and class mixing in an approved manner were all promoted by the existence of the Force. It is surely some commentary on the status of those values, as of the status of the Force, that the Volunteers were so little esteemed in their own society.

Notes

1. T.H. Hayhurst, *A History and some Records of the Volunteer Movement in Bury, Heywood, Rossendale, and Ramsbottom*, p. 140; *VSG*, 1 Oct. 1864.
2. *3 Hansard 253*, cc. 429-32, 548, 1909-10 (21 and 22 June, 8 July 1880); *4 Hansard 47*, cc. 769-82, *51*, c. 953 (16 Mar. and 23 July 1897).
3. *VSG*, 25 Feb., 14 and 18 Apr. 1860.
4. *Annual Register,* 'Chronicle', 1860, pp. 150-2; RC (1862), qq. 1739, 4593; E.A. Goodwyn, *A Suffolk Town in Mid-Victorian England*, p. 56.
5. 'Report on Reserve Forces 1868-9' by Major-General Jas. Lindsay, p. 22, WO 33/19; *The Times*, 8 Oct. 1867.
6. *The Times*, 19 Apr. 1870; *Daily Telegraph*, quoted in *VSG*, 4 Feb. 1871; see also C. Hindley, *Curiosities of Street Literature* (1st ed. 1871, repr. Seven Dials Press, Welwyn Garden City, 1969), p. 155.
7. E.A. Goodwyn, op.cit., pp. 17,29,39; J.F. Russell and J.H. Elliot, *The Brass*

Band Movement (London, 1936), pp. 121-2, 133; see also A. Howkins, *Whitsun in Nineteenth-century Oxfordshire* (History Workshop Pamphlets, No. 8, 1973), p. 33.

8. *Stamford Mercury* in Scrap Book of Lincolnshire Volunteers, Lincolnshire Archives Office Hill 12/2/1; W. Plomer (ed.) *Kilvert's Diary* (London, 1938), vol. I, p.306, vol. II, p.137.

9. A. Bennett, *The Old Wives' Tale* (London, Everyman ed., 1935). p. 61; G. Raverat, *Period Piece* (London, 1952), p. 46.

10. Frome Selwood Rifle Volunteers, Minute Book, 6 Sept. 1860, Somerset Record Office, DD/LW 25.

11. *VSG*, 6 Dec. 1862, 29 June 1861.

12. *VSG*, 25 Feb. and 12 May 1860.

13. *Punch* stressed this theme, e.g. 28 May 1859, Almanack for 1860 (Dec.), 14 July 1860; see also W.H. Blanch (ed.), *The Volunteer's Book of Facts* (London and Liverpool, 1862), p. 121.

14. *VSG*, 14 Apr. 1860.

15. RC (1862), q. 2876; *Territorial Year Book, 1909* (London, 1909), p. 6; see also *The Queen's Royal Volunteer Brigade, the Royal Scots, Chronicle*, vol. II (Jan. 1904), p. 6.

16. *VSG*, 11 Feb. 1860.

17. Placard in the Military Museum, Dorchester; [C.] Rudd, *The Early History of the 17th (North) Middlesex Volunteer Rifles*, p. 12; *VSG*, 28 Jan. 1860.

18. *Methodist Recorder*, 26 Aug. to 14 Oct. 1870.

19. *5 Hansard 56*, (HC) c. 617 (30 July 1913); H.W. Lee and E. Archbold, *Social Democracy in Britain* (London, 1935), pp. 194-201; for Ramsay Macdonald's views of Haldane's proposals, see *4 Hansard 172*, cc. 1593-1601 (23 Apr. 1907).

20. *4 Hansard 4*, c. 1424 (20 May 1892).

21. see above, pp. 20-4 30.

22. *3 Hansard 303*, c. 1508 (22 Mar. 1886), *329*, c. 493 (25 July 1888), *4 Hansard 176*, c. 389 (18 June 1907).

23. Committee (1878-9), qq. 3055, 3058; *3 Hansard 329*, cc. 457-95, *330*, c. 247 (25 July and 9 Aug. 1888); SC (1894), q. 1479.

24. *The History of the London Rifle Brigade 1859-1918* (London, 1921), p. 46; RC (1904), qq. 1115-7, 5315-24, 5397, 5649-51, 6550.

25. *4 Hansard 172*, c. 272 (4 Apr. 1907); RC (1904), q. 5598; see also *Lincoln Journal*, 15 Feb. 1870 in Scrap Book of Lincolnshire Volunteers, Lincolnshire Archives Office, Hill 12/2/2; *5 Hansard 55*, (HC) cc. 2227-8 (24 July 1913).

26. RC (1904), qq. 5498, 6117-21, 6173, 6631, but also 9151.

27. *5 Hansard 1*, (HC) cc. 412-3, 1645-62 (22 Feb. and 4 Mar. 1909), *2*, cc. 50-61, 84-8, 100-5, 131-3 (8 Mar. 1909).

28. *5 Hansard 40*, (HC) cc. 1367, 1422 (4 July 1912).

29. City of London Territorial and Auxiliary Forces Assoc., Minute Book, 22 Apr. 1913, Guildhall Library, MS 12,606, vol. II; Territorial Force Association of Kent, Minute Book of General Purposes Committee, 26 Sept. 1913, TAVR HQ, Maidstone; Col. Sir George McCrae to Seely, 16 and 28 Nov. 1913, and Bethune's comments, 27 Nov. and 6 Dec. 1913, WO 32/11242.

30. City of London T and AFA, Minute Book of Recruiting Committee, 14 Apr. 1908, 6 Jan. 1909, 13 Mar. 1912, and Minute Book, 16 June, 13 Oct., 8 Dec. 1908, 13 July 1909, Guildhall Library, MS 12,613, vol. I, and MS 12,606, vol. I.

31. T.H. Hayhurst, op.cit., 141-2, 157; E.J. King, *The History of the 7th Battalion Middlesex Regiment* (London, 1927), pp. 96-7; [C.] Rudd, op.cit., p. 40; A.R. Bennett, *London and Londoners in the Eighteen-fifties and sixties* (London, 1924), p. 42.
32. *VSG*, 12 May 1860; E.T. Evans, *Records of the Third Middlesex Rifle Volunteers*, p. 182.
33. C. Igglesden, *History of the East Kent Volunteers*, p. 7; *VSG*, 31 Mar. 1860.
34. *The Times*, 15 July 1861; *VSG*, 25 June 1864, 6 Apr. 1872.
35. G. Melly, *Recollections*, p. 107; Interview with H.P. Dawton, 10 May 1971.
36. Major Oskar Teichman, 'The Yeomanry as an aid to civil power 1795-1867', *Journal of the Society for Army Historical Research*, vol. 19 (1940), pp. 75-91, 127-43.
37. 'Copy of a Circular Letter, dated the 7th day of June 1861, addressed by the late Lord Herbert of Lea, as Secretary of State for War, to the Lords Lieutenant of Counties on the Subject of the Employment of Volunteers on the Occurrence of Civil Disturbances, and at Parliamentary Elections,' PP 1867 (153), XLI, p. 819.
38. *3 Hansard 171*, cc. 349-53 (4 June 1863).
39. HO 45. OS 7799/118-144, 167; see also Sir James Sexton, *The Life of the Dockers' MP* (London, 1936), p. 31.
40. Peel to Walpole, 20 Feb. 1867, HO 45. O.S. 8060.
41. *3 Hansard 185*, cc. 371-7, 919-30, 1550-73, 1575-81 (15 and 25 Feb., 8 Mar. 1867), *188*, cc. 728-45, 751-61 (28 June and 1 July 1867).
42. *VSG*, 25 May 1878.
43. J. Orr, *History of the Seventh Lanarkshire Rifle Volunteers*, p. 473; HO 45. OS 7322, 7326.
44. C.J. Hart, *The History of the 1st Volunteer Battalion The Royal Warwickshire Regiment*, pp. 139-42; J.H.A. Macdonald, *Fifty Years of it*, p. 149; E.J. King, op.cit., p. 55; W. Stephen, *History of the Queen's City of Edinburgh Rifle Volunteer Brigade*, pp. 49-50.
45. *VSG*, 25 May 1878. There is here a useful summary of law and practice up to 1878.
46. *The Times*, 17 June 1878.
47. Quoted in J. Walter, *The Volunteer Force* (London, 1881), pp. 38-9.
48. See e.g. Ensign Sopht [R.M. Ballantyne], *The Volunteer Levée* (Edinburgh, 1860); A. Henry, 'Illustrated narrative of a visit of Edinburgh Riflemen to Dumfries 1860', Hornel Library, Kirkcudbright; *Punch*, e.g. 6 Aug. 1859, 14 Apr. 1860.
49. *VSG*, 1 Mar. 1862.
50. Cambridge to Herbert, 19 Jan., 20 Feb. 1861, Herbert Papers.
51. W.H. Chaloner and W.O. Henderson (eds.), *Engels as Military Critic*, pp. 9-10.
52. *VSG*, 27 Apr. 1861, 1 Mar. 1862.
53. *3 Hansard 163*, c. 805 (7 June 1861); T. Hughes, 'The Volunteer's Catechism', *Macmillan's Magazine*, vol. II (July 1860), p. 193.
54. *VSG*, 22 Feb. 1862.
55. *Morning Star*, 21 July 1862, quoted in *VSG*, 26 July 1862.
56. On British military thinking in general, see J. Luvaas, *The Education of an Army* (London, 1965), and *The Military Legacy of the Civil War — The European Inheritance* (Chicago, 1959); A.W. Preston, 'British Military Thought, 1856-90', *The Army Quarterly*, vol. LXXXIX (Oct. 1964), pp. 57-74.
57. *The Times*, 21 Sept. 1864, 9 Oct. 1866, 20 Nov. 1867.

58. ibid., 25 Dec. 1869.
59. ibid., 20 and 22 Aug., 2 and 9 Sept. 1870.
60. ibid., 8 and 11 Apr. 1871.
61. ibid., 1 Apr. 27 May 1872, 15 Apr. 14 July 1873.
62. R.P. Berry, *A History of the Formation and Development of the Volunteer Infantry*, p. 492.
63. *The Times*, 27 Jan. 1869.
64. On Cardwell, see R. Biddulph, *Lord Cardwell at the War Office* (London, 1904); B. Bond, 'The Effect of the Cardwell Reforms in Army Organization 1874-1904', *Journal of the Royal United Service Institution*, vol. CV (Nov. 1960), pp. 515-24.
65. For the attitude of Cardwell, and his Under-Secretary of State, Northbrook, to the Volunteers, see R. Biddulph, op. cit., pp. 26-8, 34-5; Northbrook to Cardwell, 15 Jan. 1869, and Memorandum by Northbrook, 29 Jan. 1869, Cardwell Papers, PRO 30/48/4/18, ff. 13, 25-31.
66. *The Times*, 25 Dec. 1869, 8, 17, 20, 25 and 29 Jan. 1870, 13 Aug. 1870.
67. *VSG*, 25 Feb. 1871, 8 and 29 June 1872; *3 Hansard 212*, cc. 129-54 (24 June 1872).
68. [G.T. Chesney], 'The Battle of Dorking', *Blackwood's Magazine*, vol. CIX (May 1871), pp. 539-72. On invasion literature in general, see I.F. Clarke, *Voices Prophesying War 1763-1984* (London, 1966).
69. R.P: Berry, op. cit., pp. 131, 141-3.
70. B. Bond, *The Victorian Army and the Staff College 1854-1914* (London, 1972), p. 121; *Army List*, Dec. 1875.
71. Reports of a Committee on Army Mobilisation, Dec. 1886; Defence of England, 17 Apr. 1888; The Defence of London, 16 July 1888 in Ardagh Papers, PRO 30/40/13.
72. A.M. Brookfield, *Annals of a Chequered Life*, p. 247.
73. H.S. Wilson, 'The British Army and Public Opinion from 1854 to the end of 1873' is an invaluable survey of opinion; on Volunteer criticism of the Regulars, see J.H.A. Macdonald, op. cit., W. Lamont, *Volunteer Memories*, p. 65; on Volunteer sensitivity, E.J. King, op. cit., p. 51; *VSG*, 7 Nov. 1863.
74. B. Bond, 'The Effect of the Cardwell Reforms in Army Organization 1874-1904', loc. cit., pp. 519-20.
75. *VSG*, 15 Feb. 1868, 6 Mar. 1875; *The Times*, 19 July 1867.
76. C.J. Hart, op. cit., pp. 209-10, 354; H.A.R. May, *Memories of the Artists Rifles* (London, 1929), p. 56; T.S. Cave, *History of the First Volunteer Battalion Hampshire Regiment*, p. 434.
77. RC (1862), App. 3; J.M. Grierson, *Records of the Scottish Volunteer Force*, p. 57.
78. *The Times*, 27 May 1872; 1st Lincoln Rifle Volunteers, Minute Book, 2 May 1864, Lincolnshire Archives Office, Hill 12/1/1; C. Digby Planck, *History of the 7th (City of London) Battalion the London Regiment* (London, n.d. [1946?]), p. 3; T.S. Cave, op. cit., p. 279.
79. T.H. Hayhurst, op. cit., p. 230; J. Orr, op. cit., pp. 174-5.
80. W. Lamont, op. cit., pp. 87-8.
81. O. Anderson, 'The growth of Christian militarism in mid-Victorian Britain', *English Historical Review*, vol. LXXXVI (Jan. 1971), pp. 46-72.
82. W. Lamont, op. cit., p. 104.
83. Wood quoted in J.G. Hicks, *The Percy Artillery* (London, 1899), p. 50; RC (1904), Report, p. 13; cf. R.W. Routledge, 'A Volunteer Battalion', *Nineteenth Century*, vol. XXI (May 1887), p. 747.
84. WO 32/5974.

85. *The Times*, 23 Sept. 1857.
86. *Daily Telegraph*, 2 Apr. 1870, quoted in *VSG*, 9 Apr. 1870.
87. C.E. Callwell, *Stray Recollections* (London, 1923), vol. II, pp. 8-9.

6 PATRIOTISM AND RECREATION

Why should men join a military force which imposed on them obligations, but brought them no monetary reward? To contemporaries, patriotism was the most obvious answer. That it was this which inspired the Force was, at the time, a widespread, indeed one might say necessary belief. Speeches at prizegivings, leading articles, and other public pronouncements of the kind naturally dwelt on the patriotism embodied in the Force. Whatever the social and political benefits might be, it was in the last resort the Force's contribution to national defence, a contribution which seemed to stem from patriotism, which entitled the Volunteers to public esteem and government support. And it was the reliance for its defence on the freely offered patriotism of its people, rather than conscription, which seemed to distinguish Britain in a gratifying way from the countries of Continental Europe.

In this as in so many ways Palmerston may speak for his generation. 'The Motives which impel this Mass of Men,' he wrote to Gladstone of the Volunteers,

> cannot be mistaken. They are not as vain and childish seeking for amusement; they are not a mere Fancy for a Military Dress; the Motives which influence these men from John o'Groats House to the Land's End, are a deeply rooted Conviction that in the present State of the World, Events may at any Time happen, which would expose this Country to Danger; together with a strong opinion that our Naval and Military Establishments, though as efficient and large, as in Time of Peace, it would suit the Finances of the Country to make them, are nevertheless insufficient of themselves to repel and avert those sudden Dangers to which we might be exposed. It seems to me that this Conclusion is as demonstrable as any Proposition in Euclid.[1]

Unlike a Proposition in Euclid', Palmerston's 'Conclusion' is exceedingly difficult to test. There is no written history of British patriotism, nor indeed anything but scattered knowledge as to its political power or social location. Hopefully a study of the Volunteer Force will add to that knowledge, but there is no easy answer to the question, how far it was love of country, and a desire to defend it, which led men to join the Volunteer Force, and remain in it. Some possible approaches to an answer suggest themselves. First, an examination of the pattern of enrolment into the Force over time may give some clues to the motives of those who joined. If enrolment increased at times of national danger, we may reasonably give some of the credit to patriotism. Secondly, the political context in which volunteering occurred may indicate the likelihood of patriotism being a powerful inducement to enrolment; patriotism from the 1870s onwards was associated with Conservatism, yet the social composition of the Volunteer Force would lead one to expect that a substantial proportion of its members were Liberal. Thirdly, the statements of contemporaries can be examined to see how far they were unanimous in believing it to be patriotism which made men join. The result of such investigations casts some doubt on the notion that patriotism was the most important incentive to enrolment, at least after the first few years, and with the exception of the Boer War period.

The major part of this chapter, therefore, attempts a different approach to the question. It looks at the Volunteer Force from beneath, as it were, and asks what it meant to an individual to join the Volunteers. What kind of obligations did he assume in terms of time and finance? Could he, by enrolment, hope for any personal advantage in his employment or in society at large? What was there in the Force to attract him to it? As we shall see, the recreational facilities offered within the Force loomed larger than patriotism as an inducement to the prospective Volunteer. From the point of view of the individual, it will be suggested, volunteering was primarily a recreation.

Figure 1 shows how the number of Volunteers varied from year to year. A number of points stand out. First, the proportion of efficients to enrolled, after dropping with the introduction of stricter regulations in 1863, picked up and remained fairly constant. Secondly, there was a continuous drop in numbers from the peak of 1868 to the trough of 1873, a period which included the Franco-Prussian War. The most likely explanation for this drop, elaborated in the previous chapter, is that during these years the public was beginning to doubt the efficacy of the Force, and the Force itself was uneasy about new regulations introduced by Cardwell. By 1873 the Force was re-established on a more stable basis, and a period of renewed growth started. There was a steady rise in numbers until 1887, and then a further period of decrease, which was almost certainly caused by the introduction of stricter regulations, and a deliberate policy of not allowing the formation of new infantry corps.[2] The next notable feature was the sharp increase in recruitment at the onset of the Boer War. Part of that increase was sustained after the war, with the exception of 1908 when there was a considerable but temporary drop with the reorganisation into the Territorial Force. It seems, therefore, that normally the Force decreased in numbers when stricter regulations were introduced or when there was doubt as to its usefulness, and increased in rough accordance with the increase in numbers of the available population.

104

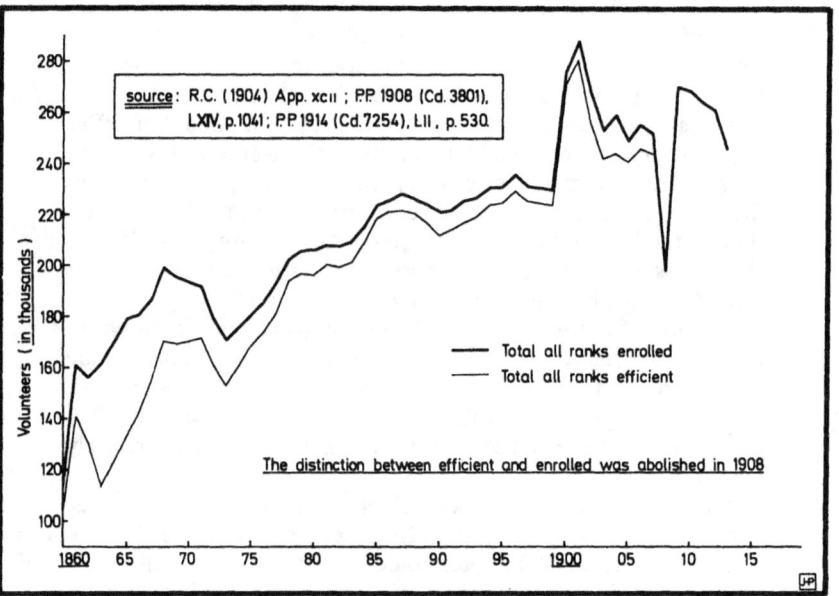

Figure 1.   Number of Efficient and Enrolled Volunteers, 1860-1913.

The exception to this generalisation is the Boer War period and the most obvious explanation for the sharp increase in numbers at that time is patriotism; at the very least there can be no doubt that the Boer War was the occasion for the increase, and if the desire for adventure or even for employment may have played a part in the recruitment, it is unreasonable to suppose that there was not also concern for the situation in which the country found itself. Although the Boer War is the most obvious instance of patriotism being reflected in recruitment, it is possible to argue that patriotism was also in part responsible for the fairly sharp increase in numbers in the second half of the 1870s, coinciding with the Eastern crisis, and in 1883-5 when General Gordon and the invasion scare of 1884 were the catalysts. Thus the *Volunteer Service Gazette* claimed that in 1878 'the moment that it appeared likely that the Regular troops would have to go and fight abroad, the Volunteers showed, in the most unmistakable manner, that they meant

105

to try to qualify themselves to fill their vacant places at home. The
ranks of every regiment were filled, and the attendances at drill,
inspection, and so on throughout the country were better, we believe,
than they have ever been since the first Establishment of the Force. And
as we have often predicted would be the case, the supply of officers
was very largely increased.'[3] This latter point is interesting as it is
suggests that the middle class was perhaps reacting more positively
than others to the threats to the country. In Edinburgh, both at the
time of the Franco-Prussian War, and in the Eastern crisis, the middle-
class corps, but not the artisan corps, increased in numbers, and in the
Boer War it has been established by Professor Price that a high
proportion of the volunteers at the beginning of the War when the
threat to the country was greatest, was middle-class.[4] There would
seem therefore to be some response to crisis which shows up in the
recruitment figures. But with the exception of the Boer War it is not
a very substantial response, and it was possibly disproportionately
middle-class.

Working-class enrolment was subject to more mundane considerations.
Economic factors could be vital. In direct contrast to the Regular Army
and the Militia, the Volunteers could expect to recruit well in times of
prosperity and lose men in times of depression. Thus in Dalbeattie,
which relied heavily on the granite trade, it was said in the 1890s that
'the strength of the Company is a fair indication whether that trade is
prosperous or not. It has often happened that when trade was brisk
in the spring that the numbers on the roll of the Company have
exceeded one hundred, but that before the drill season was half finished
trade had become dull, and numbers had left the place, and consequently
could not make themselves efficient.' Similarly in Crewe in 1871 a fall
in the number of Volunteers was said to be 'chiefly caused by the
depressed state of trade'.[5] Where the Regular Army and the Militia
gained, the Volunteers lost; the Force depended for its strength on a
supply of working men in steady jobs.

Normally that supply was good. For what is striking about the
pattern of enrolment is not so much the response to crises as the ability
of the Force to maintain itself over fifty years. The persistence of the
Force, as well as the enthusiasm for it at the outset, are what require
explanation. It will be argued that while patriotism was an essential
ingredient at the time of the Force's inception, it became less so in
time, and that the reasons for this were in part a change in the political
implications of patriotism, and in part the existence of other reasons
for joining the Force.

At the time of the invasion scare of 1859-60 there was widespread
agreement in Britain about the proper conduct of foreign affairs.
Palmerston's policy was both liberal in its support of constitutionalism

abroad and conservative in its upholding of British interests and the balance of power. Britain's power was such that there appeared to be no contradiction between the maintenance of British interests and the support of European nationalist movements. Not until 1863 was the bluff called. Then the breaking of the French alliance left Britain powerless to come to the aid of the Poles, and in the following year the climbdown over Schleswig-Holstein reinforced the impossibility of exerting influence in isolation. These humiliations led to an isolationism which sought no influence and it was the theme of Conservatives 'that the theory which connects the Tory party with war and intervention, and the Liberals with the opposite system, is founded on an utter perversion of history; that while Lord Castlereagh, Mr. Canning and the Duke of Wellington, in the years following the great peace, kept England aloof from entanglement with any contending party on the Continent, a quenchless thirst for interference, an insatiable appetite for meddling, has characterised the Liberal ascendancy.'[6] By the late 1860s that ascendancy was coming to a close, and under Disraeli the Conservatives were to put themselves forward, in a significant shift, as the party which upheld British interests. It was no longer possible for one policy to satisfy both Conservatives and Liberals. As Disraeli told his Cabinet in 1877, there must be a choice between 'the Imperial policy of England and a policy of crusade.'[7] The Conservatives in the 1870s identified themselves with the former. As was happening all over Europe, patriotism, which had formerly been a Liberal creed, was becoming a Conservative one.

The relevance of this to the Volunteer Force is clear. At the time of the formation of the Force there were only isolated Cobdenites and members of the Peace Society who objected to the notion of arming for defence of the realm against the French. There was, it is true, some working-class opposition, but, as has been seen, it arose not from belief in the pacific intentions of Louis Napoleon, but from the claim that the working man was as much entitled to a vote as to a rifle.[8] In the 1850s the articulate working man was greatly concerned to foster European nationalist movements, and as liable as anyone else to suspect the motives of Louis Napoleon in his claim to champion that cause. A sense of crusade towards Europe, a desire to help redeem it from the grip of autocracy, was a key part of mid-nineteenth-century British patriotism, and was located amongst those who thought of themselves as Liberal or Radical. As James Grant was to note as late as 1872, 'The amount of a man's patriotism has always been measured by the amount of his Liberalism.'[9] Within that decade it would be measured by the amount of his Conservatism.

Politically, therefore, it was perfectly acceptable for men of nearly all opinions to join the Volunteers in the 1860s. The Conservative could see it as an upholding of the vital British interest of defence of the shores of the country, the Liberal or Radical as a justified and patriotic response to the threat of invasion from a foreign tyrant who had come to power by an unconstitutional *coup* in the aftermath of the ruthless repression of the French working class. And in the adoption by a large number of corps of Garibaldi-style uniforms there was at least a gesture of support for European nationalism.[10]

Men of very different social rank and political opinion, therefore, could join the Force in the early years for reasons which can be described as patriotic. *Reynolds' Newspaper* criticised Napoleon III and supported the Volunteer Force in language which differed from that of *The Times* only in being more outspoken.[11] In its early years the Volunteer Force was non-political in the sense that there was no political issue concerning it. It was represented and supported on both sides of the House of Parliament. In 1868 there were no less than ninety serving Volunteer officers in Parliament, and over fifty of them were Liberals.[12] But in another sense the Volunteer Force was a highly political response to a situation in which invasion of the country seemed possible. At the formation, even in an inland county like Worcestershire, 'people thought that their property was not secure from invasion.'[13]

There is reason then to suppose that the Volunteer Force arose out of a patriotic upsurge which in the particular political situation could be shared by a wide spectrum of opinion. By the 1870s patriotism was a quality much more attached to one political party, the Conservatives. A man who joined the Force in the spring of 1878 when the Conservative Government was pursuing a highly contentious foreign policy was either consciously giving support to that policy or acting in a manner which can best be described as apolitical. It will be argued that for most people the latter was the case. There are *prima facie* grounds for believing this in that if those who joined the Force after the first decade were giving support to the Conservatives the upper working class must have been much more Conservatively inclined than other evidence would lead one to suppose.

That there were reasons other than patriotism for joining the Force receives support from the fact that there was a significant number of people within the Force who stated so in no uncertain terms. As early as 1867 a Scottish writer was claiming that 'In no instance is it pure unalloyed patriotism that retains a man in the force. Volunteering is expected to have its pleasures as well as its duties.' This was an unusually early date for such an opinion to be voiced. Later, for example in evidence given before the 1904 Royal Commission, it was a common theme. Thus the Colonel of the 3rd Volunteer Battalion of the Lancashire Fusiliers, whose men were mechanics in the cotton trade in Salford, thought that 'the bulk of my men join because they like the show, the dress, and they like the camp. I do not think they join from very high patriotic motives.' Similarly a London Cyclist Volunteer did 'not think patriotism comes in in anything like 5 per cent of them. I have a very poor opinion of patriotism as a factor in getting men either as soldiers or Volunteers. They call it patriotism, but I think it is principally a desire for sport.' And the historian of the Volunteers, R. Potter Berry, claimed in his evidence that the motive for joining the Force 'is not absolutely patriotic. I do not say that it is not so in some cases, but taking the generality of them, I do not think it is a question of patriotism.' Three years later, in a debate on Haldane's reform proposals, Viscount Castlereagh warned against putting too much weight on patriotism: 'A number joined, it was true, from a patriotic spirit, but he believed the majority joined because their friends belonged to the Volunteers, because to join was considered a good thing to do, and because members of the force had uniforms in which it was possible for them to walk out when not engaged in military duties.'[14]

Such statements are the more significant in that they come in the aftermath of the Boer War when enrolment from patriotic motives appeared to be at its height. It would of course be possible to quote statements to the opposite effect, claiming that the Force was the embodiment of patriotism. The point to be made, however, is that there were experienced Volunteers who doubted the importance of patriotism, and were prepared to go against the grain of most public pronouncements in saying so.

Patriotism, then, is clearly not in itself a sufficient explanation for the Force's size and persistence. What was there in the Volunteer Force which attracted men to it? To volunteer was no light undertaking. It exposed the citizen-soldier to the possibility of court proceedings if he was unable to pay the instalments for his uniform; it certainly entailed some financial loss through subscriptions, or paying for travel to the range, or foregoing of wages by going to camp; it might, as we have seen, lead to the loss of his job.[15] Subscriptions, it is true, became less common as government aid increased, but they were generally replaced by a signed undertaking on the part of the Volunteer that he would make himself efficient for at least three years, and on default would meet the cost of his uniform. Thus, although a Volunteer could resign at fourteen days' notice, he could only do so at financial cost to himself. There are, then, disincentives to enrolment to be considered.

On the positive side, a Volunteer would almost certainly be recognised as having joined the ranks of the respectable. Respectability, indeed, might be made a condition for enrolment as in the 3rd Somerset Rifle Volunteers whose bye-laws in 1866 stated that 'a character for respectability shall be the only test of eligibility for a member.'

Having enrolled, respectability was enhanced. 'A man's membership of a Volunteer corps', wrote the *Volunteer Service Gazette* in 1866, 'is taken to afford a well-recognized presumption of respectability.'[16] The Volunteer was a man who could be entrusted with a rifle, and who identified himself with the established institutions of the country. There is no information available on the career patterns of Volunteers, but there is at least a certain plausibility in the claim made in 1909 that 'the tendency of the ex-Territorial is to rise in the social scale.'[17] A man with social aspirations might well find it advantageous to join the Volunteers. He might gain some credit with his employer thereby, though as we have seen it was increasingly likely that this was far from the case. But whatever his employer thought, the jeers of the roughs were a constant reminder to him that he was one of the respectable.

Nevertheless, amongst the many reasons adduced by contemporaries for the numerical strength of the Volunteer Force, none that I have seen gives weight to the individual's desire to become respectable or to gain credit with his employer. These were the possible consequences of, not the reasons for, joining the Force; they were side-effects. It is to the more immediate attractions of the Force that we must look if we are to understand its strength.

A man who joined the Volunteer Force undertook to perform a certain amount of drill and rifle-shooting each year in order to make himself efficient. The formal amount required changed from time to time, with the trend towards an increase. Thus in the 1863 Regulations a recruit was required to do thirty drills, and others only nine each year. By 1881 a Volunteer was required to do at least sixty drills in all in his first two years, and could only then reduce the number to nine each year. By 1902 it was becoming something of an obligation to attend camp. Musketry requirements similarly increased. The formal requirements, however, give little idea of what actually happened. Scattered information, and some national statistics for 1904, indicate that Volunteers often did more than was required of them. Thus in the 27th Cheshire Rifle Volunteer Corps between 1878 and 1887 each man did an average of 32 drills per year. In 1884 in the 8th Lancashire the average number of drills per man was 44. And in Birmingham in 1889 recruits averaged 60 drills, old members 26. The national figures for 1904 are rather less impressive, at least as far as the Infantry, the bulk of the Force, is concerned. Whereas the Artillery averaged 34 drills per man, the Engineers 29, and the Submarine Miners 42, the Infantry averaged 19; but this was still above minimum requirements.[18]

A Volunteer, then, might spend an hour or more drilling on twenty or thirty evenings or Saturday afternoons each year. Initially at any rate, and in rural areas in particular, drill was popular. In Dunblane in Perthshire 'in the early days, drill, instead of being looked on as a hardship, was a real pleasure to the men,' and in Haddington the men enjoyed it, it was reported, because 'they had no other amusement except what they would have to pay for.' Even in London mechanics and artisans 'seem to consider drill more as an amusement for the evening, and a relaxation after the work of the day, than as a duty.'[19]

Rifle-shooting, however, was the key to the recreational attraction of the Force. Noting the decline in zeal which had set in by 1862, Frederic Leighton was still confident that 'the *shooting* will keep it together a good deal.' Lord Elcho, testifying before the Select Committee on Open Spaces in 1865, thought that 'it was not for want of patriotism that the volunteers of 1803 vanished into thin air, but that . . . there was then no prize shooting to encourage them. . . . The thing which keeps men together is the shooting and the competition at the butts.' And in 1881 Loyd-Lindsay admitted that 'that which more than anything keeps the Volunteer force together and renders it popular is the rifle-shooting, which gives as much sport to the men as pheasant and rabbit shooting does to those who can afford it.'[20] This unanimous verdict of contemporaries that rifle-shooting was essential to the persistence of the Force leaves open the question of why it should have been popular. To answer this we must look at rifle-shooting in the context of the history of leisure.

Volunteering was a pursuit undertaken in the non-work hours at a man's disposal, and could not have happened had there not been a simultaneous and progressive shortening of the hours of work. With the exception of the winter of 1859-60 when enthusiasm led to drill in the early hours of the morning, volunteering took place on weekday evenings and on Saturday afternoons. The reduction of weekday working hours, and even more the institution of the Saturday half-holiday, were therefore essential pre-requisites for a successful and widespread Volunteer Force. Later in time the beginnings of annual holidays, even if without pay, made camp a possibility.

Hours of work, especially in the textile mills, had been lengthened in the early nineteenth century, but had been brought back to the norm of ten hours work a day by mid-century by the Factory Acts. In the 1850s the building trade pioneered the campaign for a nine-hour day, but it was not until the early 1870s that there was a general and comprehensive reduction of hours to nine. Even with ten hours work, however, an enthusiast could hope to fit in an hour's drill in the evening. But shooting, parades and march-outs required daylight, and this could only be found on Saturday afternoon. In 1843 a short Saturday seems to have been confined to Lancashire and the West of Scotland, paper mills and parts of the West of England. The 1850 Factory Act directed that textile mills should cease work at 2.00 p.m. on Saturday, but there was no general extension of the Saturday half-holiday until the

111

mid-1860s.[21]

It is not surprising that there was a close connection between the Volunteer Force and the Early Closing Association. Sometimes the existence of the Volunteer Force induced employers to give their men time off; in Stafford, for example, some of the most respectable trades-men offered a weekly half-holiday to their workmen to enable them to attend drill. No one could doubt that a certain amount of available leisure time was essential for a Volunteer. As the *Volunteer Service Gazette* noted in 1861,

> ... a few years ago, before the progress of the early-closing system and the Saturday afternoon holiday, the young men employed in offices and shops — who form so large a proportion of the effective force of Volunteer corps in London and in all our large towns — could have taken no real part in the Volunteer movement. The hours which are now devoted to drill and practice were then spent at the desk or at the counter ... We think the progress of the Volunteer movement amongst the working classes must necessarily, to a great extent, depend on the progress of what may be termed in a wide sense of the expression, the early closing movement.

Important Volunteers, including Lord Elcho, and W.M.S. McMurdo, the first and popular Inspector-General of the Force, closely identified themselves and the Force with the early closing movement. As *Punch* put it, 'Those closed shutters are an addition to the Wooden Walls of England.'[22]

The Volunteers, therefore, played their part in the extension of the hours of leisure, but those hours were in any case increasing. The evidence suggests that from the late 1840s and especially in the 1850s working men were demanding leisure even at the expense of wages,[23] and moreover that they were demanding new forms of recreation to fill those leisure hours. The Volunteers found themselves in a seller's market — their wares were in demand, though with some seasonal and class variation. In London Lord Radstock found that 'in the winter the men have very little opportunity for recreation, and they are glad to have exercise. In the summer they have cricket, boating, and a variety of things which call them away.' And in Birmingham, although the middle class was gradually attracted away by other pursuits, 'the artisan has less chance of outdoor amusement, does not mind giving up his Saturday afternoons, and looks forward to the annual camp.' In Greenock, in the early days, 'football was undreamt of, and Saturday afternoon was sacred to the marchout.'[24]

At the same time, middle-class enthusiasts saw in volunteering an answer to what they had long regarded as the *problem* of leisure — how to devise a form of recreation which could safely be recommended to the working class. Since the 1820s various forms of 'rational recreation' had been established under middle-class auspices with the intention of drawing the working man away from his traditional pursuits of drink and 'brutal sports'. The Mechanics Institutes, Lyceums, Choral Societies, even in Leeds a Rational Recreation Society, had had their measure of success, but it was common to all of them that they provided recreation which was mental rather than physical, and indoors rather than outdoors. Indeed the need to provide outdoor entertainment arose only with the shortening of hours at mid-century, and the Volunteer Force seemed perfectly structured to meet that need. Volunteering took place in circumstances of discipline and under middle-class control, and was therefore a form of class mixing which could be encouraged. The physical side of it, drill and rifle-shooting, would be a 'safeguard against effeminacy' and might prove that industrialism was not incompatible with the maintenance of the physical character of the nation.[25] All in all, volunteering was likely to improve a working man rather than otherwise, and was a counter-attraction in face of other less desirable and drink-based sports which might be resorted to.

The rifle assumed an almost symbolic importance for these advocates of a new national recreation. Although invented before 1860, the growth of the rifle's popularity was so closely bound up with the Volunteer Force that *The Times* was right to point to that year in a leading article which conveys something of the significance of the new weapon: 'The change from the old musket to the modern rifle has acted upon the very life of the nation, like the changes from acorns to wheat, and from stone to iron, which are said to have revolutionised the primitive races of men. Since 1860 we have been living in a new age.'[26]

Part of the rifle's appeal was that, unlike most inventions of the industrial era, technical expertise in design and manufacture had to be matched by skill in use. Its introduction into war seemed to bring back the necessity for virtues other than discipline and brute courage amongst the rank and file. As James Walter wrote in 1881, '. . . the old musket was the arm of the masses, and the rifle is that of the individual.'[27] Individualists to a man, the middle class could agree to train for a form of warfare which required skill and intelligence, and in which, indeed, they might have an advantage; for excellence in the use of the rifle, it was thought, was proportionate to the general intelligence of the person using it.[28] Given the apparently new nature of warfare, there was nothing incongruous about the middle class serving as rank and file.

But there was more to the rifle than this. The Victorians invested it with romance, and placed it in history — it was the English longbow in modern form. No writer on the rifle could resist the comparison. 'What "the cloth-yard shaft and gray goose-wing" effected, when guided by an

English eye and an English hand at Crecy and Agincourt,' wrote Hans Busk, 'the rifle bullet will do in any future contest . . .'[29] 'What the bow was once,' *The Times* reiterated, 'the rifle should become now, a national weapon, natural to our eyes and familiar to our hands.' There was a social moral to be drawn from the comparison. Just as the longbow seemed a weapon particularly suited to the English, so was the rifle peculiarly adapted to Britain's 'national spirit of independence and self-reliance'. Success in rifle-shooting both required and inculcated '. . . moderation and temperance, a victory over the will, and a mastery over passions which hurt the soul.'[30]

A further appeal of rifle-shooting to its middle-class advocates was that it was a sport for all classes. To Martin Tupper the rifle club seemed 'an even better mode both of class-mixing and manly recreation' than cricket. The *Pall Mall Gazette*, reporting the Wimbledon meeting in 1865, was equally impressed: 'The healthy mixture of all ranks at the butts and in the tents continues to be one of the most valuable features of the gathering. Young marquises and earls and squires are there, shoulder to shoulder with strong hard-fisted men, speaking every dialect, from the roughest Scotch to the softest Devonian patois. And though several of our English games are great levellers . . . we are inclined to think that this new sport of yesterday bears the bell in this respect, even from cricket.'[31]

The annual Wimbledon meeting was the climax to the year's rifle-shooting. It stemmed from the foundation in 1860 of the National Rifle Association, an organisation which was to have the closest possible links with the Volunteer movement. The Association, explained Lord Elcho, was formed 'for the encouragement of Volunteer Rifle Corps, and the promotion of rifle-shooting throughout Great Britain.' The aim was 'to nationalize in this country a taste for rifle-shooting.' It was hoped to achieve this by holding every summer a prize competition at which the principle prizes would be open only to enrolled efficient Volunteers.[32] The Association was launched with Royal patronage, the Queen presenting an annual prize of £250 for Volunteers, and the Prince Consort one of £100 for all comers of all nations. The Queen herself opened the first Wimbledon meeting in July 1860, scoring a bull's eye with a carefully set up rifle.

The Wimbledon meeting rapidly established itself as an event in the English social calendar. By 1865 the 'At Homes' of the Chairman of the Association 'were among the select events of the London season, the arrivals in carriages being often watched by a considerable crowd.' Wimbledon remained an important social event right up to 1889 when the NRA transferred its annual meeting to Bisley. In the last years at Wimbledon, when Lord Wantage was Chairman, '. . . he and his wife kept open house and entertained freely. Their reception tents, picturesque with Eastern hangings collected abroad, were the scene of daily gatherings, afternoon parties, luncheons, dinners, and camp entertainments, at some of which the Prince and Princess of Wales, the King of Greece, and many other members of the royal family were present.'[33]

This royal patronage and social acceptance were important to the spread of rifle-shooting. Wimbledon was the climax to the rifle matches and county meetings which were taking place all over the country. Yet the popularity of rifle-shooting never quite matched the hopes of its early advocates. By the 1870s Volunteers were to complain that the counter-attractions of cricket and football were depriving them of potential recruits.[34] Shooting remained popular, and without it the Volunteer Force would probably have collapsed. But it was not a national sport in the sense that the early pioneers had hoped. They had seen it as a recreation which required individual skill, inculcated moral purpose, and encouraged the harmonious mixing of different classes. To these virtues it could uniquely add the national purpose of defence of hearth and home. It seemed heaven-sent, coming as it did at the lacuna in the history of recreation between the decline of pre-industrial and the establishment of industrial sports. But essential as it was to the Volunteer movement, it was not so popular as to satisfy those whose imagination feasted on the vision of Englishmen, peer and peasant, uniting in practice at the butts as at the time of Crecy.

The chief participants in the sport, the working-class members of the Volunteer Force, were probably little influenced by its ideology. Indeed, middle-class contemporaries, in more sombre mood, were prepared to admit as much; it was not only the rifle-shooting itself which was seen to be attractive, it was also the prizes which could be won. 'Without an inducement being held out of shooting for rifle prizes,' declared the Adjutant to the London Scottish, 'it would be almost impossible to render the force permanent.' A very large proportion of the Volunteers, thought Tom Hughes, enrolled 'from the vanity of the thing, and because there are those immense prizes held out to them.' And in far-off Kincardineshire it was the annual shooting competitions which were the greatest inducements to join.[35]

A prize may be considered both as a material reward and as an honour. Critics of the prize element in Volunteering were of course inclined to stress the former, and to see the pot-hunter as an undesirable element in the Force. Yet prizes were the only material recompense to the Volunteer for his service and his almost inevitable petty expenses in travel and so on. At the top, as we have seen, the rewards were high.[36] Elsewhere they were naturally lower, but not insubstantial. At a Grand Rifle Prize Meeting of the Wells and Shepton Mallet Volunteers in August 1864 there were 60 prizes amounting to 300 guineas, the 1st prize being £40; to be eligible for this, however, you had to pay an entry fee of at least one guinea. Sometimes the prizes were in kind. In 1860 in Hampshire the prizes included a silver cup and a writing desk; in 1864 prizes in kind were offered but the winners all chose money.[37] At Wimbledon most of the prize money came from entry fees, but the Council put some of these fees aside as a reserve, and for this incurred the criticism of the shooters who wanted more and bigger prizes. We may suspect that this kind of criticism was heard and felt in every corps, for in some it became something of an achievement not to win a prize; in Lambeth and Southwark in 1876 there were 220 prizes for 519 efficient members. In Lincoln in 1891 there were 19 main prizes ranging from a cheque for £7.7s.0d. to a brush and comb, and 95 tradesmen's and officer's prizes in the Christmas prize shoot, giving about a one in three chance of winning a prize; all these Christmas prizes were in kind, including a turkey, a goose, ale, rabbits, a lamp, coal, and so on. A Lincoln Volunteer, therefore, had a fair chance of getting some of his Christmas dinner free. Some of the prizes at Brigg in Lincolnshire in 1892 also had the wife in mind, we may suspect. Ranging in value from £3.3s.0d. to 10s. they were a marble clock, a liquor stand, a case of carvers, a fruit dish, a cruet, a teapot, an English timepiece, and a butter dish, all articles to grace a respectable English home.[38]

Prize shoots were extensively reported in the Volunteer Press and local newspapers. The annual prize-giving, normally in the winter months, was the major social occasion for any corps, again receiving extensive coverage. The prize-winner received the plaudits of his fellow-Volunteers, and could then read his name in the local paper. He won, we may suspect, the same kind of renown and much the same kind of satisfaction as the winner of a prize in a local horticultural show. He had proved himself skilled at a particular form of recreation, and received a relatively modest reward. Probably very few joined the Force to hunt for pots, but many received some satisfaction in winning them.

Rifle-shooting remained the staple attraction throughout the history of the Force. But from the very beginning there were other non-military activities which could be enjoyed within the Force. There were, for example, the theatrical shows and bazaars aimed at raising funds. There was also a custom in the early years for the Volunteers to have a dinner – the officers would entertain the men, and sometimes the men would reciprocate by entertaining the officers. As early as March 1860 the NCOs and men of the 4th Lancashire Artillery Volunteers entertained their officers 'to a splendid and sumptuous supper in the ballroom of the Zoological Gardens.' And amongst the Hampshire Volunteers in the winter of 1860-1 'convivial meetings had been the order of the day.'

The retirement of a popular officer was nearly always the occasion for the presentation of a silver salver or some other suitable gift, naturally accompanied by a dinner for the corps in question. The ardours of drill were in this way offset by activities which were purely pleasurable, and the attraction of the Force was thereby increased. The 'Volunteer Festival' at Grimston Park in 1864, for example, was clearly enjoyable (see Plate 9). Over one thousand Volunteers, after an inspection and sham fight, had been treated by Lord Londesborough to a feast in the riding school where 'a 600 gallon butt of potent Grimston ale, surmounted by the head of an ox, with a hop-bine and wheat-sheaves, was flanked by a pipe of port wine and a pipe of sherry, which were crowned with pots of vines in full bearing.'[39]

Moral purpose, however, was never far from the surface in the Volunteer Force. Enthusiastic officers began to open up reading rooms and club rooms for Volunteers in the hope of beguiling them away from the sins of the flesh. A reading room set up for the Liverpool Artillery as early as November 1859 had as its hope 'to wean young men from amusements and places tending to immorality, to make the drill room and military duty recreative and attractive.' And in Canterbury in 1863 a Volunteer Club was opened on drill nights after dismissal because the members were 'not infrequently . . . at a loss how to spend the remainder of the evenings.' The captain took the initiative, and set up a reading room, billiard and bagatelle tables, a chess board and a library.[40]

There was indeed a multiplicity of activities to be enjoyed within the Volunteer Force. Consider, for example, some of the opportunities open to anyone who joined the Hallamshire Rifles in the 1860s. There was the Hallamshire Volunteer Rifle Corps Sick and Funeral Society, subscription 9d. a fortnight, and with all but one-quarter of the proceeds distributed at the end of the year. There was a reward of a pint of beer supplied by the officers to all who were hardy enough to join in the march-out on New Year's Day 1862. There was the Volunteer Choir formed to sing at the monthly Church parade, and a Volunteer theatrical performance to raise money in 1863. In the same year, on a Monday in September, there was the possibility of going on a 'Pic Nic' to Buxton, open to members of the corps and their friends, 1s.6d. return for those in uniform. Towards the end of the decade, the athletic sports, again held on a Monday, were well-established, as was the 'Hallamshire Rifles Entertainments' 'promoted for providing a cheap, moral, and intellectual winter evening's amusement for the men and their friends, and as a means of supporting a Drum and Fife Band.'[41]

Observers could not but be impressed by this wealth of recreational activity. Its consequences were believed to be far-reaching. There had been a need, and the Volunteers had filled it. As the *Volunteer Service*

Gazette put it in a leading article addressed to parents and guardians,
'every one who had been in the habit of attending places of adult
education, or other gathering places of young men in our towns, must
have often felt, and grieved over, the exceeding difficulty of finding any
good regular exercise for them – any moderately good substitute for
the boating, cricket, etc., of the universities and public schools. This
want has been admirably met by the rifle corps.' The impact on
recreation was believed to be considerable; the *Rifleman* in January
1861 claimed that 'many publicans already complain that their
customers are falling off; that fewer young men of the commercial
classes devote their evenings to pot-house parlours and singing-clubs,
or crowd to the bars of gin-palaces to imbibe adulterated spirits and
"doctored" beer. We also understand that the fair but frail Sirens of
the Haymarket have had occasion to lament that numbers of their
friends, who have turned their attention to the more serious pursuit
of Volunteering, have lately withdrawn from the orgies of that
notorious locality.' Much publicity was naturally given to one George
Alden, a billiard table keeper, who, in the Court of Bankruptcy in 1861,
said that he was reduced to that position by losses sustained through his
principal customers having become Volunteers. As a contributor to
Macmillan's Magazine put it in 1870, 'Too much cannot be said in
favour of a pursuit which provides healthy and innocent amusement for
the youth of our cities. They reap a double advantage; they have the
positive gain of so much fresh air and exercise, and are saved the positive
loss which they would suffer were they left to fall back upon theatres
and billiard-rooms for their recreation.'[42]

Much middle- and upper-class encouragement for the Force stemmed
from this belief that it provided a solution to the problem of recreation.
A Lanarkshire adjutant noted that the Force 'received the encouragement of the leading people – first, because of the fact that healthful
employment was found for the young men during their leisure hours;
second, it was smartening up those who previously had slouched in
their gait; and, lastly, by becoming Volunteers they were not only
improving and preserving their health, but becoming more valuable
members of society.'[43] Concern with leisure seemed the primary
reason for support being given, and defence of the realm received
not a mention.

Soon, however, the positive function which contemporaries observed
in the recreational aspect of volunteering gave way to another. The
provision of leisure activities became a weapon in the hunt for recruits,
and an inducement against resignation. In 1872 in East Surrey the
officers were keeping the men together 'by social gatherings, cricket
clubs and quadrille parties.' Far away in Kinross in the 1870s it was
again social functions which 'kept the corps before the public eye,

brought recruits to the ranks and made the force worth joining.' The historian of the corps found 'a direct connection between the social functions and the prosperity of the corps . . .'[44] Particularly after 1863 when a corps' financial stability depended on the production of a sufficient quantity of 'efficients' there was a strong motive for commanding officers to resort to the provision of entertainment in order to keep their men. Thus to take East Kent examples, we find a choral society in connection with the Ramsgate Corps, a joint artillery and rifle Volunteer theatrical show at Margate in 1871, and a club room at Ashford with chess, skittles, dominoes, cards and a pea rifle range. Athletic, gymnastic, cricket, and drama clubs flourished under Volunteer aegis. As time went on they became expected and were advertised. In Liverpool by 1904 they were providing a certain amount of space for recreation, finding 'that we cannot keep the battalions together in a place like Liverpool without offering some inducement to the men in the way of club accommodation to a certain extent – rooms where they can enjoy themselves in the off season when drill is over.' A London Scottish recruiting pamphlet in Territorial Force days offered swimming, tennis, cricket, billiards, football, and running clubs, a Masonic Lodge in connection with the corps, and a reduced subscription to Wimbledon Golf Club.[45]

Thus, as rival recreational facilities increased for all classes, the Volunteers found themselves offering a kind of package deal, providing an institution within which a man could pursue any number of leisure activities. While some Volunteers saw cricket or golf or football as a leisure activity in competition with their own, others, seeing their attraction, simply offered them alongside the staples of drill and shooting. Volunteers, indeed, played no small part in spreading what were to become the most popular sports; Volunteer football clubs are prominent in a crucial phase in the history of football.[46]

It was not only on evenings and Saturday afternoons that the Volunteer Force offered recreation. In the early years the Easter Monday Field Day, and in later years camp, offered an excursion or a holiday, normally to the seaside. The Easter Monday Field Day at Brighton was, as the Metropolitan Commanding Officers recognised, unrivalled for recruiting purposes. Many Volunteers made a long weekend of it, and evidently brought their womenfolk.[47] 1872, however, was the last Brighton Easter Monday Review. The railways, with increasing custom at Easter after the Bank Holiday Act, had put up their rates, and the War Office had begun to doubt the military usefulness of the Review. Although Volunteer reviews continued to be held elsewhere, for example at Wimbledon, the end of the Easter Monday Brighton Field Day, together with the contemporaneous brigading of the Volunteers in the autumn Army manoeuvres at Cannock

119

Chase, mark the end of an era for the Volunteers. Camp began to replace the Field Day as the high point in the Volunteer's year.

Enterprising corps had held camps from the earliest days. These were normally near to Headquarters; indeed the Volunteers might go to work in the day, and return to camp in the evening. These local camps were occasions when the Volunteers could show themselves off to advantage to the community. By charging gate money on the open day they could even make some money.[48] Moreover — and this was a favourite theme for Volunteer artists — the citizen soldiers in their tents could be seen graciously receiving their admiring womenfolk. Militarily however the local camp did little more than give the Volunteer some slight experience of life under canvas.

The War Office was increasingly convinced of the usefulness of camp, and encouraged Volunteers to go further afield. But always what the military might desire had to be tempered by what the Volunteer could be persuaded to do. For almost all Volunteers camp was their holiday, and they naturally wanted some say in its planning. In Essex in the early twentieth century, 'keen Volunteers as many of them were, the majority wanted to get near the sea, and, if possible, within reach of some places of amusement when off duty.' Volunteers 'generally choose places of popular resort,' said Sir John Colomb. 'Yarmouth is one of the places which they choose, and there is a tremendous demand from the Midland and Northern counties from Volunteers to come to Yarmouth. They go into camp there in brigades, and the men give their whole time to military training, but their families are often there too, and they combine their holiday with the camp training.'[49]

The difficulty of camp, both in a military and recreational sense, was that it was expensive. A government grant in 1872 of 2s.6d. per head on the average number present, and an additional 2s.6d. in 1878 for all who remained four or more days, only met part of the expenses. It was an occasion when officers were almost invariably out of pocket, and although the men might find their expenses met, they normally had to forego their wages for the duration of the camp, and sometimes even pay for a substitute to do the work.[50] If, as in Manchester, the Volunteer camp was in Whitweek, when the works were shut down, the Volunteer was no worse off than his workmate; indeed somewhat better off, because he was maintained for the week. But it was inevitably difficult for a corps drawing on a scattered population to arrange its camp to suit everyone's holiday dates. Thus, though camp was by all accounts enjoyed by those who attended, by no means everyone could do so. The introduction of pay in camp, which was prevalent in the majority of corps by 1904, did not always solve the problem. The amount was often small; thus in Aberdeenshire the pay in camp was 1s.6d. a day, whereas a casual labourer could earn 4s.2d, and Volunteers found they still could not afford to go. Further some corps objected to pay. In the First Middlesex Engineers, the men were reported to want not pay, but (monetary) compensation for time lost.[51] And in the few middle-class corps the idea of pay was held in scorn.[52]

The financial problems associated with camp, and the difficulty of finding time for it, were probably more acute amongst working-class than clerical Volunteers. By 1904 the Sun Fire Office, Lloyds and Harrods, were all giving extra leave to those of their employees who went to camp.[53] In truth the introduction of camp was dependent on employment policies which recognised the need for holidays, and preferably paid holidays. This was of course most often to be found in non-manual occupations.

If camp was the highlight of the Volunteer's recreational year, there were still day-to-day pleasures to be found in volunteering. Despite all the club rooms and sporting facilities, we may suspect that a basic attraction was simply the companionship which volunteering offered, a companionship which found its natural focus in the pub. It is true that in the early years volunteering was thought to wean men from drink. There were, as has been seen, teetotal corps. And at the Royal Review in Edinburgh in 1860, it was claimed, 'there was none of that drunkenness for which Scotland is so unhappily notorious. Never within the memory of man has any great public demonstration taken place in the Northern Metropolis which has been distinguished by so great a freedom from intemperance, – that general bane of all holidays and excursions.'[54]

There is little evidence, however, to indicate to the historian that Volunteers were noted for their abstinence from alcohol – not that drunkenness was a common Volunteer habit, rather that drink seems to have played a not unimportant role in the life of the Volunteers. In 1861 in Northumberland the Commanding Officer of the Bellingham Volunteers 'used to lavish food and drink on his beloved Volunteers, but whisky would have been to them a much more palatable beverage than the champagne that went down their throats.' In the Working Men's College in London, where drill threatened to become more popular than lessons, it was noted that the Volunteers tended also to be those who supported the admission of beer to the College.[55] But the full significance of the pub only becomes apparent when one considers the number of pubs which adopted the name 'Volunteer' or 'Volunteer Rifleman' or simply 'Rifleman'. Readers will perhaps be able to supply their own instances, for many of them still remain. Nearly all of them date from the post-1859 period, not from the Napoleonic Wars. A search through Directories, many of them inadequate in the information they give, has revealed in England alone about 170 such pubs existing at some time in the lifespan of the Volunteer movement; doubtless this is an underestimate. It is of course possible that the name 'Volunteer' was imposed by an overbearing if patriotic brewer, or that the name never had any significance, but it seems unnecessarily sceptical to suppose so. It was more likely, surely, that the 'Volunteer' was the pub where the Volunteers were accustomed to meet, perhaps even their headquarters. The Sevenoaks Volunteers continued to use a pub as headquarters until 1898 though admittedly a Bricklayers Arms, not a 'Volunteer'.[56] We may imagine, too, that the Hastings Volunteers resorted to the 'Volunteer' which flanked their new drill hall opened in 1895. 'Beer played an important part,' writes Colonel Fazan, referring to the early twentieth-century Cinque Ports; 'fortunately it was cheap, so that even a young officer taking the chair at a recruiting smoker in the local pub could afford to order beer all round.' We may infer that this is a personal recollection.

Drink, of course, could not be confined to the pub. We hear again from Colonel Fazan that 'Field days, train journeys and prize shoots . . . were often occasions for copious libations of alcohol and light-hearted mischief . . .'[57] Sometimes the drinking got out of hand. Kilvert's Diary entry for Sunday 23 July 1871 speaks for itself: 'This morning Mr. Bevan went up to the Volunteer Camp above Talgarth, on the highh common under the Black Mountain. He is Chaplain to the Forces and attended to hold an open air service and preach a sermon to the Volunteers. When the Chaplain arrived on the Common, the Builth Volunteers were already well drunk. They were dismissed from the ranks but they fought about the common during the whole service. The officers and the corps were bitterly ashamed and scandalized.'[58]

If Volunteer drunkenness occasioned scandal, we may perhaps graciously assume it to have been rare. But social drinking was common, and the companionship it provided must be considered an important part of the recreational attraction of the Force. Men found in the Volunteer Force something of the attraction of a club. They could meet their friends there, and enrolled in order to be able to do so. 'The joining of the Volunteers,' it was claimed in 1862, 'is principally owing to friends.' 'I joined because my brother had joined,' recalled one early twentieth-century Volunteer.[59]

It would be foolish to pretend that we shall ever know exactly the reasons for the strength and persistence of the Volunteer Force. For some, like tailors hoping to get contracts for the uniforms, there may have been an element of self-interest.[60] Others may have given little conscious thought to the reasons for and implication of enrolment. 'When they sign on,' said a Volunteer Colonel in 1904, 'I do not think they know what they are signing for in ninety-nine cases out of a hundred.' What does seem clear is that the reason for enrolment was not simply patriotism. Indeed, with the exception of the early years and the Boer War period, it seems likely that patriotism was of relatively minor importance. There is much truth, we have suggested, in the assertion of a Commanding Officer in 1904 that 'the majority join primarily as a recreation.'[61]

The fact that young working and lower middle-class men should choose to fill their leisure hours in military duties is of course not without significance. It suggests that military values met with much less opposition in Victorian society than we have perhaps been accustomed to suppose. To join the Volunteers indicated a willingness to wear military uniform, to learn elementary military duties, and to both receive and obey orders. There were, as we have seen, other perhaps more attractive features of the Force to the potential recruit, but no one joining can have been totally unaware of the hard core of military activity in which he would have to engage. Similarly he cannot have been unaware that the orders he would receive would be delivered by his social superiors in civilian life, not infrequently his immediate employer. From the point of view of the history of leisure, this indicates that in their hours away from work men did not seek to escape the bonds of society. Rather they were content to see those bonds reinforced.

To suggest that volunteers was a recreation is not to deny that it might be a patriotic recreation. Moreover it may be that patriotism was a consequence of joining if not a cause of it. Young men, serving three or four years in the Force, were subjected to a stream of patriotic speech-making, from the Chaplain's sermon to the Inspecting Officer's address. They were constantly being congratulated on their patriotism, and may in consequence have felt patriotic. And for the early years when men of all classes, with no obvious compulsion, chose to assume obligations for the defence of their country, the fear of invasion and a concern that it should be guarded against was clearly an important reason for enrolment.

Such concern, in the early years at least, was perfectly compatible with a generally radical political stance. Politically conscious working men were alert to any attempts to interfere with their political views. Nevertheless we cannot ignore the fact that the Force was so structured as to emphasise the subordination of the working class. Within such a structure young working class men found recreational activities to fill their newly won hours of leisure, and increasingly joined to enjoy those activities; it is unlikely, however, that they were totally unaffected by their military experiences. Although it did not have a directly political role, the Force came to have for young men a function very similar to that of the uniformed youth movements so common in the twentieth century; it was a socialising agent designed to mould late adolescents into adherence to the dominant value system in society. As advocates of that value system were aware, it was important to control the leisure as well as the work of the working class. The Volunteer Force was one important means by which that was don. As an institutionalisation of patriotism, it had the function of both contributing to the defence of the country and of acting as a form of social control. The former function, as we shall see, was increasingly open to question.

Notes

1. P. Guedalla, *Gladstone and Palmerston* (London, 1928), p. 298
2. *3 Hansard 312*, cc. 225-6, *350*, c. 2 (Memoranda of the Secretary of State Relating to the Army Estimates 1887-8 and 1891-2).
3. *VSG*, 26 Oct. 1878; T.S. Cave, *History of the First Volunteer Battalion Hampshire Regiment*, p. 304.
4. R.Q. Gray, 'Styles of Life, the "Labour Aristocracy" and Class Relations in Later Nineteenth Century Edinburgh', *International Review of Social History*, vol. XVIII (1973), pp. 439-40; R. Price, *An Imperial War and the British Working Class* (London, 1972), pp. 201-16, 228-32.
5. *The Galloway Rifles Regimental Gazette*, vol. 1 (Jan. 1897), p. 85; A. Terry, *Historical Records of the 5th Admin. Btn. Cheshire Rifle Volunteers* (Sandbach, 1879), p.41.
6. National Union of Conservative and Constitutional Associations, Publication No. 11 (1867-8).
7. Beaconsfield to the Queen, 23 Mar. 1877, G.E. Buckle (ed.), *The Letters of Queen Victoria*, 2nd Series (London, 1926), vol. II, p. 525.
8. Ch. 2, p. 20.
9. J. Grant, *The Newspaper Press*, (London, 1871-2), vol. III, pp. 399-400.
10. For Garibaldi uniforms, see e.g. E.T. Evans, *Records of the Third Middlesex Rifle Volunteers*, p. 71; J.M. Grierson, *Records of the Scottish Volunteer Force*, pp. 150, 185, 240; C. Igglesden, *History of the East Kent Volunteers*, p. 158. For the enrolment of some Volunteers in the Garibaldian cause in 1860, and official concern, see G.J. Holyoake, *Bygones Worth Remembering* (London, 1905), vol. I, p. 245; C.T. Atkinson, *The Dorsetshire Regiment*, vol. II, p. 15; W. Lamont, *Volunteer Memories*, p. 50; Cambridge to Herbert, 2 Sept. 1860, Herbert Papers.
11. *Reynolds' Newspaper*, 13 Feb., 13 Mar., 10 and 24 Apr. 1859 for criticism of Napoleon, and references in Ch. 2, n. 37 for attitude to Volunteer Force.
12. *VSG*, 19. Dec. 1868, 2 Jan. 1869.
13. RC (1862), q. 3578; see also Victoria County History, *Worcestershire*, vol. II (London, 1906), p. 247.
14. *VSG*, 9 Nov. 1867; RC (1904), qq. 11967, 14394, 15875; *4 Hansard 172*, c. 148 (9 Apr. 1907).
15. Ch. 5, p. 76.
16. 3rd Somerset Rifle Volunteers, Minute Book, Somerset Record Office, DD/SAS/SY2; *VSG*, 22 Sept. 1866.
17. Memorandum on the Territorial Reserve, 27 Apr. 1909, WO 32/6585.
18. 27th Cheshire Rifle Volunteer Corps, *Annual Reports 1878-87;* T.H. Hayhurst, *A History and some Records of the Volunteer Movement in Bury, Heywood, Rossendale, and Ramsbottom*, p. 237; C.J. Hart, *The History of the 1st Volunteer Battalion The Royal Warwickshire Regiment*, pp. 182-3; RC (1904), App. Pt. IV.

19. G.D. Pullar, *Historical Sketch of the 4th (Perthshire) Volunteer Battalion, The Black Watch (Royal Highlanders)* (Edinburgh, 1907), p. 32; RC (1862), qq. 435, 2152.
20. Mrs. Russell Barrington, *The Life, Letters and Work of Frederic Leighton* (London, 1906), vol. II, p. 86; PP 1865 (178), VIII, p. 313; R. Loyd-Lindsay, 'The Coming of Age of the Volunteers', *Nineteenth Century*, vol. X (Aug. 1881), p. 208.
21. M.A. Bienefeld, *Working Hours in British Industry* (London, 1972), pp. 42-144.
22. *VSG*, 17 Dec. 1859, 30 Mar. 1861, 6 Dec. 1862, 22 Sept. 1866; *Punch*, 15 Sept. 1860; see also J. Latimer, *The Annals of Bristol in the Nineteenth Century* (1st ed. 1887; repr. Bristol, 1970), p. 364.
23. N.J. Smelser, *Social Change in the Industrial Revolution* (London, 1959), p. 305; M.A. Bienefeld, op. cit., pp. 86-7.
24. RC (1862), q. 252; C.J. Hart, op. cit., p. 154; W. Lamont, op. cit., p. 31.
25. A.S. Ayrton MP quoted in *VSG*, 7 Jan. 1860; see also Sir A.H. Elton, *Shall we make the Volunteer Force Permanent?* (London, 1861), p. 4 and *The Times*, 15 July 1861, 22 Apr. 1862.
26. *The Times*, 25 June 1861.
27. J. Walter, *The Volunteer Force*, p. 175.
28. *The Times*, 26 Sept. 1859.
29. H. Busk, *The Rifle: And How to Use it*, 4th ed. (London, 1859), p. 173.
30. *The Times*, 29 June 1860; *VSG*, 4 July 1863.
31. D. Hudson, *Martin Tupper, His Rise and Fall*, p. 189; *Pall Mall Gazette*, quoted in *VSG*, 5 Aug. 1865.
32. A.P. Humphry and T.E. Fremantle, *History of the National Rifle Association* (Cambridge, 1914), pp. 13-14.
33. ibid., p 103; Harriet S. Wantage, *Lord Wantage, VC, KCB*, p. 326.
34. R.P. Berry, *A History of the Formation and Development of the Volunteer Infantry*, p. 181.
35. RC (1862), qq. 1036, 1071, 3094.
36. Above p. 114, and G.B.L. Woodhouse, *The Story of our Volunteers* (London, 1881), p. 87.
37. Somerset Records Office, DD/FS Box 60; T.S. Cave, op. cit., pp. 87, 123.
38. A.P. Humphry and T.E. Fremantle, op. cit., pp. 93, 173-4; J.M.A. Tamplin, *The Lambeth and Southwark Volunteers*, pp. 40-1; 1st Lincoln Rifle Volunteers, Minute Book, Hill 12/1/3, and Brigg Volunteers, Stubbs 1-247, both in Lincolnshire Archives Office.
39. *VSG*, 10 Mar. 1860; T.S. Cave, op. cit., p. 93; *Illustrated London News*, vol. XLV (6 Aug. 1864), p. 149.
40. *VSG*, 9 Nov. 1859, 31 Jan 1863.
41. Details from the Wharncliffe Muniments, Wh. M. 459, Sheffield City Library.
42. *VSG*, 13 Apr. 1861; *Rifleman*, 3 Jan. 1861; Lt-Col. Williams and W.C. Stafford, *England's Battles by Sea and Land*, 6 vols. (London, n.d), vol. III, p. lv; F. Napier Broome, 'English Physique', *Macmillan's Magazine*, vol. XXII (June 1870), p. 130.
43. J. Orr, *History of the Seventh Lanarkshire Rifle Volunteers*, p. 446.
44. A. Larking, *History of the 4th VB East Surrey Regiment*, p. 25; E.E. Dyer, *The History of the Volunteers of Clackmannanshire and Kinross*, pp. 126, 201.
45. C. Igglesden, op. cit., pp. 76, 126, 137-8; RC (1904), q. 13222; London Scottish recruiting pamphlet in National Army Museum, MS 6911/2/21.
46. P.M. Young, *A History of British Football* (London, 1968), pp. 98-9, 108, n.6.

47. *The Times,* 22 Jan. 1872, 19 Apr. 1870.
48. G. Melly, *Recollections of Sixty Years,* p. 112; C.J. Hart, op. cit., pp. 152-3.
49. J.W. Burrows, *The Essex Regiment,* p. 20; *4 Hansard 80,* c. 1131 (16 Mar. 1900).
50. RC (1904), App. xcii and Pt. IV, q. 8406.
51. ibid., qq. 5192, 12271, 9077-8.
52. H.A.R. May, *Memories of the Artists Rifles,* p. 33; interview with H.P. Dawton.
53. RC (1904), qq. 5317, 5397, 6550.
54. For teetotal corps, see above Ch. 2. p. 19; E.R. Vernon, *A Narrative of the Royal Scottish Volunteer Review in Holyrood Park on the seventh of August 1860* (Edinburgh, 1860), p. 36.
55. L.E.O. Charlton (ed.), *The Recollections of a Northumbrian Lady 1815-1866* (London, 1949), p. 246; J.F.C. Harrison, *A History of the Working Men's College 1854-1954* (London, 1954), pp. 81-4.
56. Sir J. Dunlop, *The Pleasant Town of Sevenoaks – A History* (Sevenoaks, 1964), p. 162.
57. E.A.C. Fazan, *Cinque Ports Battalion* (Chichester, 1971), pp. 61, 63, 87-8.
58. W. Plomer (ed.), *Kilvert's Diary,* vol. I, p. 381.
59. RC (1862), q. 868; interview with H.P. Dawton.
60. *Volunteer Service Magazine,* vol. I (1892), pp. 81-2; Frome Selwood Rifle Volunteers, Minute Book 1859-60, 16 Mar. 1860 Somerset Records Office, DD/LW 25.
61. RC (1904), q. 7698 and App. Pt. IV, p. 864.
62. *VSG,* 9 Feb. 1878.

7 THE POLITICS OF REFORM, 1899-1914

The last decade of the Volunteers' existence saw the Force as much
before the public eye as it had been in the first. But whereas applause
had been the keynote of the 1860s, dispute and debate filled the 1900s.
The Boer War led to a searching examination of Britain's military
organisation, an examination which was to continue up to 1914, and
which neither the Volunteers nor their successors, the Territorials,
could escape. The early twentieth-century military reforms and debates
on strategy have begun to receive considerable attention in recent
years;[1] the account which follows focuses on one aspect only, the
extent to which these reforms were affected by the political, and in
particular the Parliamentary strength of the Volunteers. Not only the
unsuccessful Conservative reform proposals, but also Haldane's plans for
the Territorial Force, it will be argued, were greatly influenced by the
pressure brought to bear by the Volunteer interest. The citizen soldiers
used their political rights as citizens to bring to bear on government
pressure greater than that at the disposal of the Regular Army.

The Boer War affected the Volunteers in three ways. Firstly, during
the War they themselves saw active service overseas, and by volunteering
for such service raised the question both of their efficiency and of the
likelihood of their being available for overseas service in the future.
Secondly, the invasion panic which accompanied the War when Britain
was denuded of Regular troops made it clear that the public did not
have faith in the ability of auxiliaries alone to defend the country, and
enabled the Secretary of State for War to exact more in the way of
service from the Volunteers. And finally the role of the Volunteers
became part of the general debate on the Army which was the
consequence of the War.

The Boer War was not the first occasion on which the Volunteers
had offered to go beyond their terms of service, and fight for their
country overseas; nor indeed was it the first occasion when those
services were accepted. In the Eastern crisis of 1877-8 when the Russian
troops appeared to be threatening vital British interests at Constantinople,
a number of Volunteer corps offered their services. Members of the
18th Perth, for example, 'almost to a man, put down their names for
active service'.[2] There was further a proposal to form a Permanent
Volunteer Force for Active Service: this short-lived body came into
being at a meeting at Exeter Hall on 25 April 1878. Although there
were 380 unconditional volunteers, 160 of whom were Volunteers or
former Volunteers, the Force was never viable, and its inadequacies
were ruthlessly exposed by the 1878-9 Committee of Inquiry.[3] No

actual service, then, resulted from the offers made in 1877-8. But in 1882 the Post Office Volunteers, and in 1885 the Post Office and some members of the Crewe Railway Volunteers, saw service in Egypt, in both cases making use of their special skills.[4]

The general policy of the War Office, however, was clear. Volunteer offers to serve overseas should not be accepted. No encouragement was held out to those Volunteers who urged upon the authorities their willingness to serve in South Africa from August 1899 onwards. Only with the disasters of Black Week, 9-15 December, did official attitudes change. From then onwards the Volunteers found their offers of service accepted with almost too much alacrity, so much so that there was no coherent scheme for organising and utilising Volunteer troops. There were in fact three ways for a Volunteer to get to South Africa for active service.[5]

The City Imperial Volunteers were first to be authorised, the Lord Mayor of London receiving the go-ahead for the formation on 15 December. The Common Council of the City voted £25,000 towards the cost, and after three weeks' drill, the first portion of the CIV embarked for South Africa on 13 January. Their terms of enlistment were for twelve months or for the duration of the war, their pay that of the Regular soldier, one shilling a day. In total the members of the CIV numbered 1,726. They seem to have performed with credit in South Africa, and received a triumphal welcome on their return to England in October 1900.

Secondly there were the Active Service Companies, authorised by an Army Order of 2 January 1900. This provided for the raising of a 'carefully selected company' of 116 all ranks to serve with each line battalion then in South Africa, or about to proceed there, and to be an integrated part of the regular battalion in the field. The First Active Service Companies were raised without difficulty, but the response was less wholehearted to the request for Second and Third Active Service Companies in 1901 and 1902. This was partly because initial enthusiasm for the War had waned, partly because it had become apparent that most of the work required of Volunteers was unglamorous block-house duty, and partly because there were much less stringent and more financially attractive conditions in the Imperial Yeomanry. In all, nearly 18,000 Volunteers served in the Active Service Companies.

The Imperial Yeomanry also stemmed from the disasters of Black Week, and were raised by an Imperial Yeomanry Committee under War Office instructions. They varied considerably in quality, the Second Contingent sent out in 1901 being considerably inferior to the First. Nevertheless the shortage of soldiers was so acute in 1901 that these untrained men were offered five shillings a day. Not surprisingly over six thousand Volunteers chose to enlist into the Imperial Yeomanry in order to benefit from the favourable conditions of service.

In these three ways, and of course by abandoning Volunteer status and enlisting direct into the Regular Army (a course followed by between five and six thousand Volunteers) Volunteers in large numbers for the first time saw active service. Over thirty thousand Volunteers fought in one form or another in South Africa. Many more than this offered their services, but had them rejected.[6] However considered, this was a major response to the War, and the public was in general only too willing to applaud it. The experts, however, were divided in opinion as to the actual efficiency of Volunteers in action. The War therefore gave renewed impetus to the debate over the military value of Volunteers. It also raised a question of fundamental importance: was the Volunteer Force to be considered as solely an army of home defence (as it had been in the past), or should it take on new obligations as an army of reserve available for service throughout the Empire? Some of the most bitter debate of the next few years centred on this question.

It was not only those Volunteers who fought in South Africa who felt the impact of the War. From early 1900 there was considerable unease about the defences of the country, and part of the Government's policy for overcoming this was to increase the obligations of Volunteers. This was done in two ways. The first was to increase numbers and training. In presenting Supplementary Estimates on 12 February 1900 the Government both encouraged Volunteers to recruit above their Establishment, and stated that there would be the opportunity to train under canvas for one month.[7] This latter proposal met with considerable opposition, it being argued that employers could not afford to release their men for such a long period. Lansdowne quickly pointed out that the month's training was 'an emergency training special to this year. Nor did we intend that it would be obligatory on all Volunteers to spend the whole of that month in camp.'[8] Under pressure, the expectation of a month in camp was reduced to a fortnight, with the capitation grant being made in part dependent on attendance at camp; there would be a £2.2s.0d. capitation grant plus pay at Army rates for all who remained in camp fourteen days, provided at least 50 per cent of a corps attended for that period. For the first time non-attendance at camp was financially penalised. On these conditions most corps attended the special camps.[9]

The second way in which obligations were increased was through a change in terms of service. These had already been modified by the 1895 Volunteers (Military Service) Act which allowed Volunteers to offer their services and for these to be accepted in circumstances which fell short of invasion or imminent danger thereof, and further allowed the Secretary of State to call out part of corps under the 1863 Act

129

without it being necessary to mobilise the whole Force.[10] Clearly this allowed greater flexibility, but it still did not give the Secretary of State power to call out the Volunteers in the same way as he could the Militia or the Reserves, that is 'in case of imminent national danger or great emergency' and it was this which the 1900 Bill was designed to secure. Introduced in the House of Lords in May 1900, it had coupled with it a much more controversial section which if implemented would have created a Special Service Section of the Volunteers who could volunteer in advance to be available for home service in cases which fell short of emergency, and for service abroad. This attempt to create two classes of Volunteer met with considerable opposition and was eventually dropped. The idea was to be revived by both Arnold-Forster and Haldane. The first part of the Bill, however, assimilating the conditions under which Volunteers could be called out to those of the Militia, became law in August 1900.[11]

These changes in the condition of service of the Volunteers were in effect part of a larger debate involving all the armed forces. The potential and role of the Volunteers were an important element in the debate about the possibility of invasion. They had to defend themselves on a number of fronts. On the one hand there were the Blue Water theorists who, believing in the ability of the Navy to defend Britain, saw no place for a Force which was restricted to home defence. On the other extreme, and more seriously, there were those who believed in the possibility of invasion, and felt the Volunteers to be insufficient in both quality and quantity to resist such invasion. Linked with this latter group was the increasing number who foresaw a war with Germany which would be fought on the Continent, and believed both that the Regular Army was too small for such a war, and that the Volunteers could not be relied upon to offer their services overseas even in such an emergency, and in any case were inadequately trained. Although undergoing changes, including a change of name, in response to these critics (and Volunteers themselves both suggested and welcomed some of the changes), the Volunteers in their essence survived until after the outbreak of war in 1914. That they did so was due more to their political strength than their military efficacy. It is not too much to say that it was the Volunteers who made conscription politically impossible in pre-war Britain. Certainly without them the conscriptionists' task would have been much easier.

It was in the years immediately following the Boer War, years of Conservative Government, that the Volunteers felt most aggrieved. The successive Secretaries of State for War, St. John Brodrick and H.O. Arnold-Forster, tried to introduce reforms which convinced the Volunteers that they were no more understood by the War Office than they ever had been. The scheme for six Army Corps which Brodrick announced in March 1901 made provision for twenty-five specially selected battalions of Volunteers to be attached to the Corps; these battalions were to do a fortnight's camp each year and would receive a higher capitation grant.[12] The proposals, both generally and in so far as they related to the Volunteers, did not initially attract much criticism. The Volunteers, indeed, only became suspicious when Brodrick announced by Order in Council on 4 November 1901 new and stricter camp regulations for the whole Force, in effect making camp compulsory.[13] The special camp regulations of 1900, it appeared, were going to become the norm. When Parliament reassembled in 1902, there were immediate protests as to the effect on recruiting of the new regulations, and Brodrick agreed to set up a Committee of Commanding Officers under Lord Raglan 'to examine any representations they may receive as to the difficulty of carrying out the new Volunteer Regulations in different localities and to make recommendations.'[14] Brodrick, however, made it quite clear that he wanted an efficient Force, if necessary with smaller numbers; indeed, he would almost certainly have welcomed the latter.[15] Although some Volunteer representatives did not complain of the new Regulations, Sir Howard Vincent headed a strong body who objected to the treatment which the Volunteers were receiving. A revised Order in Council dealing with camp regulations on 29 May 1902, and the announcement that an Advisory Board for the Auxiliary Forces would be set up did something to allay the unrest.[16]

The announcement in early 1903 that there would be a Royal Commission on the Militia and Volunteers was seen by many MPs as simply a delaying tactic.[17] It is in fact not clear what the Government hoped from the Royal Commission, but it may be suspected that it was intended to give greater authority to Brodrick's clear belief that the Volunteers were militarily inefficient. At the very time he was appointing the Royal Commission he was proposing to the Cabinet that a memorandum signed by Lord Roberts and concurred in by his staff should be published. The memorandum stated plainly that 'the existing state of efficiency of our Auxiliary Forces is not such as to warrant the belief that the defence of the United Kingdom could be safely entrusted to them unaided.' It was further less than enthusiastic about the services rendered by the Volunteers in South Africa. The Cabinet felt it inexpedient to publish the text of the memorandum.[18] But the episode suggests that Brodrick was trying to bring about a political situation wherein reform of the Volunteers would be possible; the Royal Commission would hopefully provide the evidence.

In fact the Royal Commission was to prove a disappointment. It was dilatory. It had been hoped that it would report before the end of the summer of 1903,[19] but it did not actually do so until May 1904. Commanding Officer after Commanding Officer gave evidence, providing vital evidence to the historian, but probably saying little new to their fellow Commanding Officers who made up the bulk of the Commission. The Duke of Norfolk as Chairman was amiable, but unable to control and direct proceedings. Further, from the government point of view, the Royal Commission showed a disturbing tendency to stray outside what was considered its brief. It had been asked 'to enquire into the organization, numbers and terms of service of our Militia and Volunteer Forces; and to report whether any, and, if any, what, changes are required in order to secure that these forces shall be maintained in a condition of military efficiency and at an adequate strength.' Given the ongoing debate about the defence of the United Kingdom, the Commission seems to have been fully justified in seeking some clarification of the term 'adequate strength', but it failed to receive any satisfactory reply, and was rebuked for its pains. The Report itself was critical of the capacities of the Militia and Volunteers in ways which the Government had doubtless anticipated, but it went beyond the suggestion of piecemeal reforms to state that if there was to be a force capable of defending the country when the Regular Army was absent it could only be on the basis of conscription. This part of the Report was drafted by the military journalist and reformer, Spencer Wilkinson, who claims to have been the only member of the Commission who did not favour conscription. The section of the Report on the Volunteers was drafted by Sir Coleridge Grove. It stated roundly the Commission's agreement 'in the conclusion that the Volunteer Force, in view of the unequal military education of the officers, the limited training of the men, and the defects of equipment and organisation is not qualified to take the field against a regular army.' It suggested detailed ways in which improvements might be made, but all must be subject to the overriding consideration that 'No regulations can be carried out which are incompatible with the civil employment of the Volunteers, who are for the most part in permanent situations.'[20] The conclusion was implied if not openly stated: that no amount of improvements within the Volunteer structure could equip the Force to face a Continental army.

The particular and piecemeal reforms which the Royal Commission suggested were sensible enough, and many were already by the time of the Report under the consideration of the War Office. The suggestion that conscription was the real answer was, however, thoroughly unwelcome to the Government.[21] The only consolation, and it was a poor one, was that the Royal Commission's Report received comparatively little attention from the public. The new Secretary of State for War's reform proposals held the centre of the stage, and they were to excite much more controversy than anything emanating from the Royal Commission. Politically the Royal Commission was outdated

132

by the time it reported.

Arnold-Forster had replaced Brodrick as Secretary of State for War in October 1903. He came to the War Office with his mind already clear as to the major reforms which were necessary. He had for long studied military matters, and with some justice regarded himself as an expert. He was handicapped, however, by a quite outstanding lack of political skill. He was by no means Balfour's first choice for the post, and in the event his appointment was to weaken the already crumbling Conservative Government.[22]

From the beginning Arnold-Forster was beset by difficulties. The substantial reform of War Office organisation recommended by the Elgin Commission in July had yet to be carried out, but it was known that the execution of this reform was to be entrusted to a high-powered committee of three men headed by Viscount Esher. The consequence was that during his first months of office Arnold-Forster's authority was considerably diminished by the very existence of the Esher Committee, and by the fact that its recommendations were likely to lead to considerable changes in the decision-making process within the War Office. A politician of experience would have hesitated before embarking on major reforms of the army at a time when his own advisers were being dismissed or reshuffled at the whim of a body outside the control of the Secretary of State.[23]

Nevertheless it must be admitted that Arnold-Forster was justified in seeing the situation as one of crisis. When Brodrick had introduced enlistment for three years instead of seven he had calculated that three-quarters of the recruits would voluntarily extend their service to seven years; in fact by November 1903 less than 20 per cent of the recruits were so doing.[24] There was therefore a major recruiting difficulty which it was impossible to ignore. Arnold-Forster's solution was to abandon Brodrick's unsuccessful Army Corps plan, and, more radically, the hallowed Cardwellian scheme of linked battalions. What was needed, he believed, was a Long Service Army to meet immediate overseas needs, and a Short Service Army which would be available for service expansion in time of war, and which would be available for service overseas. Since he believed in the ability of the Navy to defend the United Kingdom against attack, Arnold-Forster had little time for any force whose services would not be available overseas. Half the Militia was to be invited to join the Short Service Army, thus significantly changing its terms of service, and the rest of it was to be disbanded. As to the Volunteers they were at root an encumbrance; as Arnold-Forster wrote later, 'It is probably true to say that no one charged with the duty of utilising the resources of the nation for the defence of the country would ever have created a force of the kind.'[25] It is not surprising, therefore, that Arnold-Forster wished to reduce both the numbers and the cost of the Volunteer Force. His sights were set high, no less than a major reshaping of the structure of the British Army and a clarification of its role. He failed to achieve his aims, and an important cause of that failure was the political opposition of the Volunteer Force.

As early as November 1903 Arnold-Forster drew up a Memorandum for the Army Board in which, while casting doubt on the military value of the Volunteers, he recognised the political difficulties of reduction. Nevertheless he proposed a reduction of the Establishment from 346,000 to 200,000, and a division within the Force between those willing to acquire a high degree of efficiency (about one-third) and those not willing (the remaining two-thirds). The Army Board was critical of these suggestions, and favoured waiting for the Report of the Royal Commission on the Militia and Volunteers before taking any action.[26] Arnold-Forster thus met with opposition from his own advisers early on.

The Cabinet was no more enthusiastic. The general reform proposals were presented by Arnold-Forster for discussion in December 1903. Arnold-Forster was doubtless hoping that he would have Cabinet backing for his proposals when he presented his Estimates in March; if so he considerably overestimated the Cabinet's capacity for decision. It was only in February that the proposals were submitted to a committee briefed to consider the financial implications,[27] and when the Secretary of State rose to present his Estimates on 7 March 1904 he had nothing very positive to say. He made it clear, however, that major reform was in the offing, and alerted the Volunteers to danger by expressing his confidence that 'the Volunteers are not fulfilling to anything like the extent they ought to fulfil the duties which the country hopes they may fulfil in time of war.'[28]

Arnold-Forster, however, still had a long battle in Cabinet ahead of him before he could secure agreement for the presentation of his reforms to Parliament. Although the Wyndham Committee on the financial implications was reasonably reassuring, the political implications of the reforms made the Cabinet cautious. As the Prime Minister reported in May, 'The Cabinet do not conceal from themselves that considerable Parliamentary difficulty will arise in connection with the Volunteers and Militia.'[29] Further consideration of the financial arrangements reopened doubts on that score, and there was only too much reason to fear the public response to the proposals. When the *Daily Express* and the *Standard* printed a preview, 'the suspicion and hostility of the Auxiliary Forces' was aroused.[30]

Arnold-Forster was determined to go ahead, and his Cabinet colleagues reluctantly agreed, urging him to make his statement to Parliament in generalities, and to leave himself the possibility of retreat, especially over the Militia proposals. And since the proposals involved

134

the abolition of much of the old Constitutional Force, it is not surprising that it was the Militia who objected most strongly and were most alarmed at Arnold-Forster's presentation of his scheme on 14 July 1904. The Volunteers at this stage were applying pressure behind the scenes. On 25 July Arnold-Forster met members of both Houses of Parliament interested in the Volunteers, and as a result of this meeting stressed to Parliament in early August how keen he was 'to proceed in this matter with the good will and the support of the Volunteer Force itself.' As a token of this he announced that he had been persuaded that it would be wrong to have two classes of efficient within the same unit; the classes would be maintained, but in separate units.[31]

It was at this stage that there emerged the first signs of open hostility to the scheme as far as it applied to the Volunteers. Winston Churchill, who had been one of a group of Conservatives who had attacked Brodrick's scheme, now, as a Liberal, found Arnold-Forster's proposals for the Volunteer Force 'instinct with all the prejudices and jealousies of the professional and Regular soldier.' He appealed to Conservatives to defend the Volunteers. Other MPs, two Liberals and one Conservative, were also critical.[32]

The summer recess, however, came to Arnold-Forster's rescue before this opposition became serious. He now had time to work out in detail his scheme, already announced to Parliament, for reducing net cost on the Volunteers by not less than £300,000 per annum.[33] As set out in a memorandum to the Cabinet in January 1905, his plan was to reduce the number of Volunteers from the current 242,000 to 180,000, to increase the number going to camp for a fortnight, and to penalise financially those who did not go to camp. He optimistically stated his belief that the Volunteers would welcome the reduction of numbers on the terms proposed.[34]

Opposition to the scheme, however, was now becoming more organised and more vocal. Immediately Parliament reassembled, Captain Norton, seconded by Major Seely, introduced an amendment to the King's Speech, claiming amongst other things that changes at the War Office had discouraged the Militia and Volunteers. A large part of the debate, as Arnold-Forster himself noted, was taken up by critics of the Volunteer proposals; they objected to the detailed proposals, they objected to the current uncertainty, and they deplored the whole principle of reduction of numbers. Some indeed, like Ivor Guest, Conservative MP for Plymouth, pleaded for more rather than fewer Volunteers. And it was another Conservative, Sir Albert Rollit, who warned the Government of the political power of the Volunteers, hoping that the Secretary of State for War 'would take into careful consideration all that had been said on this matter, and come to a wise and speedy conclusion, but if he underestimated public feeling in the matter public feeling might become a very potent factor in the solution of the question.' It was left to Churchill, rounding up the debate, to put the objections to the proposals in their most powerful form, powerful because they appealed to Conservatives more than to Liberals; for 'the natural, the inevitable effect', of Arnold-Forster's proposals, he argued, 'was that they discouraged all those spontaneous forms of patriotism in the country which had led to the creation of what was a unique force, and one which contributed largely to the greatness and security of these realms.'[35]

The effect of this debate was immediately apparent in Cabinet discussions of the proposals. Balfour was anxious that Arnold-Forster should not be unnecessarily precise in anything he stated to Parliament. He himself produced an alternative plan, but recognised as much as the exasperated Arnold-Forster that 'nothing can be done in the immediate future to carry either the one plan or the other into practical effect.' Isolated in the Cabinet, the Secretary of State's position was further weakened by the growing public knowledge that members of the Army Council were opposed to the scheme of reform.[36]

Thus when Arnold-Forster rose to present his Estimates on 28 March he was wide open to attack because he could not disguise the fact that his proposals did not have the full support of the Cabinet. They did, he claimed, have the support of nine out of ten Volunteer officers, but he made it clear that 'whether it be so or not, I have a very large amount of testimony to that effect, and I would say this, that, after all, this matter is not one that can be decided only by Volunteer officers.' The signs were, though, that the Volunteer officers and their supporters in Parliament would have a very considerable voice in settling the question. Sir John Colomb, who favoured a reduction in numbers, 'could not help asking himself whether the people of Sheffield, the Isle of Wight, Plymouth and other places represented by these Volunteer officers really believed that the Volunteers were to rule Parliament, and that Parliament was not to rule the Volunteers. It could not be denied,' he continued, 'that the Volunteer vote was an important vote, having political influences on the mind of any Government.'[37]

As the debate dragged on into early April, Balfour was induced to intervene, stating that the Government saw the Volunteers 'as an essential part of the fighting force of the country.' But while giving general support to Arnold-Forster, he surrendered what to the Secretary of State for War seemed vital ground: he conceded that any savings made on the Volunteers by a reduction of numbers would be spent on the Volunteers in improving efficiency.[38] The saving of £300,000 was at once eliminated, and with it a key element in Arnold-Forster's overall plan. He had been defeated by the political power of the Volunteer officers, a power which certain politicians were not afraid to invoke. Much more important for Arnold-Forster than the loss of £300,000 was the fact that the emphasis of Parliamentary debate on the Army was now on the Volunteers, a Force which to Arnold-Forster was of minimal use and importance. As Dilke said in the course of the debate, 'The Volunteers played in connection with the whole question of the Army a somewhat disproportionate part in the House. The cost of the Volunteers was small compared with the cost of the Regular Army, and whatever solution might be come to on the particular problem of the Volunteers would not greatly affect the difficulties of the Army question.'[39]

The Parliamentary debate over, Arnold-Forster turned his mind to carrying out the reduction of numbers. General Officers Commanding-in-Chief were to be asked to report whether they recommended any units for disbandment or absorption on grounds of inefficiency, and were to be told of the necessity of requiring from new entrants to the Force a rigid conformity to the prescribed physical standards. Further, and most important, medical officers of each corps were asked to state what proportion of their men were not up to the general physical standard required for active service in the field. All this was embodied in a circular of monumental tactlessness issued on 20 June 1905. The first paragraph read, 'Sir, I am commanded by the Army Council to invite your attention to the fact that many Volunteer units are reported upon various causes not to be in an efficient state to take the field.' Naturally this roused the wrath of the already suspicious Volunteers who could see the circular as nothing other than an underhand preparation of the way for reduction by first making out that the Volunteers were generally unfit; further both they, and in the event the War Office, had some doubts as to the legality of the attempt to enforce a medical inspection. The pressure was so great that Arnold-Forster had to backtrack. The medical examination, it was explained, was not compulsory; and the circular was reissued on 11 July in a modified and less offensive form.[40]

Arnold-Forster had had no option but to retract. The Whips 'had been very anxious,' the Secretary of State recorded in his diary on 13 July, the day of a debate on the Volunteers; 'I was told that many of our men were very discontented and would probably vote against us.' The opposition to his policy drove Arnold-Forster into increasing disillusionment with the Volunteers. At a conference with Volunteers on 28 July he found the officers 'of a much lower stamp than the Militiamen whom I met last week.' Ensuing debate about what had happened at the conference did nothing to sweeten his temper.[41] At the end of August he expressed the opinion in his diary that 'The Volunteers are an utterly undisciplined mob, run like other mobs, by Mob Law, and to make them understand the meaning of Military discipline, much more to enforce it, is practically hopeless.'[42] Neverthe-less Arnold-Forster geared himself for one final effort. In September, from Scotland, he wrote to General Douglas, the Adjutant-General, urging that now was the time to carry through reform of the Auxiliary Forces. General Douglas's reply was anything but helpful; he set out in a way damaging to Arnold-Forster what had happened to the Volunteers since August 1904, stressed the damage done by the circular of 20 June 1905, and claimed that the Army Council had had no proper opportunity to discuss the proposals.[43] Back in London Arnold-Forster found to his astonishment that both the Adjutant-General and the Financial Secretary were in favour of going to Parliament to ask for more, not less, money for the Volunteers. 'I am bound to say', he wrote, 'that neither of them thinks the expenditure is either wise or necessary, but they have apparently come to the conclusion that the "Mob" and the "Newspapers" are too strong to be resisted, and we must therefore consent to recommend this extravagance.'[44]

Having already lost his proposed financial saving on the Volunteers, Arnold-Forster now abandoned the plan for reducing numbers. In a Memorandum to the Cabinet of 11 November 1905, he set out his new policy which involved an additional expenditure of £150,000 to £200,000 per annum. The necessity for the abandonment of the policy of reduction was blamed on others: the King's telegram to the Lord Provost of Edinburgh after the Royal Review had been an incentive to men to join the Force; Balfour's speech of 9 November had been taken by the public to favour a larger Force; soldiers would not speak out in public for reduction. Further Arnold-Forster could not conceal from himself 'that in the opinion of our Whips, the policy of reduction is exceedingly unpopular and likely to be resented.' Seeing the Secretary of State eager once more to rush into reform, the Army Council had cold feet and tried to delay implementation of the policy; but Arnold-Forster overruled them. In these last days of the Government it seems that Arnold-Forster was simply trying to recoup a little popularity. As he put it in his Memorandum of 11 November, 'I think I can say with certainty that on no previous paper dealing with the Army have I referred to any Party consideration or Party advantage, but in the present instance I cannot be blind to the expediency of making any declaration we have to make on this subject without delay.'[45]

Arnold-Forster was able to declare his intentions, but the Government had collapsed before he could carry through his reforms. And those reforms, as promulgated in the autumn of 1905, involved a surrender on all important fronts to the Volunteer spokesmen: they were to get more money, not less, and there was to be no enforced reduction of numbers. It is true that Arnold-Forster had met with opposition both in the Army Council and in the Cabinet, but both these bodies had been critical of the proposals because of their political implications. Arnold-Forster had wanted to treat the Volunteers as soldiers. He had been shown all too forcefully that they were citizens more than soldiers, and citizens too with an acute political awareness.

It is important to emphasise that when R.B. Haldane became Secretary of State for War in December 1905 the condition of the Volunteers had changed considerably since the outbreak of the Boer War. Unsuccessful as the Conservatives had been in their more grandiose military plans, they had carried through some minor reforms. Volunteers could now be called out in cases of emergency, rather than simply invasion or apprehended invasion. And non-attendance at camp now met with a financial penalty. Haldane built on these trends towards improving both the use and the efficiency of the Volunteers. Where Brodrick and Arnold-Forster failed was in their desire to make the Force smaller. They shared with Haldane the prevailing orthodoxy that invasion was unlikely, and therefore could see little use for a Force which was confined to defence duties. Haldane, however, believed that a remodelled Volunteer Force could fulfil the functions of a Reserve available for service anywhere in the world; and since it was recognised by all that a large Reserve was essential, Haldane wanted more Volunteers not less. Politically this was a more enviable position to be in than that of his two immediate predecessors.

Haldane's position was further eased by the fact that his accession to office coincided with a clarification of Britain's military obligations. Since the Committee of Imperial Defence's study of the invasion problem in 1903 it had been stated policy that no invasion was to be feared; at the worst there would be raids. This conclusion lessened the necessity to devote resources to home defence, and released most of the Regular Army for what was now seen as its major role, service overseas. Until 1908 the Committee of Imperial Defence was thinking primarily in terms of overseas service in India to meet the threat from Russia. Diplomatic developments, however, were making this danger less acute, while increasing the threat from another direction, Germany. The War Office became aware of this changing focus of Britain's military problems before the Committee of Imperial Defence, and it was precisely at the time of the change of government in 1905 that the crucial steps were being taken in the form of military conversations which were to commit the British Army to fighting on the Continent of Europe in alliance with the French.[46] The problem to which Haldane had to find a solution was relatively clear. He had to provide what came to be called an Expeditionary Force whose most probable area of service would be Europe, and he had to ensure that there were forces left in Britain which would be large enough and efficient enough both to repel raids and to provide the necessary Reserves for the Expeditionary Force.

139

It was to a remodelled Volunteer Force that Haldane looked to provide both the defence force and the Reserve; his predecessors had considered it incapable of the latter role.

Many writers have contrasted the approach of Haldane to that of his two predecessors. Whereas Brodrick and Arnold-Forster are seen as trying to impose ready-made schemes on a suspicious Army and public, Haldane's proclamation of his virginity is taken at face value, and he is pictured as working with and winning the co-operation of those whom it was his task to reform. Haldane was suitably vague when he presented his first Estimates in 1906, but then so had been Arnold-Forster after a slightly longer period in office in 1904. And it is well known that Haldane had been busy planning reforms, plans which as originally set forth he was quite unable to realise. Although the aura of success hangs around Haldane's reforms, and although he was manifestly a more skilful politician than his immediate predecessor, and operating in a more favourable political environment, it will be argued that he was unable to carry through the reforms he intended, and this because of the political strength of the Volunteers. As a result in 1914 there was neither confidence in Britain that the Territorial Force was adequate to meet the danger of invasion, nor was there a large enough Reserve committed to overseas service.

Haldane, soon after his appointment to office, retreated to Scotland to fight a Parliamentary campaign and work out his reforms in the company of his private secretary, G.F. Ellison. The results of this and later deliberations were embodied in six secret memoranda drawn up by Haldane for consideration by the Army Council between January and November 1906. In the Second Memorandum, dated 1 February, Haldane made it clear that there should be two distinct armies, the Striking Force (later to be called the Expeditionary Force), and the Territorial Army (later the Territorial Force). The latter was to be administered by local Associations, an idea which, according to Ellison, was Haldane's own.[47] In the Fourth Memorandum, dated 25 April, Haldane spelt out in more detail the functions of the Territorial Army, stressing that 'the difference between the Territorial Army and the existing Volunteers will be very marked. The very essence of the conception of this army is that we have advanced a long way from the notion of the old Volunteer Force that existed almost entirely on the basis of a theory of Home defence which has now been displaced. The Territorial Army will exist for an entirely different purpose, and in numbers, in organization and conditions of service will be unlike any force we now possess.' In other words, Haldane was looking to his Territorials *primarily* as a Reserve for the Expeditionary Force, a Reserve which could be trained under cover of the Royal Navy. Whereas his predecessors had wanted more efficiency and fewer numbers in the

140

Volunteer Force so that it was able on embodiment to meet any invasion, Haldane wanted more numbers and if necessary less training for a Force which would be available for training as a Reserve after the outbreak of war. It is true that Haldane recognised that it would be a matter of time before his conception of a National Army could be realised,[48] but even he must have been disappointed that it was only a tiny minority of the Territorial Force which before 1914 committed itself to overseas service: that is to say, committed itself to being a true Reserve to the Expeditionary Force.

Indeed the public and most of the Territorial Force continued right up to 1914 to regard the Force as a Force for home defence. Ever since the Boer War there had been a running argument as to whether the Volunteers could be relied upon for overseas service. Some Volunteers, especially in 1905, had used the Volunteers' willingness to serve overseas as an argument against reduction of numbers; Arnold-Forster had openly rejected this argument.[49] Haldane accepted it, and envisaged a Force which would require a period of training, perhaps six months, before it was fit for service in the field. This was quite logical if the Force was to act as a Reserve, but if, as most people believed, the prime purpose was home defence, it was obviously going to be asked whether an enemy was going to wait obligingly for six months before invading. Increasingly, as we shall see, even Haldane backtracked from the idea of the Territorial Force as 'the grand reserve of the nation',[50] but the notion that it needed six months' training before it could take the field remained. This clearly weakened public confidence in the ability of the Territorial Force to defend the country, and played into the hands of the conscriptionists. In essence Haldane proved unable to commit Volunteers to overseas service, and was left with a Force which if it did indeed require six months' training before action was manifestly incompetent for the task of home defence.

Haldane had sketched out some of his ideas in Parliament in March 1906. Volunteers who for years had been told that they must become more efficient if necessary at the expense of numbers, were now given the impression that increased numbers with less training might be required. They felt 'more secure', but perhaps a little bemused.[51]

Having stated his general principles, Haldane now set up a Committee under the indispensable Viscount Esher 'to consider the question of how best to give effect to the principles governing the organization of the Auxiliary Forces into a Territorial Army as described in the speech of the Secretary of State on Army Estimates in the House of Commons, on 8 March, 1906.' The Committee was advisory only, and consisted of representatives of the Militia, Yeomanry, and Volunteers, and a number of other interested parties. In setting up what came to be called the Duma, Haldane hoped that he could carry through reform by agreement.

This proved impossible. The twenty-eight members met eleven times between 17 May and 15 June 1906, and then adjourned asking for further knowledge of the Mobilization Scheme, an indication of the amount of money available to the new Force, and an opinion of the work it had already done. It was never to meet again, though it was clearly intended that it should.[52] But once it was clear that representatives of the three forces involved could not agree to become one, then negotiation with each separately, and legislation, became necessary.

What worried the Volunteers was not so much the prospect of being primarily a Reserve, for few of them seem to have discerned what was in Haldane's mind, but the possibility of being placed under the control of local Associations which were to be in part at least elected. Haldane had originally envisaged, and it was an important aspect of all his reforms, a division between command and administration. The County Associations were to be responsible for the latter. Whereas radicals objected to this as an extension of landlord influence, Volunteer Commanding Officers saw it as an encroachment on their own powers. Their protests were such that as early as August Haldane was reported to be wobbling over the County Associations.[53] After meeting twenty Volunteer Colonels in September, Haig reported that 'The Volunteers won't have the Associations constituted as proposed at any price.' As Haldane's will weakened, his advisers pressed him to stand firm. Haig, Lucas, and Ellison dined with him on 15 October, and delivered a prepared onslaught. Haldane stated quite frankly that his reason for considering watering down the Associations 'is that his Volunteer Commanding Officers are so opposed to being administered by the Associations and are bringing so much pressure to bear on their MPs that he can't get the thing through.'[54] Esher was asked to apply pressure and did so. 'What I have to manage', replied Haldane, 'is the House of Commons and this requires a great deal of thought.'[55] This advice from men close to him did induce Haldane to restore some of the financial responsibility to the Associations.[56] Nevertheless the political strength of the Volunteers proved such that the Bill as presented to Parliament enshrined a considerable reduction of the powers of the Associations as Haldane had first envisaged them. The concept of a National Army having 'its roots within the people themselves'[57] was thus seriously weakened, for Haldane's compromise was to give the Associations some power, but to reduce to negligible proportions the elective element. In deference to the Volunteer Commanding Officers military members were to constitute more than half of any Association, and the powers of the Army Council in the nomination of members was considerable.

Haldane's final Memorandum, dated 23 November 1906, avoided any too specific description of the powers of the County Associations.

It re-enforced however, and stated more specifically than ever before, Haldane's belief that the purpose of the new Force was to 'provide for home defence *and for the support and expansion of the Expeditionary Force after six months of war . . .* These forces will be recognized as the main means of home defence on the outbreak of war, both for coast defence strictly and for repelling possible raids, and as the *sole* means of support and expansion of the professional army on any war engaging the whole of that army and lasting more than six months' (my italics). Recognising that the Territorial Force could not include in its terms of enlistment the obligation to serve overseas, Haldane hoped that 'from one-sixth to one-fourth of the force' might in fact undertake such an obligation − a forecast which was wildly optimistic. The Memorandum, of course, had a limited circulation only among members of the Army Council; in public Haldane never made it clear that the Territorial Force was to be the sole Reserve of the Regular Army. The reason for this was almost certainly Haldane's growing respect for the power of the Volunteer Commanding Officer − 'his susceptibilities must be very carefully regarded', he noted in the Memorandum. And in direct contrast to his two predecessors, he emphasised his hope that 'the organization proposed will render a much larger force available than we have now', though he recognised that initially, in order to appease the Commanding Officers, numbers must be 'well within the reach of the present forces'.[58]

On 4 March 1907 Haldane introduced his Territorial and Reserve Forces Bill in the House of Commons. The Bill was to absorb a considerable amount of Parliamentary time, being debated on thirteen days in the House of Commons alone. Yet it did not attract much attention. On the first reading there were only twenty-seven Liberals in the House, on the third reading only twenty-nine.[59] The House was reported to be empty during the second reading debate and after the House had been counted on one of the committee days, Sir Howard Vincent complained of the 'extremely small attendance on the Government benches throughout the discussions. The fact was that there was no driving power behind the Bill in the country.' And Sir Charles Dilke's comment during the third reading is a warning against taking the division lists too seriously: 'In Committee they had not had the advantage of the presence of those who filled the division lobbies whenever a division was taken. So much had that been the case that it was well known to all of them that many Members, after one division, on learning what they had voted for, expressed the deepest regret for the vote they had given, and some of them had carried their Parliamentary conscientiousness so far as to vote against the Government in a later division when the Government happened to be perfectly right. The House generally had not followed the details of the Bill with much care.'[60]

This was indeed true. The Bill was complicated and long, and its content was of little interest to most MPs. The participants in the debates, and in all subsequent army debates up to the outbreak of war, were nearly all identifiable as speaking for some interest, the Militia, the Yeomanry, the Volunteers, and the conscriptionists being the main protagonists. With the possible exception of the last group their vision was myopic; they were concerned simply to defend a vested interest. It was the Militia and Yeomanry spokesmen who appeared to have most to defend in the Territorial and Reserve Forces Bill. The Yeomanry were asked to come into the Territorial Force on terms which, initially, seemed financially disadvantageous; and the Militia had either to join the Territorial Force (involving a major change in the terms of service), or become Reservists as drafts rather than as units, and this was something they had long fought against. For the Volunteers, however, the only major changes were, firstly, that administration and financial responsibility would pass from the Commanding Officer to the County Association, and, secondly, that on mobilisation they could be called up for a period of training which was taken to be six months. Only after such training, was the implication, would they be fit to face foreign troops.

As we have seen, the six months' training only had logic if the Territorial Force was seen as a Reserve. Haldane more than anyone knew this, yet in his opening speech he declared that the 'primary purpose' of the new Force was 'to defend our shores.' No other purpose was spelt out. There was provision in the Bill for volunteering for service abroad, 'but the scheme and provision is for a force for home defence.'[61] The Conservatives moved an amendment opposing the Bill, and it was noticeable that their chief spokesmen, Wyndham, Arnold-Forster, and Balfour were all aware of the need for a reserve for service abroad, and critical of the ability of the Territorial Force to supply it. Yet although this point was raised, it was not pressed home.[62] Later, as the Bill passed through its various stages, only Sir Charles Dilke in the House of Commons and Viscount Monkswell in the Lords noted the change of emphasis in the ostensible purpose of the Force from Reserve to defence. As Dilke put it, 'The Secretary of State played into his assailants' hands by speaking of this force over and over again as one intended for home defence. That it was not, and it was a mere sham to pretend that it was . . . All the earlier speeches of the Secretary of State pointed to the view held by the Elgin Commission and the Esher Committee, that this force was intended to be one on which we could draw for the support of the fighting force across the sea.'[63] The only possible reason for Haldane's retreat on this vital issue is his awareness of the political difficulty of making Volunteers available for service overseas. Militarily, the retreat

144

made a nonsense of the whole scheme.

The bulk of the debates, however, was taken up with the attempts of the various interests to secure concessions; they achieved considerable success. The Volunteers secured a strengthening of military control of the County Associations, the Yeomanry a postponement of the implementation of the new conditions of service, the Militia the continuing existence of their units, the Labour Party the concession that no public money should be spent on cadets under sixteen. It was the revolt of the Militia interest in the House of Lords which had been most feared, but 'it soon became apparent that the number of its members interested in the Militia was extremely small. Most of the peers were much more concerned with driving the best bargain they could for the Yeomanry and the Volunteers on their becoming part of the Territorial Force.'[64] They could in the main be satisfied that the bargain was a good one.

The passage of the Bill into law was secured by concessions in Parliament and by successful Liberal attempts to persuade the Opposition leaders not to wreck it.[65] It also required an unremitting effort on the part of Haldane to explain his ideas to the parties concerned in the reform. Thus in the month of January 1907 alone he 'got some valuable "spadework" done with the Commanders of the Glasgow Volunteer Corps', and also visited Volunteers in Liverpool, Manchester, Sheffield and London. In early February he again dined with London Volunteers. 'I am rather weary of it, ' he explained to his mother, 'but it has to be done.'[66] This effort did not end with the passing of the Bill. The months immediately before and after the inauguration of the new Force in April 1908 were clearly crucial, and Haldane's optimism in the future of his creation gave him strength to devote considerable time, energy, and tact to its organisation.

His main task in the autumn of 1907 was to get the County Associations established. In essence this meant persuading Lords Lieutenant that the Territorial Force was something to which they should devote their names and their time. The formal steps towards this were, firstly, a letter from Haldane to Lords Lieutenant on 7 August, asking them to become President of their County Associations, and, if they were agreeable, proposing to address them in the first instance for advice as to the personnel of the Associations; and, secondly, in the same month, some suggestions issued from the War Office on how best to set up an Association. Final control, it was made clear, rested with the Army Council, and a small committee, once again under Viscount Esher, was set up to discuss schemes with any county which might so wish.[67]

More important than this, however, was Haldane's personal evangelising. A letter to Viscount Esher from Blair Atholl indicates his

145

approach:

> We have had an excellent Meeting of about nine Lords
> Lieutenant here — Duke of Atholl, and Richmond, Aberdeen,
> Strathmore, etc. They came suspicious and I think there is
> no doubt that they have gone away with wholly new views
> and keen. What astonished them was to find everything
> thought and prepared even to minute detail, and I think
> your Committee's work has been much lightened so far as
> the Highlands are concerned. I will try to get Lord Derby
> to arrange another great Meeting, and I think we ought to
> have one in London — for the Southern Lieutenants — and
> one in Wales. Bron [Lord Lucas] is going on a round of
> visits to Rosebery and others — and Mackinnon [Director-
> General of the Territorial Force] who is here also is to see
> others.[68]

The climax to this activity was an invitation to Lords Lieutenant
to Buckingham Palace on 26 October 1907. In this way the King
became identified with the new Force. Sir Almeric Fitzroy reported on
the day before the Buckingham Palace meeting that Haldane 'is full of
hope for the success of his army scheme, and has great confidence in the
spirit with which the County Associations are likely to undertake their
work.' Immediately after the meeting Haldane himself told his sister
how 'The King's intervention has produced the requisite steam for the
engine, and I am working day and night to take full advantage of the
moment.'[69] Haldane's aim in all this work was clear. He concentrated
such social pressure as he could muster on the Lords Lieutenant in the
hope that they in turn would exert such pressure on the elite of their
counties. If the Territorial Force was to be the Nation in Arms, there
was no question in Haldane's mind but that it should be under its
'natural leaders.' His success could not be questioned. By 1909 no
fewer than one hundred and fifteen members of the House of Lords
were serving on County Associations. As Halévy wrote, the 1907 Act
'may be briefly described as the establishment of the governing classes
in the very centre of his new organisation, to act as its mainspring.'[70]

The creator of the new Force was full of enthusiasm at the moment
of its birth. On 2 April 1908, he reported to his mother, 'the recruiting
for the Territorial Army is better than we ventured to hope for.' On 3
April, 'the Territorial Force goes on well. It is wonderful how smoothly
the new and intricate machine is working.' And on 7 April, 'the
Volunteers are pouring in and it is not too much to hope that the
critical point is now passed, and that the new Army is going to be a real
success.'[71]

Such enthusiasm was, alas, unjustified. If Haldane had hoped that
once the new Force had become established its existence and function

would be accepted and non-controversial, he was to be disappointed. Up to and beyond the outbreak of the First World War the Territorial Force was near the centre of the debate about Britain's military requirements. Figures for enrolment into the Force were awaited and interpreted with a keenness which later politicians would reserve for trade or employment figures. The attention paid to the Force arose chiefly because of renewed anxiety about the defensive capacity of the nation. Haldane's planning of the Territorial Force had been based on the modified Blue Waterism which allowed for raids but not invasion. But it was precisely at the time when the reform of the Auxiliary Forces was being carried through that new concern about the likelihood of invasion was being aroused. The main instigator of this new concern was the National Service League with Lord Roberts as its President. Roberts and the powerful journalist Repington secured the setting up of a sub-committee of the Committee of Imperial Defence to reconsider the question of invasion. First meeting in November 1907, it reported in October 1908, The Report confirmed the policy of 1903, and was in that sense a defeat for the National Service League. But it also recognised that it was now Germany more than France which was to be feared, and called for an expansion of the Territorial Force.[72]

More important than the reaffirmation of the unlikelihood of invasion was the fact that concern was aroused rather than laid to rest by the Committee of Imperial Defence's Report. During the winter of 1908-9 speculation about invasion reached its height. Thereafter the National Service League in particular never allowed politicians to forget the invasion question.[73] Propagandists for conscription were necessarily ambivalent about the Territorial Force. 'A more praiseworthy or more patriotic body of men does not exist in this or in any other country,' as Roberts recognised. And yet it was a necessary part of the conscriptionists' case that the Territorial Force was inadequate in both numbers and training for the defence of the realm. Recruiting after the spring of 1909 proved disappointing to the authorities. General French, as Inspector-General of the Forces, was to note that some placed the blame for this on the activities of the National Service League; others replied that the National Service League had helped recruiting.[74] At bottom, the National Service League's attitude was hostile, and towards the end of 1912 there was a concerted effort to compel the Government to resort to some form of conscription by demonstrating the inefficiency of the Territorial Force. Professional soldiers, few of them ever enthusiastic about Haldane's creation, became openly critical or reluctant to be associated with the new Force. Haldane's engagement of Sir Iain Hamilton to write a defence of the voluntary system landed him in a political storm, and did little to advance the cause. Even Esher began to desert the ship. Of the leading soldiers only

147

Haig was thoroughly loyal to the Territorial Force.[75]

The re-emphasis on home defence meant a corresponding decline in the concern to build up the Territorial Force as a reserve available to fight overseas. Lord Lucas, representing his chief, Haldane, in the House of Lords, was to claim in November 1908 in a travesty of the truth that 'the Territorial Force has never been considered in any other light than as a home defence Army.' In 1910, however, members of the Territorial Force were invited to accept liability to serve overseas. Three London corps refused to accept anyone who would not so engage, but in general 'the suggestion was either entirely ignored, or treated with a kind of pained resentment.' In January 1913 only 1,152 officers and 18,903 NCOs and men were under the engagement to serve abroad on mobilisation.[76] The truth was that the Territorial, though eager enough to serve overseas when the need arose, was reluctant to commit himself in advance. The Force remained what the Volunteers had been, primarily a force for home defence.

There can be little doubt that the Territorials had a somewhat tarnished image at the outbreak of war. Although there were reports to suggest that they were militarily more effective than the Volunteers,[77] a mere glance at the debates in Parliament is sufficient to show that they were the objects of a barrage of criticism, and felt to be incapable of even defending the country against raids, much less a full invasion. Members of the Territorial Force itself were often openly critical of it, even supporters of conscription.[78]

The final blow to the Territorial Force's battered pride was dealt by Kitchener in August 1914. Fresh to Whitehall, and with a remarkable ignorance of the organisation of defence in Great Britain, he refused to recognise that the expansion of the Territorial Force, supported by the County Associations, was the natural way to raise more soldiers in a voluntary system. Instead he appealed direct to the people. The Territorials found themselves fighting for recruits, and more than ever misunderstood in Whitehall. Only the pressure of events was to restore their position to one of some dignity. By Christmas 1914 twenty-two Territorial Battalions had joined the BEF in France.[79]

If the Territorials felt that their organisation and achievements were treated with scant respect, they could perhaps take some satisfaction in contemplating the ways in which they had helped to shape Britain's military structure. Through their spokesmen in Parliament, amounting in 1912 to fifty-seven Conservative and thirty-seven Liberal MPs who were members of the Territorial Force,[80] they had exerted considerable influence to frustrate both Brodrick and Arnold-Forster, and to cause Haldane to reshape his plans. An essential part of those plans was that the Territorial Force should be available for service as a reserve. In fact this could not be enforced, and was only voluntarily accepted by a small

148

minority of Territorials. Thus the Territorial Force, in the eyes of its own spokesmen, and by 1908 evidently of the Government also, was a force which was admitted to need months of training before it was adequate to meet Regular troops, and yet was seen by authority as the main defender of the shores against invasion or raid. The opponents of the Force ruthlessly exploited this yawning credibility gap, some of them hoping that the failure of the Force would be the inevitable prelude to conscription. But despite the criticism, numbers in the Force maintained, if precariously, a level, and the advocates of conscription were unable to press home their advantage. The Volunteers and their Territorial successors, by their numerical strength and by their voting power in the country and in Parliament, were able to survive and frustrate the plans both of those who wanted conscription and of those who wanted them to be available for service overseas.

Notes

1. See esp. S.R. Williamson, Jr., *The Politics of Grand Strategy* (Cambridge, Mass., 1969); M. Howard, *The Continental Commitment* (London, 1972), Chs. 1 and 2; H.R. Moon, 'The Invasion of the United Kingdom: Public Controversy and Official Planning' (London University unpublished Ph.D. thesis, 1968); N.W. Summerton, 'The Development of British Military Planning for a War against Germany, 1904-1914' (London University unpublished Ph.D. thesis, 1970); B. Bond, *The Victorian Army and the Staff College*, pp. 181-298; N. d'Ombrain, *War Machinery and High Policy* (London, 1973).
2. G.D. Pullar, *Historical Sketch of the 4th (Perthshire) Volunteer Battalion, The Black Watch (Royal Highlanders)*, p. 14; *VSG,* 2 Mar. 1878; *Echo,* 14, 21, 23 Mar. 1878.
3. Committee (1878-9), qq. 130-461, App. I; see also Cantab, *The Proposed Volunteer Force for Active Service* (London, 1878); *Daily Telegraph,* 26 and 27 Apr., 14 May 1878.
4. *Regimental Record of the 24th Middlesex (formerly 49th Middlesex) Post Office Volunteers from 1868 to 1896* (London, n.d.), pp. 60-4; G. Williams, *Citizen Soldiers of the Royal Engineers Transportation and Movements and the Royal Army Service Corps 1859 to 1965* (Ashford, n.d.), p. 11.
5. For an account and analysis of volunteering in the Boer War, see R. Price, *An Imperial War and the British Working Class*, pp. 178-232.
6. For debate about the numbers who served or offered to serve, see *Spectator,* vol. 94 (11 and 25 Mar., 8 and 15 Apr. 1905), pp. 360-1, 436, 508-9, 549.
7. *4 Hansard 78,* c. 1267.
8. *4 Hansard 79,* cc. 42, 145-8, 158, 160 (15 Feb. 1900), c. 257 (16 Feb. 1900), cc. 397-8 (19 Feb. 1900).
9. *4 Hansard 80,* cc. 612-13 (12 Mar. 1900), *86,* c. 1532 (27 July 1900).
10. 58 and 59 Vict. c. 23.
11. *4 Hansard 83,* cc. 532-6, 1419-32 (18 and 28 May 1900), *84,* cc. 577-8, 1279-86

(21 and 28 June 1900), *86*, cc. 344-85, 925-65 (18 and 23 July 1900), *87*, cc. 233-44, 583 (31 July, 3 Aug. 1900).

12. *4 Hansard 90*, cc. 1066-8, 1076 (8 Mar. 1901).
13. J.K. Dunlop, *The Development of the British Army 1899-1914* (London, 1938), pp. 142-3.
14. *4 Hansard 101*, cc. 304, 956 (20 and 27 Jan. 1902); for the Committee, see WO 33/221.
15. *4 Hansard 104*, cc. 392-3 (4 Mar. 1902); Brodrick to Hicks-Beach, 9 Apr. 1901, Midleton Papers, PRO 30/67/7, ff. 377-8.
16. *4 Hansard 104*, cc. 606-64 (6 Mar. 1902), *111*, cc. 607-14 (17 July 1902). The Advisory Board was short-lived, being wound up in 1904 – see WO 32/6453-4.
17. *4 Hansard 119*, cc. 188, 217, 223-4 (9 Mar. 1903).
18. 'Condition of Auxiliary Forces', Printed Paper for Cabinet, 10 Mar. 1903, CAB 37/64/17; Balfour to the King, 10 Mar. 1903, CAB 41/28/5.
19. *4 Hansard 119*, c. 209 (9 Mar. 1903).
20. H.S. Wilkinson, *Thirty-five Years 1874-1909*, pp. 263-6; RC (1904), Report.
21. 'Remarks on Report of RC on Militia and Volunteers', Printed Paper for Cabinet, 30 May 1904, CAB 37/71/73.
22. A. Tucker, 'The issue of army reform in the Unionist Government, 1903-5', *Historical Journal*, vol. IX (1966), pp. 90-100; M. Arnold-Forster, *The Right Honourable Hugh Oakley Arnold-Forster* (London, 1910).
23. C.E. Callwell, *Field-Marshal Sir Henry Wilson Bart* (London 1927), vol. I, pp. 54-6.
24. M. Arnold-Forster, op. cit., p. 235.
25. H.O. Arnold-Forster, *The Army in 1906* (London, 1906), p. 211.
26. Memorandum dated 24 Nov. 1903, Arnold-Forster Papers, Add. MSS 50303, ff. 139-46.
27. Balfour to the King, 14 Dec. 1903, 26 Feb. 1904, CAB 41/28/27 and 41/29/4.
28. *4 Hansard 131*, cc. 345-6 (7 Mar. 1904).
29. Balfour to the King, 19 May 1904, CAB 41/29/16; see also same to same, 14 and 26 Apr., 10 May 1904, CAB 41/29/11, 13, 15.
30. Balfour to the King, 14 and 15 June, 5 and 13 July 1904, CAB 41/29/19, 20, 23, 25.
31. 'Notes of a Conference of both Houses of Parliament interested in the Volunteers', 25 July 1904, Arnold-Forster Papers, Add. MSS 50303, ff. 83-8; *4 Hansard 139*, cc. 1386-7 (8 Aug. 1904).
32. *4 Hansard 139*, cc. 1416-9, 1435-6, 1445 (8 Aug. 1904).
33. Arnold-Forster to Sir Guy Fleetwood-Wilson, 19 Nov. 1904, Arnold-Forster Papers, Add. MSS 50312, ff. 79-80.
34. 'Volunteers' Establishment and Pay', Printed Paper for Cabinet, 13 Jan. 1905, CAB 37/74/7.
35. *4 Hansard 141*, cc. 911-64, 1113-1204, esp. 1177-8, 957-9, 1166, 1197 (22 Feb. 1905).
36. Balfour to the King, 10 and 28 Mar. 1905, CAB 41/30/7, 12.
37. *4 Hansard 143*, cc. 1415-6, 1552 (28 and 29 Mar. 1905); see also *144*, cc. 372-3 (4 Apr. 1905).
38. *4 Hansard 144*, cc. 513-20 (5 Apr. 1905).
39. *4 Hansard 144*, c. 192 (3 Apr. 1905).
40. WO 32/6377; 'Copy of Circular Letter Addressed to General Officers Commanding-in-Chief' and 'Copy of Circular Letter Addressed to General Officers Commanding-in-Chief, in Substitution for that of 20th June, 1905', PP 1905 (Cd. 2437, 2439), XLVI, pp. 905-11; *4 Hansard 149*, cc. 579-646

(13 July 1905).

41. Diary, 13 and 28 July 1905, Arnold-Forster Papers, Add. MSS 50349, ff. 69-70, 145; and Add. MSS 50312. ff. 167-209.
42. Diary, 29 Aug. 1905, Arnold-Forster Papers, Add. MSS 50350, f. 65.
43. Arnold-Forster to Douglas, 20 Sept. 1905, Douglas to Arnold-Forster, 26 Sept. 1905, Arnold-Forster Papers, Add. MSS 50312, ff. 346-61.
44. Diary, 30 Sept. 1905, Arnold-Forster Papers, Add. MSS 50350, f. 139.
45. 'The Volunteers', Printed Paper for Cabinet, 11 Nov. 1905, CAB 37/80/170; Arnold-Forster Papers, Add. MSS 50312, ff. 64-73.
46. M. Howard, op. cit., pp. 22, 33-47.
47. 2nd Memorandum, Esher Papers, 16/8; Sir G. Ellison, 'Reminiscences', *The Lancashire Lad,* vol. XVII (Feb. 1936), p. 9.
48. 4th Memorandum, Esher Papers, 16/8.
49. *Spectator,* vol. 94 (11 and 18 Mar., 8 Apr. 1905), pp. 360-1, 400-2, 502-3.
50. Haldane used this phrase in the 4th Memorandum, Esher Papers, 16/8; see also, *4 Hansard 160,* cc. 1114, 1117-8, 1166 (12 July 1906).
51. *4 Hansard 153,* cc. 676-8, *154,* cc. 1608-10 (8 and 29 Mar. 1906).
52. Reports of Territorial Army Committee, Esher Papers, 16/8; M.V. Brett (ed.), *Journals and Letters of Reginald Viscount Esher* (London, 1934), vol. II, pp. 163-4, 167-9.
53. M.V. Brett (ed.), op. cit., p. 174.
54. Haig to Esher, 9 Sept. 1906, Lucas to Esher, 16 Oct. 1906, Esher Papers, 10/27.
55. M.V. Brett (ed.), op. cit., pp. 195-6; Haldane to Esher, 18 Oct. 1906, copy, Haldane Papers, MS 5907, f. 108.
56. Lucas to Esher, 22 Oct. 1906, Esher Papers, 10/27.
57. 4th Memorandum, Esher Papers, 16/8.
58. Final Memorandum, Esher Papers, 16/8.
59. *4 Hansard 170,* c. 596, *176,* c. 566 (4 Mar. and 19 June 1907). For an account of the passage of the Bill through Parliament, see J.K. Dunlop, op. cit., pp. 266-90.
60. *4 Hansard 172,* c. 172, *176,* cc. 239, 503 (9 Apr., 17 and 19 June 1907).
61. *4 Hansard 170,* cc. 508, 514 (4 Mar. 1907).
62. *4 Hansard 172,* cc. 83-98, 235-48, 1627-8 (9, 10 and 23 Apr. 1907).
63. *4 Hansard 175,* c. 713, *176,* cc. 1081-6 (5 and 25 June 1907).
64. Sir G. Ellison, 'Reminiscences', loc. cit., p. 9.
65. S.E. Koss, *Lord Haldane – Scapegoat for Liberalism* (New York and London, 1959), p. 53; P. Fraser, *Lord Esher* (London, 1973), pp. 195-6; Repington to Haldane, 19 Apr. 1907, Haldane to mother, 18 July 1907, Haldane Papers, MS 5907, ff. 144-5, 5978, f. 25.
66. Haldane to mother, 12 and 29 Jan., 1 and 8 Feb. 1907, Haldane Papers, MS 5977, ff. 5, 7, 37, 43, 55-6.
67. WO 32/8820-1.
68. Haldane to Esher, 15 Sept. 1907, Haldane Papers, MS 5907, f. 201.
69. Sir A. Fitzroy, *Memoirs* (London, n.d.), vol. I, p. 333; Haldane to sister, 1 Nov. 1907, Haldane Papers, MS 6011, f. 36.
70. *5 Hansard 4,* (HL) c. 925 (24 Nov. 1909); E. Halevy, *The Rule of Democracy – A History of the English People in the Nineteenth Century,* vol. VI, Book 1, 2nd revised ed. (London, 1952), p. 181.
71. Haldane Papers, MS 5979, ff. 146, 148, 154.
72. H.R. Moon, op. cit., pp. 330-78.
73. D. Hayes, *Conscription Conflict* (London, 1949), pp. 1-146; D. James, *Lord Roberts* (London, 1954), pp. 412-64.

74. Field-Marshal Earl Roberts, *Fallacies and Facts* (London, 1911), p. 10; 'Report of the Inspector-General of the Forces on the Territorial Force', PP 1911 (Cd. 5998), XLVII, p. 658; *5 Hansard 14* (HC), c. 1871, *35,* (HC), cc.116-7 (11 Mar. 1910, 4 Mar. 1912).
75. C.E. Callwell, op. cit., vol. I, p. 120; N. d'Ombrain, op. cit., p. 220, n. 38; I' Hamilton, *Compulsory Service* (London, 1910); Esher, 'The Voluntary Principle', *National Review,* vol. LVI (Sept. 1910), pp. 41-7; D. Sommer, *Haldane of Cloan* (London, 1960), pp. 367-70.
76. *4 Hansard 196,* c. 830 (16 Nov. 1908); E.J. King, *The History of the 7th Battalion Middlesex Regiment,* pp. viii-ix, 149-50; 'Territorial Force and National Reserve: Statistics Relating to Strength and Efficiency', PP 1912-3 (Cd. 6616), LI, p. 953.
77. 'Report of the Inspector-General of the Forces on the Territorial Force', PP 1911 (Cd. 5598), XLVII, p. 658.
78. *5 Hansard 14* (HC), cc. 1824-8, *18,* (HC), c. 754 (11 Mar. and 27 June 1910). I am indebted to Michael Allison who first alerted me to this point.
79. M.V. Brett (ed.), op. cit., vol. III, pp. 176-7; Viscount Esher, *The Tragedy of Lord Kitchener* (London, 1921), pp. 36-7, 62-4; L.S. Amery, *My Political Life* vol. II, (London, 1953-5), pp. 21-35; M. Middlebrook, *The First Day on the Somme, 1 July 1916* (London, 1971), pp. 5, 15-6; Midleton Papers, PRO 30/67/25.
80. *5 Hansard 41* (HC), c. 298 (16 July 1912).

CONCLUSION

This history of the Volunteer Force began as a study of patriotism. At the outset there seemed logic and force in the contrast evoked by the Mayor of Leicester when he administered the oath oath of allegiance to the local Volunteers in 1859: 'In the great majority of cases of voluntary enlistment into the line the parties enlisting enter rather from some pressing uneasiness at home or in a spirit of adventure than from any high or enlightened feeling of patriotism; but in your instance, the motives that have induced you to enlist are of the highest and purest patriotism.'[1] A social history of the Force, it seemed, might be the single best way of coming to an understanding of the strength of patriotism in Victorian Britain. Yet the patriotism of the Volunteers has proved to have the quality of a vapour; it eludes the grasp. The motives which induced men to enrol quickly began to appear more complex than those mentioned by the Mayor of Leicester. At the same time it was obvious that the Force had an interest and significance much wider than had been originally foreseen. The relationships both within the Force and between the Volunteers and society illuminate many aspects of social life.

It is, however, the role of patriotism in the Force which deserves some concluding comment. What is remarkable about the Force is its ability to sustain itself when the praise of the earlier years had turned to criticism and disparagement. A military organisation so dependent on public opinion might in the circumstances have been expected to fade away. But, with the exception of the years 1869-73, the numbers in the Force generally increased year by year. At the same time the social composition of the Force changed. The middle class left as the criticism of the Force mounted, returning only in times of crisis. The working class remained. The Volunteer movement became the Volunteer Force, an institution which proved to have a remarkable ability to survive times both of neglect and abuse. The reason for this seems to be that for most members of the Force volunteering had an instrumental value which was unaffected by doubts in military circles as to its value for the defence of the country. For its members the Volunteer Force provided recreation.

Middle-class contemporaries were not unaware of this, and it made them somewhat uneasy. For although they were much conerned with the way leisure time was spent, they knew there was something odd about a Force which was publicly proclaimed to be the embodiment of patriotism, while its actual role was to provide recreation for the working class. The *Volunteer News* illustrates the doubts which were felt;

153

subtitled 'A Weekly Journal devoted to the Volunteer and Reserve Forces and a Record of all Healthful Exercises and Recreations,' it felt obliged to urge in a leading article in 1868 the importance of impressing 'on every Volunteer that the service they are engaged in is a grave and serious one, and at the same time not incompatible with a great deal of enjoyment. Patriotism is never frivolous, and if the Volunteer movement has not patriotism as its leading and guiding motive, it is more than a sham — it is a delusion and a snare.'[2] Patriotism and enjoyment could be combined, but the writer was clearly worried that enjoyment was too predominant. We have seen reason to think that he was correct in his diagnosis, and that a desire for recreation was the prime motive which led working men to enrol. And just as patriotism was certainly not the sole cause of the Force's strength, so also it seems simplistic to suppose that for more than a minority it was a consequence of having served.

Yet if the conclusions about working-class patriotism which can be gleaned from a study of the Volunteer Force are somewhat negative, it seems possible that more can be said about middle- and upper-class patriotism. Here was an institution orginally designed so that the middle class could play their part in the nation's defence. And yet, after initial enthusiasm, they left its ranks, and treated it with a tolerant smirk. It was 'looked upon by most people as a good enough amusement for "those who liked that sort of thing".'[3] The Volunteer Force had insufficient recreational attraction for the middle class who had an increasingly wide range of leisure opportunities to choose from. And patriotism was not in itself enough to induce them to enrol in a Force, membership of which brought no social advantages.

The low status of the Force is the more remarkable in view of the royal and elite support which gave the Volunteers such a dramatic birth. All too soon the unanimity of praise, praise it is true often from contradictory standpoints, gave way to criticism. Spreading from the urchins and professional military journals, it entered the columns of *The Times* and the drawing rooms of Society. And the criticism, it is clear, was not simply of a technical and military kind. It was largely social in nature, a disparagement in particular of a Force whose officers were not obviously gentlemen. To upper-class Victorians the Volunteer Force, the embodiment of patriotism in a military institution, was something to be patronised at annual prize-givings, and called upon for service in times of crisis. Of course there were exceptions to the rule, aristocrats who were deeply committed to the Force, but in general the day-to-day business of drilling and shooting practice and march-outs was found both boring and slightly embarrassing. For soldiering was traditionally an aristocratic calling and lower-class way of life, and the intrusion into it of bourgeois and artisan respectability, with its odd blend of duty and pursuit of enjoyment, seemed out of place. Patriotism, to the upper class, was more acceptable as an ideal than a reality, and its manifestation in the Volunteer Force was repellent enough to send them instead to the grouse moors and golf courses; or, if soldiering was in their blood, to the more socially acceptable Yeomanry.

One consequence of the low status of the Volunteers has been that only those in some way connected with the Force have, until recently, paid any attention to its history. This neglect would have astonished the Victorians, particularly those who knew the Force in its early days. To them the Volunteers were one of the finest expressions of public spirit; they brought an end to panics, and brought the classes together; a symbol of social peace, they served the cause of international peace. 'The emphatic and ardent loyalty to the land of their birth of these masses,' wrote the *Volunteer Service Gazette* in 1863, '. . . will render the Volunteer movement of 1860 memorable through all future English history.'[4] History, however, has ignored the Volunteers, and mistakenly so. The inception of the Force is a testimony both to the fear of the French and the necessity felt for a respectable class-mixing form of recreation, and its structure and persistence suggest a substantial working-class acceptance of existing social differentiation. Volunteering was a recreation enjoyed by the working class, and acceptable to the middle class, for it took place under their control, and was stamped with the seals of patriotism and respectability. No military planner would have created such a Force if his sole aim had been the defence of the realm. And no politician proved strong enough to carry through any substantial reform of a Force so embedded in the social life of the community.

Notes

1. *VSG*, 9 Nov. 1859.
2. *Volunteer News*, 7 Nov. 1868.
3. C.J. Blomfield, *Once an Artist always an Artist* (London, 1921), p. 6.
4. *VSG*, 8 Aug. 1863.

APPENDIX

THE IRISH AND THE VOLUNTEERS

There was no Volunteer Force in Ireland. In 1859-60, however, the Government seriously considered extending the Force across St. George's Channel: their fear, of course, was that the Irish would use their weapons in internecine quarrels. The solution, as it seemed to Palmerston and Cardwell, was to offer the Irish artillery but not rifles. Artillery guns, Palmerston hoped, 'could not be applied to any bad purpose.' Swords also might be permissible as 'a man would hardly think himself a soldier if he had not some weapon besides a Cannon Ram Rod.'[1] By July 1860, however, when the matter was raised in Parliament, the Government had evidently decided not to authorise the Force in Ireland. Government spokesmen stressed their belief in the loyalty of the Irish people, but argued that weapons might be used in internal strife.[2]

The Irish could not be excluded from Volunteer corps in Britain. There was a highly respectable London Irish Corps to match the London Scottish in the capital, and in other areas of Irish immigration there were corps with a heavy preponderance of Irish. In Liverpool, for example, as early as January 1860, a corps was reported 'to be infected with Orange fever to an alarming extent.' Trouble resulted.[3] It was in Liverpool, too, that there was suspicion that Volunteer arms were being hoarded for Irish nationalist purposes.[4] These difficulties highlight the necessity for an environment of social peace if a Volunteer Force is to be viable. With the exception of Irish immigrants such conditions existed to a sufficient degree in Great Britain.

At periodic intervals Irish MPs demanded to know why the Force was not extended to Ireland. The most serious attempt to win authorisation for the Force in Ireland was in 1879 when the Government was not actively hostile to the idea, but the Bill was defeated in the House of Lords. The question was also raised in, for example, 1863, 1877-8, 1881, 1890-1, and 1897; but never with success.[5]

Notes

1. Palmerston to Cardwell, 1 Dec. 1859, to Herbert, 19 Dec. 1859, Palmerston Papers, Add. MSS 48581, ff. 84-5, 96; Cardwell to Herbert, 3 Dec. 1859, 22 Jan. 1860, Herbert Papers.

2. *3 Hansard 159,* cc. 2106-10, *160,* cc. 428-41 (18 and 31 July 1860).
3. De Grey to Herbert, 12 Jan. 1860, Ripon Papers, Add. MSS 43533, ff. 85-6; *3 Hansard 171,* c. 336, *286,* cc. 1796-7 (4 June 1863, 7 Apr. 1884).
4. See above p. 80-1.
5. *3 Hansard 171,* cc. 332-343 (4 June 1863); Volunteer Corps (Ireland) Bills were given First Readings on 9 Feb. 1877, 21 Jan. 1878, and 7 Jan. 1881, but made no further progress. For 1879 see *3 Hansard 245,* cc. 1903-36, *249,* cc. 368-87 (7 May and 7 Aug. 1879); *3 Hansard 346,* cc. 935-6 (7 July 1890), *354,* cc. 1521-5 (25 June 1891), *4 Hansard 45,* cc. 843-4, *46,* c. 822 (29 Jan. and 19 Feb. 1897).

BIBLIOGRAPHY

A.S. White, *A Bibliography of Regimental Histories of the British Army* (Society for Army Historical Research, London, 1965) contains a substantial section on the Volunteer Force, the entries being arranged by county. Anyone who wants to know what published material exists on the Volunteer Force can do no better than turn to White's book. Its existence obviates the necessity for a comprehensive bibliography here. Although White lists only specifically military histories, omitting those more general works in which the Volunteers appear incidentally, it would serve no useful purpose to group together here such a disparate collection of books. A glance at my notes will indicate those to which I am most indebted. This bibliography, therefore, is confined to manuscript sources which I have consulted.

Aberdeen Public Library
> Minute Book, Aberdeen Rifle Volunteer Battalion, 1860-5. Not much of general interest, except disputes over appointments to the commissioned ranks.

Army Museums Ogilby Trust
> H. Spencer Wilkinson Papers. Some correspondence with Roberts about Volunteers, but otherwise disappointing.

British Museum
> Arnold-Forster Papers Add. MSS 50275-50357. Essential for an understanding of his projected reforms.
> Gladstone Papers. I have consulted Add. MSS 44118-20, 44637-41. Not much on the Volunteers.
> Palmerston Papers Add. MSS 48417-48589. Only occasional but often interesting references to the Volunteers.
> Ripon Papers Add. MSS 43510-43644. De Grey played an important part in the early history of the Force, but this is only reflected to a limited extent in his manuscript papers.

Carlisle Record Office, Carlisle
> Minute Book, 7th Cumberland Rifle Volunteers 1868-74, D/Cu/1/44. Of minor interest.

Churchill College, Cambridge
> Esher Papers. Essential for the 1907-8 reforms.

Dorset Military Museum, Dorchester
> Some interesting early posters.

Guildhall Library, London
> London Rifle Brigade Papers, 1859-1939. Of particular rather than

general interest.
Regimental Orders and muster roll books of the Post Office
Volunteers, including occupations and ages of all recruits 1870-1909.
Minute Books and papers of the City of London Territorial and
Auxiliary Forces Association. These give a very full idea of the
problems of the Territorial Force.

Hornel Library, Kirkcudbright
'Illustrated narrative of a visit of Edinburgh Riflemen to Dumfries
1860', a sketch-book by the Edinburgh gunsmith, A. Henry, an
excellent example of Volunteer self-mockery.

Kent County Archives, Maidstone
Muster roll book, 15th Kent Rifle Volunteer Corps, 1860-70, U 120.
07. Gives ages and occupations of Volunteers.

Lewisham Archive Depository
Minute books and papers of the Sydenham Rifle Corps, 1859-70,
A 58/6/1-10. Full information on an interesting corps.

Lincolnshire Archives Office, Lincoln
Minute, scrap, and muster roll books of the 1st Lincolnshire Rifle
Volunteers, Hill 12/1/1-3, 12/2/1-3, 12/3. Very full records.
Brigg Volunteers in the 1890s, Stubbs I-247, a miscellaneous box
containing posters, minute books, and letters.
Minutes of Lincolnshire Territorial Association, TA 1/1.
Minute books of officers (1883-1907) and non-commissioned
officers (1882-92), Lincoln Volunteers, TA 1/4-5. Some interesting
debates as to who should be allowed in the respective mess-rooms.

Middlesex County Record Office
Letters and Papers of George Cruikshank, Acc 534/1-14. Full, but
scrappy, records of Cruikshank's somewhat unhappy venture in
teetotal Volunteering.
Clerk to Lieutenancy Records, L 40-86. Contain letters on the
establishment of working men's corps in London, occupations and
ages of officers by corps, rules, and some muster roll books.

National Army Museum
A few miscellaneous records, the most substantial being those of
the London Scottish, MS 6911/2.

National Library of Scotland
Minute Books and correspondence of the Advocates Volunteer Rifle
Corps, 1859-65, Adv. MSS 81.2.11-38. Not very full records of an
early middle-class corps.
Haldane Papers MSS 5901-6109. Essential for his reforms.

New Hayters, Aldington, Kent
Deedes Papers, vol. 3. Of marginal interest for the Volunteers.

Public Record Office
HO 45. Used particularly for the employment of Volunteers in

disturbances.

HO 51/96-9. Information on attempts to form Volunteer corps before 1859.

WO 32. The main, but inadequate source for official policy. The bulk of the material is from the early twentieth century.

WO 33. Some miscellaneous committee and other reports on the Volunteers.

WO 43/88. Contains information on the Victoria Rifles 1853.

WO 70. Muster roll book and other records of the 36th Middlesex Rifle Volunteer Corps.

CAB 37. Papers Printed for Cabinet 1880-1914. Comparatively few in the early years, but important for the twentieth-century reforms.

CAB 41. Copies of Cabinet letters in the Royal Archives. Again very little mention of the Volunteers until the twentieth century. Essential for the reforms.

PRO 30/40/13. Ardagh Papers. Contain mobilisation plans 1886-90.

PRO 30/48. Cardwell Papers. Read for his period as Secretary of State for War. Some, but not detailed, material on the Volunteers.

PRO 30/67. Midleton Papers. Contains some information for his period as Secretary of State for War, and also on the attempt to recruit through Territorial Associations in 1914.

Scottish United Services Museum, Edinburgh

An archive rich in material, the most valuable for the Volunteers being the minute books and papers of the 77th Lanarkshire Rifle Volunteers, MS 6323. Also papers of the 1st Aberdeenshire Rifle Volunteers (75/92 V. 861. 1), and the Glasgow Territorial Force Association (26/90 V. 884. 1).

Sheffield City Library

Wharncliffe Muniments, Wh. M. 459. Some interesting material on Sheffield Volunteers in the 1860s.

Somerset Record Office

Minute book and records of the 3rd Somerset Rifle Volunteers, DD/SAS/SY2 and DD/FS, Box 60. Some general interest for the 1860s and 1870s.

Minute books of the Frome Selwood Rifle Volunteers, 1859-62, DD/LW 25-6.

Somerset County Rifle Association Papers 1876-7, DD/FS, Box 70. Of minor interest.

TAVR Headquarters, Maidstone

Minute book, Territorial Force Association of the County of Kent, 1908-15. Gives some insight into the work and problems of the Territorial Associations.

Wilton House, Wilton
Herbert Papers. No full record of the early years when Herbert was Secretary of State for War, but some interesting letters, especially from the Duke of Cambridge.

INDEX

Aberdeen, 4th Earl of (1784-1860), 5
Aberdeen, 7th Earl of (1847-1934), 146
Acland, T.D., 3
Active Service Companies, 128
Akroyd, Edward, 3
Alden, George, 118
Alliance Assurance Company, 77
Alton Locke, 28
American Civil War, 87
Annual Register, 1, 4
Ardagh, J.C., 92
Aristocracy; attitude to Volunteers, 9, 154; members of Volunteer corps, 10, 55; criticism of in Crimean War, 11; support of necessary for Volunteers, 15, 19-21, 83; role in Territorial Force, 145-6
Armed Associations, 8
Army, *see* Regular Army
Army Board, 134
Army Council, 136-8, 140, 142-3, 145
Army Enlistment Act, 1870, 90
Army List, 92
Arnold, Matthew, 3, 55
Arnold-Forster, H.O., 130-1, 133-41, 144, 148
Artillery, 2, 14, 110, 156
Atholl, 7th Duke of, 146

Balfour, A.J. 133, 136, 138, 144
Bands, 59, 71, 117
Band of Hope, 79
Bank Holidays Act, 1871, 119
Battle of Dorking, 92
Baxter, Dudley, 15
Bazaars, 68, 71-3, 116
Bennett, A.R., 78
Beresford, Marcus, 21, 91
Berry, R. Potter, 109
Bethune, E.C., 77
Birkenhead, 3
Bisley, 114
Blackburne, J.G., 20
Boer War, 2, 46, 87, 96, 104-6, 109, 122, 127-31
Bousfield, Nathaniel, 10, 27
Boyle, Hon. Mrs. Richard Cavendish, 72
Brackenbury, C.B., 61

Brackenbury, Henry, 92
Bright, John, 28, 86
Brighton, field days at, 70, 85, 89, 94, 119
British Expeditionary Force, 148
Brodrick, St. John, 130-1, 133, 139-40, 148
Brookfield, A.M., 58, 93
Brunner, J.T., 75-6
Bucknill, Dr. J.C., 9
Burgoyne, Maj.-Gen. Sir John, 6
Bursley Wakes, 71
Bury, drill club in, 10
Bury, Viscount (1832-94), 34, 55, 85, 96
Busk, Hans, 10, 114

Cadets, 59, 75, 145
Cambridge, 2nd Duke of (1819-1904), 10, 62, 78, 84-6, 93
Camp, 59, 76-7, 84-5, 94, 109-11, 119-21, 129, 131, 139
Campbell-Bannerman, Sir Henry, 3, 69
Canning, G., 107
Cannock Chase, Army manoeuvres at, 119-20
Cardwell, E., 90-1, 104, 133, 156
Carlile, Lt-Col. E.H., 75
Castlereagh, Viscount (1769-1822), 107
Castlereagh, Viscount (1878-1949), 109
Cave, Col. T.S., 40
Chamberlain, Joseph, 19
Chartism, 1, 8, 27-8
Cheltenham, drill club in, 10
Cherbourg, 7
China, 74
Choral singing, 33, 113, 117
Churches, attitudes to Volunteers, 19, 68-70, 74-5, 117, 122-3
Churchill, Winston, 135-6
Churston, Lord (1799-1871), 9
City Imperial Volunteers, 128
Clarendon, 4th Earl of (1800-70), 19
Class relationships; book contributes to study of, 4; Volunteers seen as improving, 1, 22-4, 27-8, 72, 82,

98, 113-5, 155 (*see also* Aristocracy, Middle class, Working class)
Cobden, Richard, 6, 86, 107
Cobden-Chevalier Treaty, 1
Cockermouth, attempt to form Volunteer corps in, 8
Colomb, Sir John, 120, 136
Commanding Officers, 12, 26, 54-5, 60, 62-3, 82, 91, 95, 121, 131, 142-4
Committee of Imperial Defence, 139, 147
Committee of Inquiry into the Financial State and Internal Organisation of the Volunteer Force in Great Britain, 3, 34, 59, 61, 76, 96, 127
Conscription, 2, 83, 130, 132, 147-9
Corn Laws, 5
County Associations, 77, 140, 142, 144-6
Cricket, 19, 59, 114-5, 118-9
Crimean War, 6-7, 11, 14, 95
Cross, R.A., 3
Crowfoot, W.M., 56
Cruikshank, George, 3, 19

Daily Express, 134
Daily Telegraph, 10, 70, 86
De Grey, Earl (1826-93), 15, 24, 61, 158
Derby, 15th Earl of (1826-93), 70, 82-3
Derby, 16th Earl of (1841-1908), 146
Dilke, Sir Charles, 137, 143-4
Discipline, 13, 52, 62-4, 79, 87
Disraeli, Benjamin, 107
Disturbances, role of Volunteers in suppressing, 8-10, 80-2
Donegal, Marquis of, 55
Douglas, Gen., 138
Drill, 64, 78, 110-11, 113, 154
Drill clubs, 10
Drink, 1, 29, 113, 118, 121-2
Drummond, Henry, MP, 19
Drunkenness, *see* Drink

Early Closing Association, 112
Easter Monday, field day on, 70-1, 85, 88-9, 91, 119
Ebury, Lord (1801-93), 19
Edinburgh, rifle club in, 10

Edward VII, 71, 115, 147
Egypt, Volunteers serve in, 128
Elcho, lord (1818-1914), 15, 23-4, 26, 28, 38, 55, 89, 111-12, 114
Elgin Commission, 133, 144
Ellice, Gen., 89, 94
Ellison, G.F., 140, 142
Employers; and Volunteers, 1, 3, 21-2, 28-30, 55, 64, 75-8, 110, 129
Enfield, Viscount (1830-98), 55
Engels, F., 62, 85
Engineers, 2, 59, 110
Esher, Viscount (1852-1930), 133, 141-2, 144-7

Factory Acts, 111
Fenians, 80-2, 156
Fitzroy, Sir Almeric, 147
Football, 59, 115, 119
Forster, W.E., 3, 62, 81
Fortifications, 5, 7
France, 5-7, 14, 107-8, 139
Franco-Prussian War, 86, 88, 104, 106
Freemasons, 19
French, Gen. J., 147

Galloway Rifles Gazette, 36
Garibaldi, G., 81, 87, 108
Garvock, Sir John, 88
Germany, 130, 139
Gladstone, W.E., 103
Glasgow Sentinel, 30
Gordon, Gen., 105
Grant, James, 107
Grey, Sir George, 8-9
Grimston Park, Volunteer Festival in, 117
Grosvenor, Earl (1825-99), 55
Grove, Sir Coleridge, 132
Guest, Ivor, MP, 135

Haig, Gen. Sir Douglas, 142, 148
Haldane, R.B., 2, 59, 75, 77, 109, 127, 130, 139-48
Halévy, E., 146
Halifax, 3
Hamilton, Sir Iain, 147
Hardwicke, Earl of (1799-1873), 18
Harrods, 121
Hastings, rifle club in, 10
Hay, Sir Hector, 35
Henry, Alexander, 21

163

Herbert, Sidney, 14, 18, 26, 52, 80
Holms, John MP, 40
Home, Col. Robert, 92
Hughes, Thomas, 3, 27, 86, 115
Hyde Park, review in, 1, 78
Hythe, rifle-shooting at, 62

Imperial Yeomanry, 128-9
India, 10, 74, 139
Indian Mutiny, 6
Infantry, 2, 104, 110
Invasion, fear of, 2, 5-7, 14, 103,
   108, 123, 127, 129-30, 140, 147,
   155
Irish, 80-1, 156-7
Ironclads, 7
Italy, 7

Joinville, Prince de, 5
Jones, Lloyd, 30

Kilvert, Rev. F., 71, 122
Kingsley, Charles, 28
Kitchener, Viscount (1850-1916),
   148
Knight, F.W., MP, 56
Knowsley, review at, 70

Labour Party, 145
Laird, John, 3, 29
Lamont, Col. W., 96
Landsdowne, Marquis of (1845-1927),
   129
Leigh, Lord (1824-1905), 18
Leighton, Lord (1830-96), 3, 111
Leisure; effects of volunteering on,
   1-2, 29, 117-8; book contributes
   to study of, 4; volunteering seen
   as leisure activity, 3, 75, 104,
   108-9, 123-4, 153-5; leisure
   facilities within Volunteer Force,
   110-22; middle-class attitudes to,
   112-3; implications of volunteering
   for history of, 123-4
Light Horse, 2, 60
Lindsay, Col. C.H., 91
Liverpool, drill club in, 10
Lloyd George, David, 3
Lloyds Bank, 121
Londesborough, Lord (1834-1900),
   117
Lords Lieutenant, 9, 12-13, 18-19,
   24, 26, 52-5, 75, 81, 90, 145-6
Louis Napoleon, 6-7, 15, 107-8

Louis Napoleon, 6-7, 15, 107-8
Louis Philippe, 5
Loyd-Lindsay, R., 55, 111, 114
Luard, Lt-Col. R., 94
Lucas, Lord (1876-1916), 142, 146,
   148
Lyceums, 113
Lytellton, Lord (1817-76), 70

Macaulay, T.B., 4
Macdonald, J.H.A., 42, 62, 82
Macgregor, John, 28
McIver, Col., 29
Mackinnon, Maj.-Gen., 146
Macmillan's Magazine, 118
McMurdo, W.M.S., 70, 112
Malmesbury, 3rd Earl of (1807-89), 1
March-outs, 68, 72, 79, 111-12, 154
Mathews, William, 28
Mechanics Institutes, 113
Melly, George, 62-3, 79
Mentana, Battle of, 87
Methodist Recorder, 74
Metropolitan Commanding Officers,
   84-5, 119
Middle class; Volunteer Force
   originally intended for, 2, 14, 18,
   83; thought dangerous to arm, 9;
   desire for military role, 11;
   attitude to aristocracy, 11, 55;
   middle-class corps, 18-19, 23, 25,
   35, 42, 57; attitude to admission
   of working class, 22-4, 27, 30;
   difficulty in keeping up numbers,
   30, 41-2, 153; as ideologues of
   Volunteer Force, 72-3, 115;
   enrolment of in crises, 105-6;
   and leisure, 112-3; and rifle,
   113-4
Millais, J.E., 3
Militia; revival of, 5-6; in Napoleonic
   Wars, 8; as alternative to Volunteers,
   9, 14-15; Volunteers compared
   to, 11, 13, 25, 38, 40-1, 71, 76,
   92, 106, 130; *The Times'* support
   for, 88; Volunteers train with,
   52, 91; country gentlemen as
   officers, 58; attempted reforms
   of, 133-5, 141, 144-5
Monkswell, Viscount (1845-1909),
   144
Morning Herald, 86
Morning Star, 86
Morocco, 5

164

Mounted Rifles, 2

Napier, Gen. Sir William, 9
Napoleon III, *see* Louis Napoleon
Napoleonic Wars, 5,7
National Artillery Association, 96
National Association for the Promotion of Social Science, 28
National Rifle Association, 94, 114
National Service League, 75, 147
Navy, Royal, 5-7, 130, 133, 140
Neilson, Capt., 54
Nice, 7
Nineteenth Century, 35
Non-commissioned officers, 63-4
Norfolk, Duke of (1847-1917), 132
Norton, Capt., 135

Observer, 86
Oddfellows, 19
Officers, Volunteer, 52-65; election
   of, 2, 21, 52-5; mode of
   appointment, 13, 21, 52;
   employers as, 21-2, 64; trade a
   bar to a commission, 53, 55-6;
   occupations of, 55-9; peers as,
   55; previous service in ranks of,
   57-8; education at public
   schools and universities, 58-9;
   cost of being, 59-60, 120; low
   status of, 60-2, 64, 154; proposed
   exemption from jury service of,
   61, 66; military qualities of, 62,
   132; proficiency tests for, 62,
   90-1; regular soldiers as, 62;
   Arnold-Forster's opinion of, 137;
   (*see also* Commanding Officers)
Orsini, F., 7

Pakington, Sir John, 7
Pall Mall Gazette, 88, 114
Palmerston, 3rd Viscount (1784-
   1865), 6, 24, 103, 106, 156
Panmure, Lord (1801-74), 10
Parliament, and Volunteers, 26-7, 56,
   63, 68, 75-7, 81, 86, 90-1, 108,
   127, 131, 134-7, 141-6, 148-9,
   156
Patriotism, 1, 3-4, 11-12, 50, 73,
   83, 98, 103-9, 122-4, 153-5
Paxton, Sir Joseph, 86
Peace Society, 19, 107
Peel, Gen. J., 12-14, 81

Peel, Sir Robert, 5
Percy, Lord Algernon, 40
Permanent Volunteer Force for
   Active Service, 127
Pettie, John, 28
Physique, volunteering thought to
   improve, 1, 82, 113, 118
Plymouth, defence of, 92
Price, Prof. R.N., 106
Prince Consort, 13-14, 71, 92, 114
Prince of Wales, *see* Edward VII
Prizes, 115-6
Prostitution, 1, 118
Public opinion, and Volunteers,
   19-20, 27-30, 64-5, 68-72,
   86-9, 91, 98, 117-8, 127, 153-5
Public Record Office, 4
Punch, 84 112

Quakers, 19, 74

Radstock, Lord (1833-1913), 55, 112
Raglan, Lord (1857-1921), 131
Ranelagh, Viscount (1812-85),
   23, 55, 84-6, 93
Rational Recreation Society, 113
Recreation, *see* Leisure
Regent's Park, inspection in, 79
Regular Army; Volunteers'
   identification with, 2, 61, 63,
   94-5; overseas role of, 5, 93, 139;
   and law and order, 8; *The Times'*
   attitude to, 11; Volunteers'
   relation to, 13-14, 84-98;
   compared to Volunteers, 25,
   38, 40-1, 71, 106, 137;
   Volunteers train with, 52, 85,
   89, 91-4, 131; role in
   appointment of Volunteer
   officers, 54; effect of
   Volunteers on, 68, 95-8;
   attitudes to Volunteers, 68,
   84-5, 93-4, 96-8; mutiny of, 81
Repington, C. a C., 147
Respectability, 3, 30, 109-10,
   154-5
Reynolds' Newspaper, 30, 108
Richards, A.B., 10-11, 24
Richmond, 7th Duke of (1845-
   1928), 146
Rifles and rifle-shooting, 26, 30, 78,
   80-1, 87, 94, 110-11, 113-16
Rifle clubs, 10, 27

165

Rifleman, 118
Roberts, Lord (1832-1914), 131, 147
Rochdale Observer, 20
Rochdale Pilot, 27
Rokeby, Lord (1798-1883), 19
Rollit, Sir Albert, 135
Rosebery, Earl of (1847-1929), 146
Roughs, and Volunteers, 78-80, 110
Roupell, William, MP, 21
Royal Commission on the Militia and Volunteers, 1904, 3, 33, 57-8, 76-7, 96, 108, 131-4
Royal Commission on the Volunteer Force, 1862, 3, 25-8
Royal Review, Edinburgh 1860, 21, 121
Royal Review, Edinburgh 1905, 138
Royal Review, Hyde Park 1860, 1, 78
Russell, Lord John (1792-1878), 6, 8
Russia, 7, 139

St James's Park, inspection in, 78
Sala, G.A., 4
Salisbury, Marquis of (1830-1903), 24
Savoy, 7
Seely, Major, 135
Selborne, Earl of (1859-1942), 41
Select Committee on Open Spaces, 1865, 111
Select Committee on Volunteer Acts, 1894, 3, 54, 61, 76, 94
Shelley, J.V., MP, 24
Silver, Hugh, 21
Social control, 1, 20-2, 27-30, 123-4, 155
Social Democratic Federation, 75
Social mobility, 3, 46, 61, 110
South Africa, *see* Boer War
Special constables, Volunteers as, 82
Special Reserve, 41
Standard, 134
Strathmore, Earl of (1855-1944), 146
Submarine mining engineers, 2, 110
Sun Fire Office, 121
Surrey, drill club in, 10
Swan, John, 21
Sydney, Lord (1805-90), 53

Tahiti, 5

Taillefer, N., 60
Tennyson, Alfred, 12
Territorial and Reserve Forces Bill, 143-5
Territorial Force, 2, 59, 77, 79, 104, 119, 127, 140-9
Territorial Force Associations, *see* County Associations
Territorial Year Book, 74
Thorne, Lt-Col., 76
Three Panics, 6
Times, The, 10-12, 23, 62, 67, 70, 79, 82, 87-9, 97, 108, 113-4, 154
Trade Unions, and Volunteers, 74-5
Truro, Lord (1816-91), 55
Tupper, Martin, 19, 27, 114

Uniform; cost of, 23-4, 26, 59-60, 109; style and colour, 46, 84, 94-5, 108

Verulam, Earl of (1809-95), 19
Vickers, Sons and Maxim Ltd., 76
Victoria, Queen, 1, 21, 52, 114
Victoria Rifle Corps, 9
Vincent, Sir Howard, 63, 75, 131, 143
Volunteer Act, 1863, 27, 80, 129-30
Volunteer Act, 1895, 129
Volunteer Act, 1900, 130
Volunteer Force; age of members, 42-3, 45-6, 50, 124; apathy towards, 19, 65, 68; attitudes to Regular Army, 61-2, 84-6, 91, 93-5, 98; club-like atmosphere of, 2, 23, 54, 63; cost of being a member, 2, 9, 12-13, 19, 22-4, 26, 109, 115, 120-1; court proceedings against members, 23, 52, 109; enrolment in, motives for, 3, 30, 103-24, 153-5; 'Father of', 10; finances of, 89-90; fines for members, 12, 52; geographical spread, 46-50; government attitude to, 2, 5, 7-10, 12-15, 18, 26-7, 80-1, 89-93, 119, 128-49; length of service of members, 42, 44, 50; links with local community, 68-72, 120; members join Regular Army and Militia, 38, 40-1, 129;

Members of Parliament and, 3,
19, 83, 86, 108, 136, 148; military
role of, 2, 12-14, 84-98, 129-30,
140-9; in Napoleonic Wars, 7-8;
numbers in, 1-2, 15, 49-51, 91,
104-5, 134, 138-41, 147-9, 153;
obligations of members, 12, 26,
52, 76-7, 87, 104, 109-10,
129-31, 139; occupations of
members, 25, 33-42; opposition to,
19-20, 30, 68, 78-80, 107;
overseas service for, 10, 127-31,
140-1; patronage of by aristocracy
and wealthy, 15, 19-21, 83;
political effects of, 24, 28;
political implications of being a
member of, 28, 103-4, 106-8,
124; political reform and, 19-20;
political strength of, 2-3, 68, 127,
130-49; Reserve for Expeditionary
Force, 2, 139, 140-5, 148; in
rural areas, 4, 14, 21, 25, 35,
40-1, 46-50, 55, 71, 83, 92;
self-mockery of members, 4,
83-4; social effects of, 27-30,
117-8; spectators of, 70-1, 73;
status of, 3, 60-1, 68, 83-4, 98,
154-5; teetotalism in, 19, 121; in
urban areas, 4, 14, 22, 25, 35,
40-1, 46-50, 55-6, 61, 83, 92;
Volunteer Decoration, 61-2 (see
also Aristocracy, Bands, Bazaars,
Cadets, Camp, Churches,
Commanding Officers, Discipline,
Disturbances, Drill, Drink,
Employers, Leisure, March-outs,
Middle class, Non-commissioned
officers, Officers, Parliament,
Patriotism, Prizes, Public
Opinion, Rifles, Roughs, Trade
Unions, Uniform, Women,
Working class)

Volunteer News, 153

Volunteer Service Gazette, 3, 15, 27,
42, 54-5, 61, 63, 65, 72, 76, 86,
91, 94, 105, 110, 112, 117-8,
155

Volunteer and Territorial units in:
Aberdeenshire, 46, 120;
Airdrie, 63, 69; Argyll, 21;
Ashford, 119; Ayrshire, 47;
Bath, 73; Beccles, 56, 70-1;
Bedfordshire, 18; Berkshire, 55;

Birkenhead, 21, 29, 64, 81;
Birmingham, 19, 40, 53, 64, 81,
94, 110, 112; Bristol, 42, 70;
Buckinghamshire, 58; Builth,
122; Bury, 69, 78; Caithness, 82;
Cambridge, 18, 71; Canterbury,
79, 117; Carlisle, 70; Chatham, 53;
Cheltenham, 9; Cheshire, 64,
110; Chester, 19; Chesterfield, 81;
Cinque Ports, 93, 122; Crewe,
106, 128; Cumberland, 42;
Cumbernauld, 74; Dalbeattie,
106; Derbyshire, 34-5, 38, 92;
Devon, 41; Dorset, 21; Dunmow,
74; Durham, 25, 29, 64, 74;
East Surrey, 40, 118;
Edinburgh, 18-19, 22, 25, 34,
42, 54, 57, 61, 64, 73, 82,
106; Essex, 120; Evesham, 56;
Exeter, 9-10; Eye, 73; Galloway,
33, 35-6; Gartness, 21, 64;
Gillingham, 53; Girvan, 55;
Glamorgan, 35, 38, 60;
Glasgow, 18, 21, 25, 29, 40,
53-4, 145; Grantham, 79;
Greenock, 8, 112; Guildford, 19;
Haddington, 25, 111;
Hampshire, 40-1, 94-5, 116;
Hastings, 122; Hay, 71;
Hereford, 19; Hertfordshire, 60;
Highgate, 54; Huddersfield, 20;
Hull, 9, 69; Inns of Court, 23;
Kent, 42, 56; Kidderminster, 69;
Kincardineshire, 21, 115;
Kinross, 118; Lambeth, 21, 60,
116; Lanarkshire, 21, 59, 95, 118;
Lancashire, 20, 25, 60, 110, 116;
Leeds, 8; Leicester, 153;
Lincoln, 21, 33, 36-9, 42-5, 51,
71, 95, 116; Liverpool, 25,
27-9, 34, 60, 80-1, 117, 119,
145, 156; London, 8, 10, 19,
24-5, 28, 35, 42, 55-7, 77-9,
94-5, 109, 111-12, 115, 119,
145, 148, 156; Lyncombe, 55;
Manchester, 21, 25, 61, 82, 120,
145; Margate, 119; Middlesex,
23, 25, 29, 33, 35-9, 42-5, 51, 57,
59-60, 62, 74, 78, 82, 121;
Monmouthshire, 22, 40;
Newbury, 79; Northumberland,
58, 121; Oldham, 19-20, 25;
Osborne, 21; Perthshire, 110, 127;

For Product Safety Concerns and Information please contact our EU
representative GPSR@taylorandfrancis.com
Taylor & Francis Verlag GmbH, Kaufingerstraße 24, 80331 München, Germany

www.ingramcontent.com/pod-product-compliance
Lightning Source LLC
Chambersburg PA
CBHW052125300426
44116CB00010B/1781